M000275447

War against Saddam Hussein

SPECIAL FORCES IN IRAQ

Eric MICHELETTI

Translated from the French by Gerard DREVILLE

Histoire & Collections - Paris

SPECIAL FORCES IN IRAQ

A new
Special War   4

The Coalition Forces
attack Iraq   6

The Green Berets ahead
of the operations   32

The Rangers' mission:
to secure
western Iraq   56

PSYOPS assault
the iraqi hearts
and minds   66

The Civil Affairs mission
was to "win Iraqi's
hearts and minds"   74

The 160th SOAR
"Night Stalkers"   80

Task Force 121
manhunts the 55
most wanted Iraqis   88

The CIA Commandos
at the heart
of the iraqi regime   100

SEAL come
from the Sea   110

SPECIAL FORCES IN IRAQ

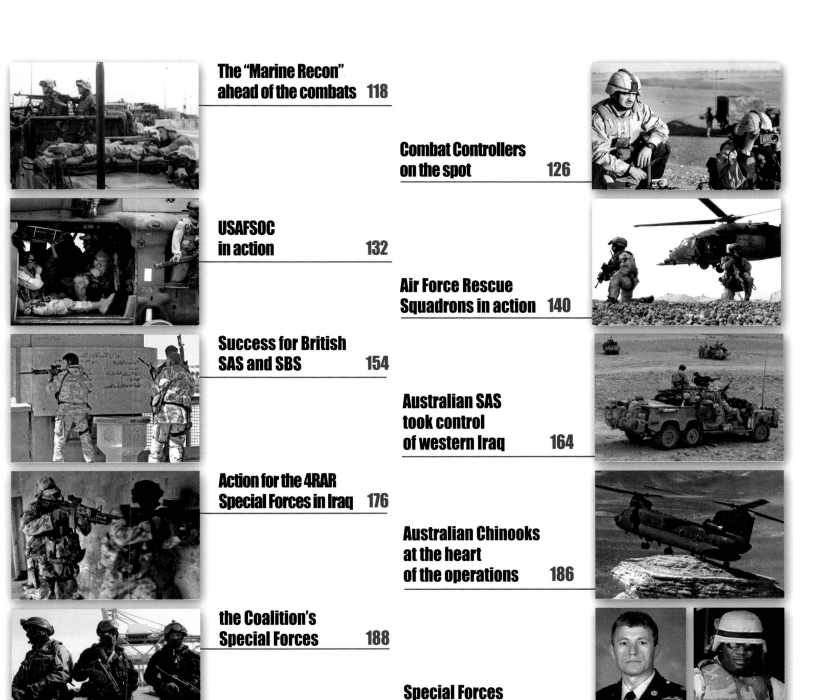

The "Marine Recon" ahead of the combats 118

Combat Controllers on the spot 126

USAFSOC in action 132

Air Force Rescue Squadrons in action 140

Success for British SAS and SBS 154

Australian SAS took control of western Iraq 164

Action for the 4RAR Special Forces in Iraq 176

Australian Chinooks at the heart of the operations 186

the Coalition's Special Forces 188

Special Forces deaths in Iraq 198

Several experts consider the specific Special Forces employment during operation *Iraqi Freedom* (OIF) as revolutionary. For the first time, special units substituted for conventional forces, fought an armoured and mechanized enemy and what's more, won the battle.

A few months prior to launching the ground forces against Iraq, the coalition thought two combined special units could conduct a series of operations in northern and western Iraq; and that these units would have enough strength to carry out large scale operations, in support of the conventional forces which would attack from Kuwait.

That is why C/JSOTF-West special units infiltrated into Iraq from Jordan and Saudi Arabia. Their mission was to seize airfields in the desert, and to hold and block the communication roads from the Jordanian and Syrian borders so as to prevent Baath party leaders from fleeing. The other major mission for the American, Australian and British special units was the tracking down of the Iraqi ballistic missiles, to avoid them being set on Israel and Jordan. Iraqi Freedom planners' estimates were that Special Forces deployment in northern and western Iraq would allow to isolate Baghdad.

These decisions proved to be correct and victory has been achieved. On the other hand, the post-war has been " another story ".

However, for the first time, American Special Forces played a significant role in the ground operations in Iraq. This was the result of all the efforts devoted to the integration of SF teams into the conventional forces in the field, and to the willingness of the Special Operations Command to cooperate and to jointly work with the other Iraq-based Commands as well as with Central Command based in Tampa, Florida.

For the first time at such a level, conventional forces provided support to special units, allowing the latter to carry out combat operations, in-depth reconnaissance and special missions. In return, SF provided combat units with intelligence they had never had before.

Heliborne or airlifted Special Forces traditionally work in the depth of the battle field to carry out short term operations. However, during OIF, Special Forces teams were integrated in the various combat brigades, even during the final combats in Baghdad.

Relationships were " positives " as all reports say, in spite of the very different cultures SF and conventional forces have and which was the source of certain issues. *Iraqi Freedom* Special Forces HQ quickly understood the best way to infiltrate into Iraq was with the help of the mechanized units. Even if some within the conventional forces have said special units received more than they gave in return, one has to acknowledge SF detachments ahead of the front line units provided a better understanding of the situation, thanks to the enemy and local population localisation.

For the first time also, SF liaison Officers were integrated in the various HQ, and were part of the design of operations in which SF were involved, something which had not been possible so far. Thus, during the first days of OIF, SF provided first hand intelligence that conventional units would not have known otherwise.

There is no doubt that the SF - conventional units reciprocal support was a key factor in the success of this large scale operation, an operation which can be seen as a milestone in the American strategy.

❑

A NEW SPECIAL WAR

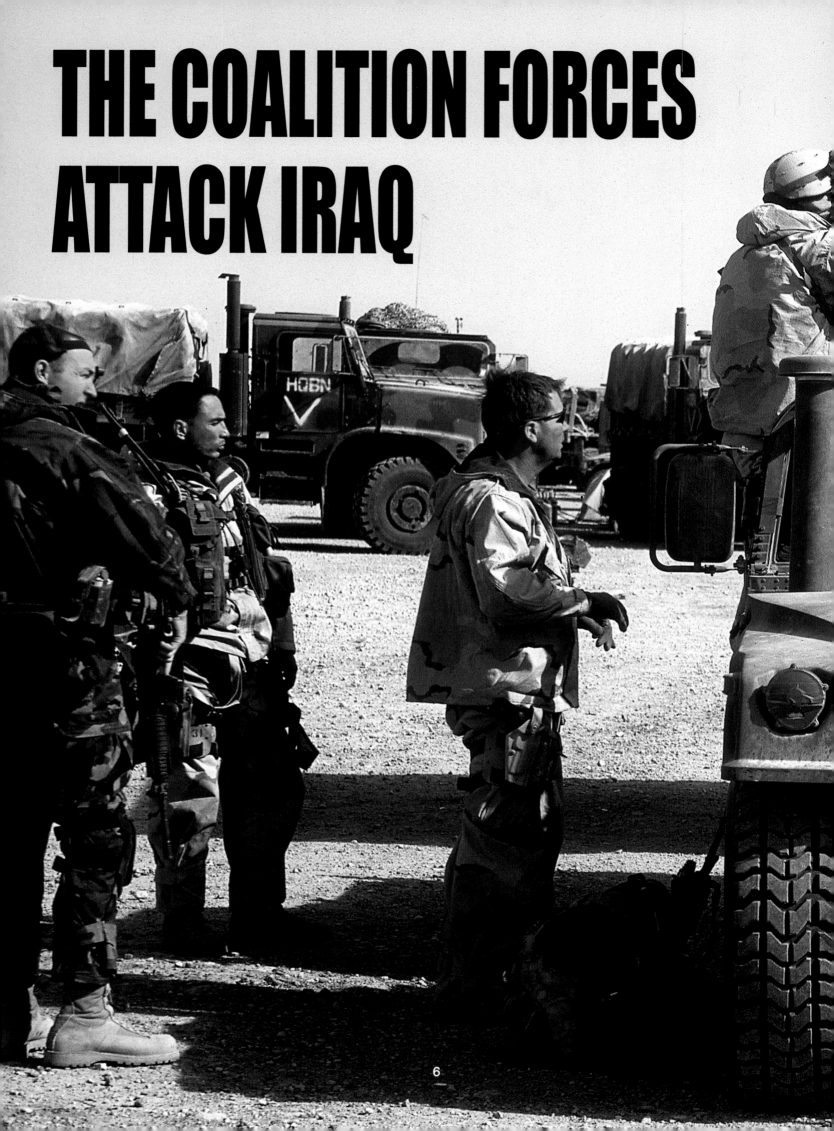

THE COALITION FORCES ATTACK IRAQ

200 kilometres in Iraq, a 9th PsyOps Battalion Special Forces' team attached to Task Force "Tarawa" during Operation *Iraqi Freedom*, prepares to set up a satellite link with its parent unit command. *(Photo Yves Debay)*

Left.
In the heart of the oil-rich fields, after 24 hours of firefight
in the far south of Iraq, a pair of Marine Recon of the 1st Marine
Recon, 1st Marine Division, wait for the orders to continue its advance.
(Photo USMC)

Bottom left.
On 20 March, Marines of the 1st Marine Division prepare
to assault a building Iraqi soldiers still defend, outskirts of Rumaylah.
(Photo USMC)

showed some limits, especially at the Tora Bora fight (from 1 to 7 December 2001): relying on a friendly auxiliary force did not prevent Taliban's and Al-Qaeda leaders to successfully flee.

The overall framework of OIF was the following: a ground operation launched from Kuwait to overcome the Iraqi forces, and isolate the government in Baghdad or in Tikrit, the Baath party home city, if necessary; once the major combats over, security operations would take place. The main ground effort was to be sustained by huge aerial operations, but also - and it was a first - by Special Forces.

On its side, Special Operations command (SOCENT) had drawn lessons from the Kosovo, and certainly from the Afghan operations. Thus, OIF planners put an emphasis on the north, where American Special Forces and the Kurds' would have to pin down the major Baghdad's units behind the "green line" which parted the Kurd region from the rest of Iraq. This force could then attack towards the southern region of Tikrit, while stabilizing the Kurdish region.

On the other hand, SF would conduct operations in western Iraq aiming at preventing Iraqi forces from launching ballistic missiles against Israel, Jordan or Turkey. For the Ira-

Operation Iraqi Freedom (OIF) is the first conventional forces-special forces combined operation since the Korean War in 1950. According to some experts, this large scale operation was the result of all those carried out in the Balkans and in Afghanistan.

Enduring Freedom in Afghanistan is certainly a milestone in the American concept of waging war. What is true is that the US Army participation, which meant support to the Special Forces (SF) — at least in the first part of the campaign — was limited. Combats began on 7 October 2001 with an aerial campaign whose aim was to gain air superiority.

Lessons learnt from Afghanistan

As of 15 October, the Army Special Forces were in the field, shoulder to shoulder with the Afghan opponents. By combining modern and ancient vectors — horse and target laser designator — American and Afghan forces successfully overthrew the Taliban regime when Mullah Omar fled on 6 December 2001. This campaign led by Special Forces also

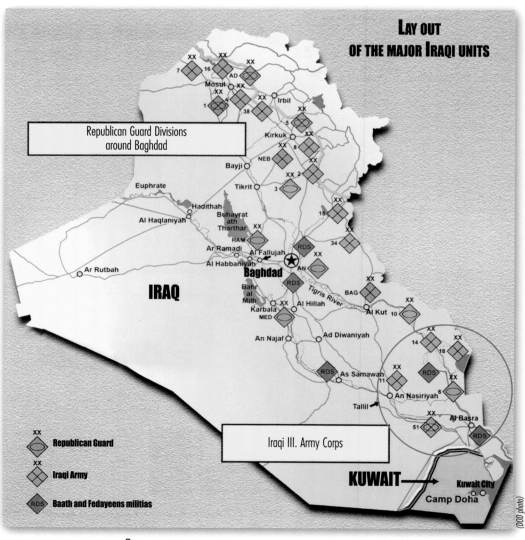

LAY OUT OF THE MAJOR IRAQI UNITS

Republican Guard Divisions around Baghdad

Mosul · AD · Irbil · Kirkuk · NEB · Bayji · Tikrit · Euphrate · Hadithah · Buhayrat ath Tharthar · Al Haqlaniyah · HAM · Ar Ramadi · Al Fallujah · RDS · Al Habbaniyah · AN · **Baghdad** · Ar Rutbah · **IRAQ** · Bahr al Milh · RDS · BAG · Karbala · Al Hillah · MED · Al Kut · An Najaf · Ad Diwaniyah · Bahr al Milh · RDS · As Samawah · An Nasiriyah · RDS · Tallil · Al Basra · RDS · Tigris River

Republican Guard

Iraqi Army

Baath and Fedayeens militias

Iraqi III. Army Corps

KUWAIT · Kuwait City · Camp Doha

SADDAM HUSSEIN'S MISSILES

On 19 March 2003, prior to the beginning of the operations in Iraq, American and British intelligence services did say Bagdad had twenty Al-Hussein ballistic missiles (a 650-km range modified Scud) and some Al-Samoud and Al-Ababil-100 ballistic missiles (the specialized media spoke of missiles Al-Abbas, but nobody seemed to be in agreement on what the range of these various missiles was: 200 km range?). At the time, intelligence analysts maintained these missiles could have chemical and biological war heads. The fear was that they could be used against the coalition's forces, but that they also could reach Israel.

According to the American-government-created Iraq Survey Group (ISG), in 2000 Saddam Hussein had ordered the development of missiles capable of reaching a target within 1,000 km range. Iraqi documents seized later on, revealed that in 2002, Baghdad had allocated $ 10 millions to North Korea to acquire a 1,300 km range No Dong missile. However, North Korea knew it was being watched by the Americans and therefore, the missile was never delivered nor the money given back!

ISG's final report, contradicting its 2003 analysis, finally concluded that Iraq had no longer modified Scud missiles; they had no programme to develop 1,000 km range missiles; projects of vectors capable of scattering chemical or biological agents had been abandoned in 2001; and lastly, the various UN inspections carried out since 1991 had really ended all these programmes.

Only seventeen Al-Samoud and Ababil-100 ballistic missiles, as well as Frog-7 rockets were launched during the coalition's offensive. No Al-Hussein missile was launched. □

qi Freedom HQ, this mission was a *"Scud big game hunting"*, more visible than the Desert Storm one eleven years before. Then, SF would have to conduct reconnaissance actions far behind the Iraqi lines, for the combat units benefit.

Beginning of 2003, SOCENT formed two Joint Special Operations Task Forces: JSOTF-West and JSOTF-North. Special operations command responsibility within Iraqi Freedom was to be led by the Combined Forces Special Operations Com-

Above.
In a HH-60 Pave Hawk, pararescuemen of the USAF's 301st Rescue Squadron carefully watch the Iraqi desert during a rescue mission on 6 April 2003. *(Photo USAF)*

Below.
Near Bassorah, a sniper of the British 1st Armoured Division watches the Iraqi soldiers. British soldiers took control of Iraq southern oil fields in forty eight hours.

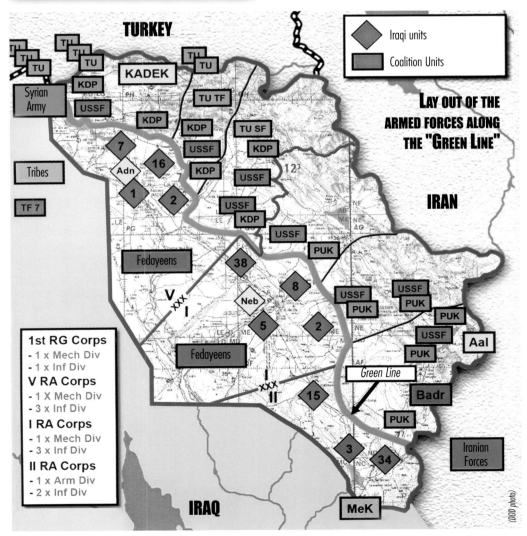

LAY OUT OF THE ARMED FORCES ALONG THE "GREEN LINE"

Iraqi units

Coalition Units

1st RG Corps
- 1 x Mech Div
- 1 x Inf Div
V RA Corps
- 1 X Mech Div
- 3 x Inf Div
I RA Corps
- 1 x Mech Div
- 3 x Inf Div
II RA Corps
- 1 x Arm Div
- 2 x Inf Div

ponent Command (CFSOCC) formed from the Special Operations Command-Central (SOCCENT) HQ. CFSOCC had command and control over C/JSOTF-West and C/JSOTF-North.

Because Turkey had denied overflying rights at the last minute, the six C-17 aircraft had to fly over the Iraqi air defence over the night of 22 to 23 March 2003: an aircraft was hit and had to return. The brigade-size C/JSOTF-North comprised some 5,200 men. It had three Special Forces battalions, the 2nd and 3rd battalions of the 10th Special Forces Group (SFG), and the 3rd battalion of the 3rd SFG, making a total of nine companies of Special Forces, which meant 45 ODA. 14th Infantry's 2nd battalion of the 10th Mountain Division added to the Special Forces, as well as 1,000 paratroopers of the 173rd Airborne Brigade, and two battalions of light Infantry and an armoured unit.

The three C/JSOTF-North SF battalions mission (also called Forward Operating Bases or FOB) was to fix thirteen divisions of the Ist and Vth Iraqi Corps, then to break them thanks to the combination of the ground and air operations, and finally to move toward Mosul and Kirkuk. Based on the SF

experience gained during operation Enduring Freedom in Afghanistan, coalition planners strongly thought Special Forces could play a major role in operation Iraqi Freedom.

JSOTF-North command was manned by the Officers also commanding the 10th SFG. They had a hard game to play: while attacking the Iraqi enemy forces, they would have to take care of two touchy elements of this northern region of Iraq, the two rival Kurd parties and the Turkish army. To conduct their operations American SF would be supported by 60,000 Peshmegas.

The hunt for the Scuds continue

On its side, JSOTF-West was manned by the 5th SFG HQ. The primary mission of its combat detachments was to infiltrate into Iraq from Saudi Arabia and Jordan, to capture all air bases in western Iraq and to use them as Forward Operating Bases.

Then, American, Australian and British SF had to screen western Iraq to find the ballistic missiles launch pads. Then, they had to block the communication routes from and to the

other countries, before capturing (as was possible) all Iraqi leaders willing to flee.

American planners relied on the 4th Infantry Division deployment in northern Iraq to block the Iraqi army. However, the 4 ID's units had to embark in 40 transport ships and once on the ground had to cross Turkey. But by mid-February, Ankara denied the division the rights to cross its territory. In the meantime, the 10th Special Forces Group teams of JSOTF-North, under Colonel Cleveland command, were ready to deploy in Kurdistan. Because of the Turkish position, General Tommy Franks gave the transport ships the order to urgently sail to Kuwait through the Suez Canal. JSOTF-North had to be airlifted to northern Iraq with SOC's

(DOD photo)

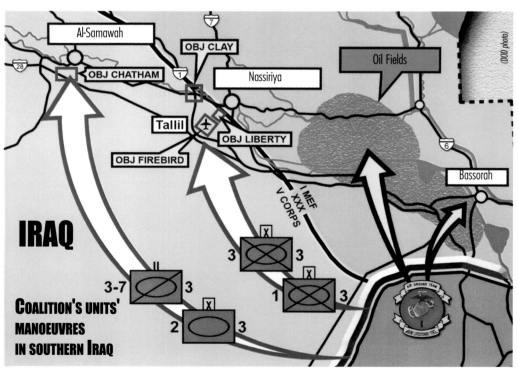

IRAQ

COALITION'S UNITS' MANOEUVRES IN SOUTHERN IRAQ

THE HQ STRESS

HQ's stress comes from several levels of frustration. The first one comes from the gap between knowing an event occurs and the number of information collected about that event. A threat you don't see but you feel.

Then, there is the counter-guerrilla context: cadre in contact have the right feeling while HQs feel *"dispossessed"* of the information. Most of the commitments, even the problems to solve don't go further than the platoon level, while necessitating immediate reactions. In order to lower this stress, the temptation is strong to harass the lower level of responsibility with many requests of reports.

" On the other hand, There is a new phenomenon which has appeared with the modern intelligence or communications assets (drones with gyro stabilized camera for instance). It is the anxiety of the *"higher level of inaction"* and *"the lower level of decision"* which means that there is a tendency to have the final decision go up the hierarchy chain. It is not rare in Iraq that Generals make a decision that should be taken by a Captain.

Extract from *"War after the war. Lessons learnt from twenty months of stabilization operations in Iraq "*, by Major Michel Goya", French Doctrine magazine of CDEF (Centre for Force Employment Doctrine).

Left page. Often taken for the US Air Force Special Operations Command helicopters, 160th Special Operations Army Regiment's rotary wings carried out many missions for the Joint Task Force-West between March and April 2003. They took off from Jordan. (Photo SOCOM)

Below.
On 19 March, a Land Rover Defender of the British 1 Battalion Irish Guard advances in the oil-rich and highly strategic zone of Rumaylah. (Photo MOD)

Right. This 9th PsyOps Battalion Special Force soldier in southern Iraq has a high morale. It is 22 March and Iraqi units offer little resistance. (Photo Yves Debay)

C-130, without flying over Turkey, but therefore flying over Syria and the Iraqi air defences. Eventually Turkey allowed limited overflying rights some weeks later, but for logistics aircraft only.

The American command estimate was that the SF forces strength in Kurdistan was not sufficient. It therefore decided to airborne two battalions of the 173rd Airborne Brigade based in Vicenza, Italy, and to airlift a M1A2 Abrams and M2 Bradley Company as well as a M113 Company.

The spectre of wells burning

While the American units of the Vth Corps units, 1st Marine Expeditionary Force (I MEF) and Task Force " Tarawa ", and the British 1st Armoured Division were packing up along the Iraqi border, 5th SFG motorized teams opened the barriers marking the country's limit and crossed the Iraqi-made huge earth and sand levee on 19 March, around 0200. The objective was to reconnoitre the oil fields and to make sure Iraqi had not sabotaged or booby-trapped them.

There was no way they were going to let the Iraqis to destroy the oil wells as they did it in 1992 during operation Desert Storm in Kuwait where hundreds of wells burned for months.

However, images from a Predator drone taken at first light showed higher flames from the wells than the previous days. There was no doubt in the Joint Term Fusion Cell specialists' minds that Iraqi had started to sabotage the wells [1]!

At 0830 Major General Marks asked the cell leader: " *Do you think Iraqi sabotage their wells? ".* " *Yes, Sir. - I want to*

be sure before launching 60,000 Marines in the area! - Yes, I am sure! "

In the following minutes, the order to pull forward operation Iraqi Freedom by twenty four hours was given.

The ground offensive was launched at 0600 on 21 March. While the 3rd Infantry Division (3rd ID) Brigades and I MEF fast paced to the north, the British 1st Armoured Division

---

1. *Actually, only nine wells out of 1,000 of the oil field were set on fire by the Iraqi troops. They thought they had more time, as in 1992 the air campaign had lasted thirty days.*

seized the oil fields and began advancing toward Bassorah.

To prevent any sabotage of the oil terminals, the coalition had also decided to seize them during the first hours of the attack. A joint complex operation was setup with US Navy SF, British Navy SBS, ships of the US Navy, Coast Guards as well as elements of the US Army.

At 2309 on 21 March, two LCU (landing Craft Utility) type crafts tied up at the *khor* Al-Amaya platform. 24 coast guards disembarked and quickly secured the platform, before discovering a SEAL team which had just arrived, climbing the platform's legs, a few minutes earlier. An hour later, another LCU did the same at another terminal, but this time with a 22 Marine team.

At the same time, SEAL and SBS teams supported by Polish GROM Special Forces, seized the Rumaylah oil terminals and refineries. SEAL members of Team 8, with 56 Polish SF entered Umm-Qasr port and took control of the port facilities without any loss.

Hundred and sixty kilometres in a day

On their side, the various 5th Special Forces Group teams which crossed the earth and sand levees dividing the two countries twenty four hours before went on, to reconnoitre

the Talil air base as well as the defences around Nassiriya, and then those of Samawah.

Behind them, the I MEF units worked a series of breaches (seven in total) in the earth levee to allow passage to the Vth Corps's 10,000 vehicles, as well as those of Task Force "Tarawa". The latter crossed with the 3rd ID to attack in the Nassiriya region. Several tens of kilometres ahead, SF reconnoitered Talil air base whose defences were almost abandoned (3rd ID captured 200 prisoners).

The American command had planned to use it as a forward air base. In the mean time, 1st and 3rd Brigades of the 3rd ID fast paced over 140 kilometres to capture a bridge on the Euphrates River, north of Nassiriya that they handed over to TF "Tarawa" on 23 March.

In less than twenty four hours, 3rd Infantry Division, the Vth Corps spear head, had already crossed more than 160 kilometres in Iraq, meaning one third of the distance to Baghdad.

More in the north, 210 kilometres from the border, 3-7 Cavalry Squadron, 2nd Brigade, 3rd ID faced aggressive Iraqi units vicinities of Samawah. The coalition's HQ understood that the Americans were not welcome as liberators.

However, 23 March remained a black day for the coalition's forces as a convoy of the 52nd Air Defense Artillery

Above.
On 23 March, a 332nd Air Expeditionary Wing A-10 Thunderbolt II ground attack aircraft returns from a close air support mission in southern Iraq. Some days later, this aircraft operated from one of the captured Iraqi bases in the southern and western Iraq.
(Photo USAF)

went in an ambush during that morning: eleven soldiers were killed and several captured. Among the latter was Private First Class Jessica Lynch, who would be rescued later on, during a Special Forces operation.

The night of 23 to 24 also saw the failure of the 11th Attack Helicopter Regiment's AH-64 Apache-led attack in the depth against the "Medina" division, stationed before Baghdad. Beside the loss of two helicopters, all Apaches were hit.

On its side, 3rd ID decided to by-pass the Chiit city of Najaf. But it had to cross a plateau defended by some units of the Republican Guard, militiamen and Artillery to achieve that objective. Supported by coalition's aircraft, it destroyed the enemy positions one after the other in a few hours. That day, coalition's aircraft were from USAF, US Navy, USMC and the RAF, and were guided by Tactical Air Controllers.

As of 23 March, Iraqi forces opposed some resistance.

The battle of Najaf (25 to 28 March 2005)

Najaf is located along the Euphrates River, as is Samawah. Its bridges are strategic and Route 9 goes along the

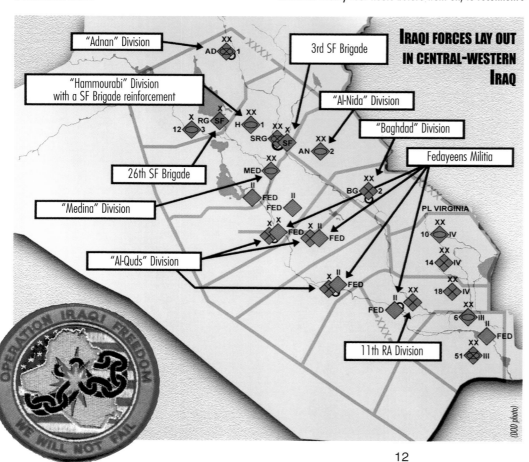

"Adnan" Division

"Hammourabi" Division with a SF Brigade reinforcement

3rd SF Brigade

"Al-Nida" Division

"Baghdad" Division

Fedayeens Militia

26th SF Brigade

"Medina" Division

"Al-Quds" Division

11th RA Division

IRAQI FORCES LAY OUT IN CENTRAL-WESTERN IRAQ

(DOD photo)

Right. For the first time in the United States military history, the American command engaged thousands of Special Forces in a major operation. They were given strategic and tactic missions with the conventional forces and this unlike what happened during the first Gulf War when SF had only played a low-key role.
(Photo Yves Debay)

west of the city. Iraqi troops in the city could block any V Corps action toward Karbala which is further north. However, 3rd ID decided to by-pass Najaf instead of seizing it, and to capture the north and south of the city two bridges. It is then that 3-7 Cav. units discovered in a cloud of dust (visibility was twenty metres or so) that SF vehicles had already taken position near the southern bridge, nicknamed Objective Floyd.

The bridge was easily captured, but when Abrams and Bradley move up along the eastern bank of the river Euphrates, they went under fire of hundreds of militiamen who turned around the column aboard 4x4 vehicles. As meteo conditions did not allow air support, they had to fight on their own.

Below. On 26 March 2003, paratroopers of the 173rd Airborne Brigade board a C-17 in Italy. They had a non-stop flight over Kurdistan before jumping and support the Special Forces to hold northern Iraq.
(Photo USAF)

SURGICAL ACTION AGAINST CLEARLY IDENTIFIED TARGETS

Intelligence was a challenge in such a complex environment where the enemy disappeared among the population and occupied holy sites, schools and hospitals. How to differentiate a militia from an innocent civilian? How to drag the enemy toward combat zones? That is why it was vital to make the population leave the cities. Once the target was spotted, (political leader, cache of weapons, strong point), a zone blocking could begin.

During such an operation, everything depended on the decision making process and therefore, on the downstream intelligence. Three sensors were often used: unmanned aerial vehicles provided images in real time; war dog teams in particular for the caches of weapons; the unit leader (a sensor?) at troop or platoon level. ❑

The northern bridge was nicknamed Objective Jenkins. There the situation was no better. Taking advantage of the low visibility, the militiamen assaulted by waves. At midnight, the 3-7 Cav. Returned to its starting point after a quasi non-stop fight of hundred and twenty hours. The 2nd BCT successfully " cleaned " the eastern and northern routes of Najaf.

On 29 March, Command approved General Wallace's request to have 3rd ID relieved in line by the 101st and 82nd divisions. While Vth Corps moved north toward Baghdad, I MEF carried out a series of ground and amphibious operations around Bassorah, supported by the British 1st Armou-

SPECIAL FORCES UNITS DURING OPERATION IRAQI FREEDOM
ORDER OF BATTLE as of 1 May 2003

V Corps [OPCON]

— 2nd Battalion, 5th Special Forces Group (ODA 521, ODA 522, ODA 523, ODA 525, ODA 531, ODA 534 ODA 581)
— 19th Special Forces Group (ODA 916)
— 308th Civil Affairs Brigade (OPCON)
— 432nd Civil Affairs Battalion
— 490th Civil Affairs Battalion (OPCON)
— 9th PsyOps Battalion (OPCON)
— 346th Tactical PsyOps Co.
— 3rd PsyOps Battalion (Public Information Detachment)
— Two companies of the " Free Iraqi Forces "

● 3rd INFANTRY DIVISION
— ODA 916,
— Co. C of the 9th PsyOps Battalion
— 3rd PsyOps Co. (Print Production Team)
— Detachments 1550 and 1560/346th Tactical PsyOps Co.
— 315th Tactical PsyOps Co.
— Detachment 1270/3rd Tactical PsyOps Co.
— Detachment/318th Tactical PsyOps Co.
— 422nd Civil Affairs Battalion
— B Co./411th Civil Affairs Bn.

● Task Force Iron
— Team 1093/9th Tactical PsyOps Bn.
— 431st Civil Affairs Bn.

● 4th INFANTRY DIVISION
— HQ/Teams 1670, 1671, 1680, 1681/362nd Tactical PsyOps Operations Co.
— HHC/General Support Co/Team 10/418th Civil Affairs Battalion
— 1st Brigade, 4th Infantry Division
— Teams 1670, 1671, 1672 Detachment 1670th/362nd Tactical PsyOps Co.
— Teams 1, 5, 7/718th Civil Affairs Bn.
— 2nd Brigade, 4th Infantry Division
— 1690th Tactical PsyOps Det/362nd Tactical PsyOps Co.
— Teams 2, 6, 8/418th Civil Affairs Bn.
— 3rd Brigade, 4th Infantry Division
— 1680th Tactical PsyOps Det./362nd Tactical PsyOps Co.
— Teams 3, 9/418th Civil Affairs Bn.
— 4th Brigade, 4th Infantry Division
— Team 623/362nd Tactical PsyOps Co.

● 101st AIRBORNE DIVISION (Air Assault)
— ODA 915 of 19th Special Forces Group
— 318th Tactical PsyOps Co.
— 1st Brigade, 101st Abn. Div.
— Detachment of the Tactical Air Control Party/19th Air Support Ops Squad. (USAF)
— Detachment 1070/318th Tactical PsyOps Co.
— Team 4/B Co./431st Civil Affairs Bn.
— Detachment of the " Free Iraqi Forces "
— 2nd Brigade, 101st Abn. Div.
— Teams HQ, 3, 4, 7, 8/431st Civil Affairs Bn.
— 3rd Brigade, 101st Abn. Div.
— Co. B/431st Civil Affairs Bn.
— Detachment of the " Free Iraqi Forces "
— Task Force " Rakkasan "
— Team 6/Co. B/431st Civil Affairs Bn.
— Detachment of the " Free Iraqi Forces "
— 101st Support Command (DISCOM)
— Detachment 1080/318th Tactical PsyOps Co.
— One Company of the " Free Iraqi Forces "

● 82nd AIRBORNE DIVISION
— Elements of 301st Tactical PsyOps Bn.

— 96th Civil Affairs Bn.
— Two companies of the " Free Iraqi Forces "
— 82nd Division Support Command (DISCOM)
— 301st Tactical PsyOps Bn.
— 12nd Aviation Brigade
— Detachment of B Co./411th Civil Affairs Bn.
— Detachment of the 361st Tactical PsyOps Co.
— 3rd Armored Cavalry Regiment
— Detachment of the 361st Tactical PsyOps Co.
— A Co./411st Civil Affairs Bn.
— Detachment of the 490th Civil Affairs Bn.
— 18th Military Police Brigade
— Detachment of the 362nd Tactical PsyOps Co.
— 377th Theatre Support Command (OPCON)
— B Co./13th Tactical PsyOps Bn.
— HHC/304th Civil Affairs Bn.
— 414th Civil Affairs Bn.
— 486th Civil Affairs Bn.

JOINT SPECIAL OPERATIONS TASK FORCE-SOUTH
(Kuwait)

— SEAL Team 8
— SEAL Team 10
— Detachment of Polish Special Forces "GROM"
— Detachment (rear base) of the 9th PsyOps Operations Bn.
— Detachment (rear base) and plans of 308th Civil Affairs Bn.
— Detachment (rear base) and plans of 414th Civil Affairs Bn.

MARINE EXPEDITIONARY FORCE

● 1st Force Recon (reinforced),
consisting of 2nd Recon Bn. of the 2nd MEB of the 1st Marine Div.
ODA 554, 5th Special Forces Group
— 3rd Civil Affairs Group
— 358th Civil Affairs Brigade (elements)
— 402nd Civil Affairs Battalion (elements)
— 9th PsyOps Batt. (detachment)

● 1st MARINE DIVISION
1st Force Recon (reinforced)

● 2nd MARINE EXPEDITIONARY BRIGADE
(Task Force "Tarawa ")
— Co. C of the 4th Recon Battalion (reinforced)
— 4th Civil Affairs Group (detachment)
— One Company of the " Free Iraqi Forces "

● 1st ARMOURED DIVISION (United Kingdom)
— 402nd Civil Affairs Battalion (detachment)
— 358th Civil Affairs Brigade (elements)

---

1. Combined Forces Land Component Command. (HQ of the ground forces)
2. Tactical Control.
3. Marine Central Command.
4. Operational Control.
5. Special Forces Operations Detachment Alpha.

JOINT SPECIAL OPERATIONS TASK FORCE-NORTH
(Kurdistan)

— 10th Special Forces Group
— 404th Civil Affairs Bn.
— Detachment 443rd Civil Affairs Bn.
— 930th Tactical PsyOps Det.

JOINT SPECIAL OPERATIONS TASK FORCE-WEST
(Jordan - Saudi Arabia - Iraq)

— 3rd Bn./75th Ranger Regiment
— Special Forces Group
— 160th SOAR
— Australian SAS
— 4RAR (Commandos)
— British SAS/SBS Detachment

US CENTCOM Air Forces
(Kuweit-Saudi-Arabia)

— 57th Rescue Squadron (H-60) (50)
— 58th Rescue Squadron (75)
— 66th Rescue Squadron (110)
— 301st Rescue Squadron (50)
— 20th Special Operations Squadron (MH-53M)
— 21st Special Operations Squadron (MH-53M Pave Low IV)
— Elements of the 193rd Special Operations Wing (EC-130E)

● Incirlik Turkey
129th Rescue Squadron (C-130 and HH-60G)
711th Special Operations Squadron (C-130)
● Masirah, Oman
4th Special Operations Squadron (6 AC-130U)
8th Special Operations Squadron (MC-130 E)

CFLCC [1]

— Civil Affairs Tactical Planning Team/A/352nd Civil Affairs Command (TACON) [2]

MARCENT [3]
(Djibouti)

— Civil Affairs Tactical Planning Team/A/354th Civil Affairs Brigade (OPCON) (3)
— 352nd Civil Affairs Command (OPCON)
— 402nd Civil Affairs Battalion
— 407th Civil Affairs Battalion
— " Free Iraqi Forces " Unit

Right.
On the first day of the combats, Marine Recons of the 1st Marine Recon try to spot Iraqi enemy movements. American combat units faced all the range of Iraqi forces, from elite units of the Republican Guard to paramilitary combat groups in the urban areas, including some "second hand" combat units.
(Photo USMC)

red Division. At the same time, the coalition's units successfully seized the oil facilities. On their side, at the south edge of Iraq, American, British and Polish Special Forces captured the port of Umm-Qasr.

British units began to surround Bassorah from the west while the Marine secured the oil fields which the SF had reconnoitered forty eight hours before.

During all these operations, SF were there to reconnoitre the terrain and to report any information gathered.

In western Iraq, elements of JSOTF-West already took control of huge portions of the Iraqi desert, hunting possible sites of ballistic missiles launchers.

Australian SAS in the centre, British SAS/SBS in the north, and Green Berets in the south, had the mission to capture H1, H2 and H3 airfields allowing the coalition's aircraft to use them.

To cross the Euphrates river

On 23 March, Samawah had become the next objective on the road to Baghdad. The city is a crossroads on the Euphrates River, and its two bridges would be used to transit 60% of the 3rd ID's logistics. SF reconnaissance, as well as drone-provided images showed a series of defences outside the city, but also numerous strong points inside the built-in area. On 23 March, 3-7 Cav. with its M-1 and Bradley moved to the first objective, *Objective Pistol*, when its crews found a group of light heavily-armed American-flag-bearing vehicles. It was one of the SF units sent forward to Samawah several days before to reconnoitre the objectives. SF's

OPERATIONS OF THE IRAQI CAMPAIGN (MARCH-APRIL 2003) WERE ORGANIZED IN FOUR PHASES

Phase 1
Set the neighbouring countries " in condition " and search international support, weaken the Iraqi regime, establish an airlift and secure the communications vectors in preparation for the military operations, deny Baghdad's tactical missiles deployment, deploy the American forces and lay them out in attack posture. To sum up, meet all conditions aiming at neutralizing the Iraqi forces.

Phase 2
Seize the space of the battle field, first degrade the command cells and the security forces, and seize strategic points in the field with the support of the Special Forces units.

Phase 3
Launch the major offensive operations with the conventional ground and air units, in the southern and northern parts of the country. End of this phase with the occupation of Bagdad and the replacement of Saddam Hussein's government.

Phase 4
It is the transitioning between combat and stabilisation operations, humanitarian aid and rebuilding assistance. During OIF, the time difference between phase 3 and phase 4 "was measured for the first time in only a few kilometres". Civil Affairs began their mission once the combat units had fulfilled their actions. ❑

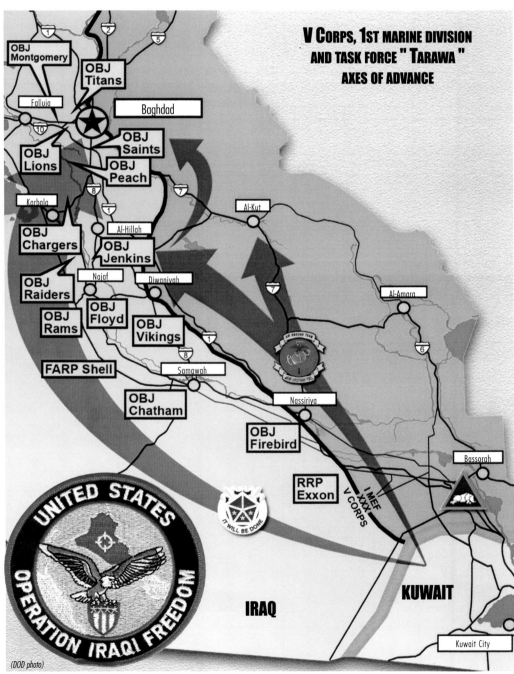

V CORPS, 1ST MARINE DIVISION AND TASK FORCE "TARAWA"
AXES OF ADVANCE

(DOD photo)

SADDAM'S FORCES

Saddam had seventeen combat divisions and six Republican Guard divisions to defend Iraq.

The latter had better equipment and were better trained. In Baghdad, the 15,000 man special Republican Guard had the mission to defend some strategic points. In addition to these forces, were the Baath party militia and as well as the Saddam's Fedayeens militia.

Air forces were almost inexistent and the Navy was nocount. Only the Republican Guard units had some helicopters capable of ground attacks. ❑

Special Forces Operational Detachment Alpha (ODA) made itself known through a signal sent to the Special Forces Liaison Elements (SFLE) attached to the 3rd ID Brigades, then announced that the bridges were intact and had no explosive charges. However, the presence of troops of the Republican Guard (500 to 1,000 men), and paramilitary forces was reported.

Despite a significant resistance, 3-7 Cav. troopers, supported by OH-58D, successfully took control of the bridges, after they killed more than 550 Iraqi soldiers, and destroyed 30 light vehicles and 30 light air defence artillery guns.

3rd Brigade (3rd BCT) of the 3rd ID fought at Samawah until it was relieved in line by the 2nd Brigade of the 82nd Airborne. The 3rd BCT was to advance up toward Najaf and prepare to fight at Karbala where the " Medina " Division of the Republican Guard was.

As of 24 March, the first elements of JSOTF-North of the 10th Special Forces Group were in place in the north. They had two missions to fulfil at this time: together with the Kurd forces, pin point a maximum of Iraqi units on the " Green Line ", and prevent a Turkish military intervention in the Kurdistan.

While the coalition's forces advanced up to Baghdad, SF crossed and screened Kurdistan. They were accompanied by Peshmegas, when they found a suitable site for a massive air drop of paratroopers and an unprepared landing.

It was 2000 and dark for a long time at the air base of Vicenza, Italy, when a C-130 took off with a USAF Tactical

Right and below.
Pararescuemen of the USAF's 301st Rescue Squadron at a Forward Operations Base. They are to carry out an operational mission and intervene if necessary. On 21 March, H2 and H3 Iraqi air fields were captured by the American, Australian and British SF of the coalition. Three days later, 75th Rangers Regiment's Rangers jumped over the designated H1 air field which would become a Forward air base for the SF aircraft.

Air Controllers aboard and ten elements of the 74th LRS Detachment of the 173rd Airborne Brigade. The landing location was Constanza air base in Romania, where this forward detachment was to join 10th SFG teams in order to jointly jump over Iraq. On 25 March, all of them boarded a MC-130 Combat Talon of the USAF special operations. After Turkey granted its overflight rights, the Combat Talon dropped them in the middle of the night, under heavy rain and cold air. On the ground, they were welcomed by the SF who had already arrived. LRS could begin their mission which was to materialize the dropping zone.

On Wednesday, the 26th of March, after a four hours and a half hour flight, 965 paratroopers of the 173rd who had boarded in Italy jumped and achieved the first American airborne assault since operation Just Cause in Panama in 1989 (it was the 44th airborne assault jump of the American military history).

It took a day for the paratroopers of the 1-508th Infantry Regiment (Airborne) and 2-503rd Infantry Regiment (Airborne) to be fully operational. The next day, the first C-17 of the twelve transport aircraft landed and started to unload Abrams tanks, VCI Bradley and M-113 (2). Coalition's HQ felt more at ease, for a visible and credible conventional force was now in Kurdistan to fight the Iraqi army.

To capture the Karbala pass

From 25 to 27 March, all the coalition's units were pinned down by a huge sand and dust storm, and so were the Iraqi's. American forces took advantage of it to rest. But SF actions continued as CENTCOM and the Vth Corps command

2. Paratroopers of the 173rd and armoured took part in the ultimate actions against the Iraqi army in the north.

wanted to know where the Iraqi conventional forces were really located between Nassiriya and Karbala. Intelligence Officers thought they were more in the north, defending the outskirts of Baghdad. If the Republican Guard special division was still in the capital to defend the government buildings, the " Hammourabi ", " Medina " and " Al-Nida " divisions of the Guard had been moved from west to east. In the north, on the " Green Line " there were still two fifths of the Iraqi army, also including two divisions of the Republican Guard, plus some Fedayeen units and militiamen of the Baath party.

Americans were surprised by the lack of response of the conventional units. In fact after five days of war, only the militia really fought. However, as they were not formed into real units, their attacks were more suicide actions.

From 25 to 29 March, all the units stopped their advance to Baghdad. The aim was to secure the supply routes from the Kuwait border up to the outskirts of Najaf. Simultaneously, I MEF had finished securing Nassiriya.

After the Karbala plateau was seized, V Corps prepared the final assault on Baghdad. All intelligence units, and obviously all SF which still worked ahead of the forces, were

requested to spot the " Medina " division and its tanks as it was not the Karbala area.

And the 101st Airborne helicopters failed to fulfil their mission which was to destroy the T-72.

Operation " Viking Hammer "

On 28 March, operation Viking Hammer began at the far east of Kurdistan. The mission was to destroy a Kurd terrorist group called Ansar al-Islam, which had created an "enclave" in Kurdistan. According to the Americans, this Islamic group was alleged to have links with Al-Qaeda. Viking Hammer began with a series of cruise missiles striking the Islamic group's positions and causing heavy casualties. This obliged Ansar al-Islam to leave the mountains and to settle in the small city of Khurma. Its 700 elements were supplemented by 1,500 combatants from the so called *"Komali i-Islami Kurdistan"* Islamist group.

They dug foxholes around the small city. On Friday, some 6,000 Peshmegas and a thirty or so members of Special Forces assaulted the Ansar al-Islam guerrilla's strong point. Every unit of Peshmergas, which meant about 400 men, had

two Green Beret and a Combat Control Team in charge of liaising with the Special Forces command in Sulemanieh and to designate targets for air strikes.

True is the fact that at the beginning, the relative strength ratio was one to ten for the pro-American Kurds as their enemies had been worn out by endless night bombardments of F-14, F-18, B-52, and their positions stricken by AC-130 gunships. With the exception of some firefights, Peshmegas reoccupied the " enclave " in less than a day, capturing ten or so Ansar al-Islam elements handed over to the CIA for interrogation.

Crushed down in the south and pinned down in the north

SF teams reported regularly Republican Guard units tried to reinforce the " Medina " division in southern Baghdad. However, the Iraqis did not take advantage of the sand-storm enabling days of rest, to really reorganize. Therefore, on 31 March at dawn, the Vth Corps commander launched five simultaneous attacks: 2nd Brigade of the 82nd Division attac-

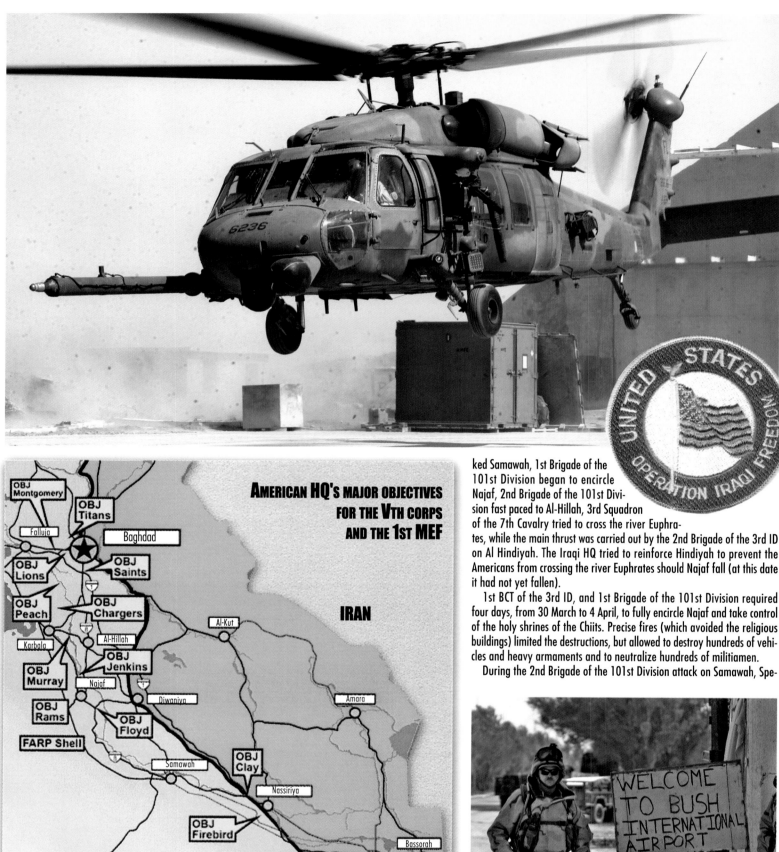

(DOD photo)

Map labels

OBJ Montgomery
OBJ Titans
Falluja
Baghdad
OBJ Lions
OBJ Saints
OBJ Peach
OBJ Chargers
Al-Kut
Karbala
Al-Hillah
OBJ Jenkins
OBJ Murray
Najaf
Diwaniya
Amara
OBJ Rams
OBJ Floyd
FARP Shell
Samawah
OBJ Clay
Nassiriya
OBJ Firebird
Bassorah
RRP Exxon
I MEF XXX V CORPS
KUWAIT
Kuwait City
IRAN

AMERICAN HQ'S MAJOR OBJECTIVES FOR THE VTH CORPS AND THE 1ST MEF

ked Samawah, 1st Brigade of the 101st Division began to encircle Najaf, 2nd Brigade of the 101st Division fast paced to Al-Hillah, 3rd Squadron of the 7th Cavalry tried to cross the river Euphrates, while the main thrust was carried out by the 2nd Brigade of the 3rd ID on Al Hindiyah. The Iraqi HQ tried to reinforce Hindiyah to prevent the Americans from crossing the river Euphrates should Najaf fall (at this date it had not yet fallen).

1st BCT of the 3rd ID, and 1st Brigade of the 101st Division required four days, from 30 March to 4 April, to fully encircle Najaf and take control of the holy shrines of the Chiits. Precise fires (which avoided the religious buildings) limited the destructions, but allowed to destroy hundreds of vehicles and heavy armaments and to neutralize hundreds of militiamen.

During the 2nd Brigade of the 101st Division attack on Samawah, Spe-

18

Left.
On 3 April 2003, a HH-60 Pave Hawk of the of the USAF's 301st Rescue Squadron takes off for an operational mission. At this time, there are tens of aircraft flying over Iraq. Risks that they may be shot down or have technical problems are high. This is why Rescue units are on a permanent alert status. They carried out more than 55 rescue operations and save 70 people. *(Photo USAF)*

Previous page, bottom.
On 28 March, USAF personnel of the 621st Air Mobility Group take possession of the Talil air base in the south of the country. Thus, the coalition has a forward base for its SF's aircraft and other fighter aircraft. *(Photo USAF)*

Right.
In Kurdistan, facing tens of Iraqi divisions, the Green Berets advance on the "Green Line" while MH-53 Pave low IV helicopters of the 21st Special Operations Squadron drop SF teams in Iraq and supply the units close to the front line. *(Photo USAF)*

cial Forces followed in quasi real time the enemy movements in the zone and identified twenty mortars in the city. AC-130 and A-10 continuously flying over in the sky destroyed those mortar positions, as well as the Baath party HQ: Iraqi attacks stopped.

Northern and western special units continued on harassing the Iraqi forces, preventing them from moving toward Baghdad. On 30 March, JSOTF-North Special Forces carried out a series of attacks, along with the Kurds, against the 4th Iraqi Division, the day after against the 2nd ID, and on 2 April against the 8th and 38th ID.

Searching the desert

The well media-covered operation to rescue Private Jessica Lynch in Nassiriya took place on the 1st of April. On their side, JSOTF-West elements continued on methodically destroying all Iraqi units stationed in an area 100 kilometres deep toward the Jordan border. They literally searched the desert looking for ballistic missiles launchers. Moving further in central Iraq, Task Force 20 captured the Hadithah dam in order to prevent the Iraqis from destroying and subsequently flooding the Euphrates River valley. For almost three weeks, Rangers of the 3rd Battalion of the 75th Ranger Regiment fought against determined Iraqi units to keep that objective. It was not until 19 April that the 1st compa-

ny, 502nd Infantry Regiment, 101st Division, relieved the Rangers in line.

JSOTF-West's operations success decided the coalition's command to amplify the on going actions: C Company, 2-70 Armour Regiment, 3rd ID was sent hundreds of kilometres from its parent unit to H-1 air base in western Iraq for the benefit of the coalition's Special Forces. Thus, on 2 April, USAF C-17 airlifted ten M1 tanks, three M-113, a FST-V air

(Continued on page 22)

For the first time with such amplitude, PsyOps of the Special Forces were at the heart of the operations, working with the front line units to convince the Iraqi soldiers to surrender. Here is a 9th PsyOps Battalion's Humvee near Rumaylah.
(Photo Yves Debay)

RECAPTURING THE REBELS' CITADELS

Phase 1 consisted in encircling the rebel cities. Entrances had to be controlled and outskirts to be watched. To block a city of several hundred inhabitants, the Americans rarely employed more than one Brigade, reinforced with Iraqi forces, artillery and helicopter units, and specialized groups. Thus, Task Force Iron Dukes assumed a COIN mission in Najaf for five weeks in April and May 2004. The TF consisted of four combined-arms manoeuvre "Teams". It had 30 Abrams tanks and a hundred or so armoured Humvee; one Military Police company, one combat Engineer company, as well as a Special Forces detachment, a PsyOps team, two war dog teams, and two Civil Affairs teams. Concerning Artillery combat support, there were six 155 mm self-propelled Paladin guns and four 120 mm mortars. Lastly, the Task Force also integrated aerial scout weapons teams (OH-58D Kiowa Warrior) and several F-16 and AC-130 Gunships.

From the positions around the city, artillery fired on all enemies spotted by the target designation teams, but also by combat controllers in helicopters, and obviously by UAVs.

During the siege of Fallujah, from October to November 2004, air strikes were combined with drops of PsyOps-created flyers and messages delivered by speakerphones inviting the population to leave the city. Within less than a week, two thirds of Fallujah population had left. The rebellion had lost its best protection.

After the outer city action ended, did the inner city operations began. They aimed at taking control of the political and administrative centres, to divide up the built up area in different zones classified as friendly, enemy or uncertain, and then treated accordingly. Americans systematically used armoured columns supported by low-flying helicopters, mid-altitude AC-130 Gunships and F-16 at more than 3 000 metres. They entered into the urban part of the city and blasted all strong points of spotted resistance.

In Fallujah, Marines combined mounted combat with armoured columns, and dismounted fights, often taking place on the roofs. Thus, in less than an hour, armoured columns could penetrate several kilometres into a dense and defended built in area.

They could even perform zone blocking actions against precise objectives. ❐

On 21 March 2003, a combined team of members of the 9th PsyOps Battalion and British soldiers watch the evolution of the combats between Safwan and Bassorah. From the lessons learnt of the first Gulf War, the Iraqis set up a fibber optic network to secure their communications. As a priority target for the coalition's forces, this network was deciphered, and then bugged with IT worms before being destroyed.
(Photo Yves Debay)

support vehicle, three tank lorries and three transport vehicles. The armoured company was then attached to the 1st Battalion, 75th Ranger Regimen, moving east towards Baghdad. The mission was to destroy the Iraqi units' vicinities of Bayji-Tikrit. In addition to that mission, C Company had to support SF which controlled Route 1 to Syria (3). The objective was to prevent Baath party leaders from fleeing to Syria.

Facing Baghdad

On 2 April, 1st BCT and 3rd BCT of the 3rd ID crossed the Karbala plateau which was lightly defended - while American expectations were that the " Medina " Division would make a strong point of this strategic position. In mid-afternoon vanguard units crossed the Euphrates River. On 3 April,

the Iraqis tried a counter-attack with the 10th Armoured Brigade of the " Medina " Division, supported by a commando battalion of the Republican Guard. In an hour, 2nd BCT destroyed 15 T-72 tanks and 30 M-113. The first Iraqi attempt to stop American forces had failed.

On 4 April, V Corps continue its advance. Coalition's forces were surprised to see buried tanks with their guns aiming south while American armoured vehicles arrived from the south-west. By the end of the day the 2nd BCT had reached its objective, the Routes 1 and 8 crossroads before Bagdad. It had destroyed 33 T-72, 19 T-55, 2 T-62, 12 MTLB, 50 Artillery pieces, 6 BM-21, 127 lorries, and killed some 700 enemies.

3rd ID units' commanders ordered to speed up and to make a hasty attack to capture Baghdad airport. SF gathe-

Above.
During the March and April 2003 operations the coalition had five USAF Rescue Squadrons. In addition it also had two reserve units of the Navy, the Helicopter Rescue Squadron 4 and the helicopter Rescue Squadron 5, meaning a total of 180 personnel and eight HH-60 Seahawk helicopters. The Marines also had several rescue teams called Tactical Recovery of Aircraft and Personnel (TRAP) flying CH-53. TRAP worked for the 1st Marine Division. Lastly, the Army had Assistance Response Teams "DART" called Raptor, formed from the 5th Battalion of the 158th Aviation Regiment, flying UH-60L.
(Photo DOD)

Below, left. Two USAF Combat Controllers Teams arrive to see "the results" in one of the Republican Guard barracks not far from Baghdad International Airport, one day after the zone was seized. As what they had done in Afghanistan in 2001, CCT made a huge work during *Iraqi Freedom.*
(Photo USAF)

red intelligence of the region reported that the 17th Brigade of the Division that had blocked the road between the airport and the capital could be in the vicinities.

But other intelligence reports said the 8th Brigade of the " Hammourabi " Division was in northern Baghdad, while a special Battalion of the Republican Guard and two Light Infantry Brigades supported by about fifteen thousand paramilitary troops were still in the city. At 0038 on 4 April, armoured vehicles of Task Force 3-69 Armoured Regiment were on Baghdad international airport runway. Beginning of the morning, various Iraqi points, including some held by Saddam's Special Forces, were " cleaned " one after the other.

On 3 April, 1st BCT moved west towards Routes 1 and 8 crossroads in order to protect the 3rd ID western and northern flanks. It had to fight an armoured battalion of the Republican Guard which abandoned twenty T-72 some fifteen minutes later.

3. It remained along with the Special Forces from 2 to 24 April 2003.

Left.
Navy mine clearers, attached to SEAL teams during Iraqi Freedom, watch the local population around the runway of Irbil in Kurdistan. In April, during the last week of the operations, several SF detachments were deployed in Kurdistan from Jordan to attack the Iraqis from the north.
(Photo USAF)

Below.
At the end of March 2003, a Green Beret detachment has just entered in an urban area in central Iraq. The local Iraqis seems surprised to see coalition's soldiers so far from Kuwait, as Baghdad was saying it at this time.
(Photo SOCOM)

ces which worked west of the capital and advanced in all directions.

At 0538 on 7 April, 2nd BCT moved toward Baghdad. The objective was to capture the official buildings in the centre of the capital. Iraqi defence was totally disorganized and American armoured columns were attacked by groups of soldiers and paramilitaries firing RPG and mortars only. SF vehicles had joined the armoured units.

Special Forces mission was to arrive first at the official buildings, to try to capture the Baath party leaders who had not fled yet, and to retrieve as many documents as possible. By the end of the afternoon they'd reached their objective,

Armoured raid in the capital

At this stage V Corps was ahead of its schedule: it had captured the airport and secured the southern and western positions.

The next day, Task Force 1-64 Armored Regiment of the 2nd BCT carried out an armoured reconnaissance in Baghdad, known as Thunder Run. The aim was to perform a vast encircling movement along Route 8 " to get the enemy layout ", then to link up with the 1st Brigade stationed at the airport. This superb operation was successfully carried out in two and a half hours at the cost of one death, one M-1 destroyed and several Bradleys damaged. The American HQ knew then the Iraqi defence could be broken through.

On 6 April, 3rd BCT carried out a vast encircling movement around Baghdad to block the path to the Euphrates River. The Brigade ended the day by encircling the Iraqi capital after it had defeated Special Forces, " Hammourabi " Division elements and Artillery units of the Republican Guard.

While V Corps units and Marines of I MEF, who had crossed the river Euphrates at Nassiriya, prepared to assault Baghdad, coalition's aviation efforts focused on Special For-

THE SOLDIER STRESS FACTORS

Soldiers have multiple stress factors. Theatre of almost all combats, the urban area is quelling, and because of its 3D characteristics it offers multiple origins of possible danger. Threats are often invisible: snipers, IEDs, mortar shells and ambushes; and enemy fire often arrive as a surprise.

The main offensive operations may last for a long time, several weeks in a row, and go on by day and night. They also include rapid changes of posture according to the location and time.

Thus, the same troop may carry drastically different missions within the same day, searching an area in the morning, providing humanitarian aid in the afternoon and carrying out an offensive patrol during the night. The short notices prevent from understanding the why of each mission.

The population attitude itself, which often seems unrewarding or plays a double game, may lead to a great frustration for an armed force which feels as an "outsiders".

Extract from *"War after the war. Lessons learnt from twenty months of stabilization operations in Iraq "*, by Major Michel Goya", French Doctrine magazine of CDEF (Centre for Force Employment Doctrine). ❐

Previous page, at the top.
Impressive alignment of MH-53M Pave Low IV of the 21st Special Operations Squadron on one of the runways of Irbil air field in Kurdistan. The airlift set up from Romania as of 22 March allowed the massive arrival of Special Forces and heavy equipment.
(Photo SOCOM)

Right. A Special Forces arrive to see the "results" in one of Saddam Hussein's residence during the conquest of Iraq in April 2003. To avoid aerial bombardments, the Iraqis scattered their forces, hiding them in palm tree fields and in urban areas. Several times, Artillery guns or armoured vehicles were placed near schools, mosques or houses.
(Photo DOD)

Previous page, at the bottom.
American Special Forces command also decided to deploy Civil Affairs units on the front line. They participated in the operations (as the PsyOps), trying to explain what the *Iraqi Freedom* nature was to the population.

Previous page, Inset. Famous picture of Private Jessica Lynched the SF rescued at the Nassiriya hospital on 1 April 2003, during a Army/Air Force/Navy combined operation.
(Photo DOD)

the avenue where the military parades took place.

In the night, at 0415, Iraqi forces made a counter-attack attempt (with units of the Republican Guard and paramilitaries) crossing the river Euphrates. But it was beaten off at the price of severe casualties.

While the media focused on the Spartan Brigade (2nd BCT) which was already in central Baghdad, Hammer Brigade (3rd BCT) was going to fight the hardest urban battle of this campaign. The Iraqis attempted to recapture a bridge on the Tigris River on route 1, by combining an artillery barrage and a counter-attack.

During the whole night of 6 to 7 April, with a surge of intensity around 0600, tens of armoured and hundreds of soldiers tried to capture the bridge.

Combats went on for forty eight hours, preventing 3rd ID to link up with the marines as it had been planned to do so within ten hours.

On 8 April, after three days of fights, 3rd BCT carried out its last attack of the campaign on the right bank of the Tigris River along Route 1, and " cleaned " the last Iraqi positions.

In the south, Australian and British combat divers proceeded with the mine clearing of the Umm-Qasr port waters and maritime accesses.

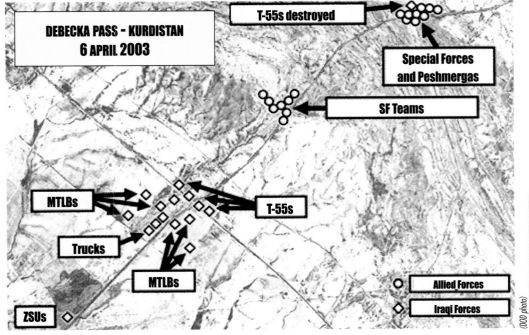

DEBECKA PASS - KURDISTAN
6 APRIL 2003

T-55s destroyed

Special Forces and Peshmergas

SF Teams

MTLBs

T-55s

Trucks

MTLBs

ZSUs

◇ Allied Forces
◇ Iraqi Forces

(DOD photo)

SF COMMANDS

SF had four chains of command involved in operation *Iraqi Freedom* under the lead of General Tommy Franks, CINC of Central Command:
- Special Operations Central Command,
- Combined Joint Special Task Force-West,
- Combined Special Task Force-North,
and Naval Special Warfare Task Force. ❐

" Special Forces " crushed Iraqi armoured

One of the last coordinated operations the Iraqi forces carried out took place on 6 April on the " Green Line " against a strong point held by Green Berets. Nicknamed " Alamo " and located on the Debecka hills, this position overlooked a wide valley the Iraqi wanted to use to try their break through. Although outnumbered by their assailants, Special Forces were over equipped:.50 calibre machine guns, Mk-19 automatic grenade-launchers, 60 mm mortars, not forgetting the brand new Javelin missile-launchers. Moreover, they had USAF and Navy CAS as they had laser target designators. The Iraqis launched their attack with a T-55 platoon, two mechanized platoons aboard armoured vehicles and additional troops aboard heavy vehicles.

To support this attack, the Iraqi command had decided to crush the American position with Artillery 122 mm guns, 120 mm mortars and 57 mm air defence pieces. Then, armoured vehicles attacked straight to " Alamo " from the road. Simultaneously armoured vehicles scattered in the valley around the road. Javelin anti-tank missiles proved very effective against the Iraqi tanks which, despite their superiority, were not able to reach a sufficiently close distance to open fire. In the meantime, Infantry had dismounted with heavy machine guns and grenade-launchers. Besides, all supporting positions were systematically crushed by the coalition's aviation. In less than an hour everything was over. Special Forces had stopped an armoured attack without any casualties: Javelin effectiveness had been devastating for the T-55. One member of the Special Forces became the " first Javelin ace " with a record of two ICV (Infantry Combat Vehicle) and three transport vehicles destroyed.

This attack was the last sudden burst of the northern Iraqi forces. JSOTF-North units continued in their advance. They seized Irbil on 1 April and Kirkuk on 10 April, whose airport had been captured by 10 SFG elements along with Peshmegas some days before. In a second phase, they opened the way to I MEF units as well as 101st Airborne Division's in charge of securing Mosul.

Close the borders

On 7 April, a statement announced the coalition had gained full air superiority over Iraq. Task Force 20 launched its motorized detachments to secure the Syria-Iraq border the next day. The aim was to prevent Iraqi leaders from fleeing. At the same time, 1st Marine Division entered into Baghdad. The day after, Army and Marine units linked up at the heart of the Iraqi capital.

North of the country, 173rd Airborne Brigade paratroopers fought for the first time when they entered into Kirkuk with SF on 10 April. They faced Republican Guard units still resisting. In Baghdad, any organized resistance had ended.

On 11 April, on the motorway to Jordan, Rangers stopped a bus and arrested 59 Iraqis. In a briefcase were $ 630,000 and a document saying that a $ 1,000 reward would be awarded for any American soldier killed.

That same day, Central Command published the famous Iraq's 55 most-wanted deck of playing cards (on 28 May, 27 of them surrendered or had been captured). At this time combats had virtually come to an end.

Post war

Several Generals of CENTCOM have said that operation Iraqi Freedom stabilisation phase had not been extensively

THE IRAQI GUERILLA

First Iraqi guerrilla attacks began as early as the second half of May 2003. At the time they were small groups of some people, including criminals or unemployed persons paid " by the action " by former security services members called moubhabarak. These teams came from the various tribes and families Saddam Hussein relied on.

These insurgents' objective was to undermine the GI's morale and to recover some prestige with the Sunnit population affected by the political turmoil. By no means were these not-tactically-significant actions able to beat the American army, but 200 to 300 American soldiers were killed or injured by these attacks.

Subsequent to the lack of strength: Syrian and Iranian borders were totally crossable - a situation not in favour of the Syrian, Iranian, and even Saudi governments' ambiguous policy. However, abandoned armament stocks were so numerous that the guerrilla had no need to get its "supply" from abroad, with the exception of money. The situation was also true for men: no lack of combatants - even though American intelligence services pretended for a long time that hundreds of foreign volunteers fought in Iraq.

The guerrilla's command network was more complex than the Americans had first thought. As a matter of fact, there were family or tribal link networks during the first months. But, over time, it changed to a more ideological aspect with Jihadists, followed by foreigners, and then opponents of all sorts. The Sunnit guerrilla was of a decentralized type: It had no supreme leader or a dominant ideology, hence the difficulty to destroy these cells which multiplied and varied according to the action.

By the end of August 2003, guerrilla groups were active in the entire Sunnit triangle. Thanks to the Arabic television channels and to some networks of Mosques (one has to admit it), the

Photos.
The American Special Forces fight platoon or section level Iraqi paramilitary groups. The latter are armed with RPG, heavy machine guns and air defence civilian-vehicle-mounted pieces.
Their favourite tactics are: Mortar and small calibre weapon attacks, ambushes with RPG along the supply axes.
The American soldiers always have difficulties to spot the Iraqi rebels as they fight in civilian clothes and drive civilian cars.
(Photos MAMS)

guerrilla organizations had succeeded in taking the minds over. However, if Iraqi rebels had won a " psycho-political victory ", their losses were huge. That is why they tried to organize themselves and to create regional command cells to better plan their actions. On 3 September, a 4th Infantry Division's unit was attacked by a hundred or so insurgents armed with heavy machine guns, RPG and mortars. GIs were able to disengage only thanks to some attack helicopters and aviation help.

Then came the time of mass attacks with suicide car bombs: destruction of the UN office in Baghdad on 19 September, attack in Najaf on 29 September, with 80 deaths… Then were harassments of snipers, followed by mortar attacks and IED along the roads that the logistics convoys used. On top of that were political actions, with assassinations and high jacking; economical actions, with sabotages of strategic sites (pipelines, power station, etc.) and destructions of civilian enterprises; psychological actions, with retaliations against " collaborators ", but also through aid actions.

By the end of October, the Americans had put their actions relatively on hold. Therefore, the rebels took advantage of the situation to launch an offensive in the Sunnit triangle. Coalition's losses doubled in some months (one third of the losses were

in convoys). Insurgents took advantage of the medium and low flying altitude of the American helicopters to shoot them down.

Insurgent motivations were diverse. Many unemployed Iraqi paid for their actions against the Americans did it only for money. On the contrary, others were led by revenge or despair, such as the religious fanatics and the nationalists. Behaviour was more and more aggressive, even suicidal. And cases multiplied such as insurgents with no precise objective driving suicide attacks against an Iraqi police building or close to an American vehicle where it would blast.

As of April 2004, rebels moved to a next step in their war against the Americans. Zones like Fallujah, Latifiya, Koufa, Najaf, Ramadi, Sadr City, Samarra, Tall Afar and Tikrit, were created and entirely ruled by the insurgents. These strong points were a threat to the coalition's logistics routes from Kuwait or Jordan. Thus, in Fallujah during a screening of an area, 1st MEF's Marines faced relatively well-armed organized units that held the city. Several days of fight were needed, including the aviation help, to overcome it. But the news was that the Chiit resistance appeared in the " *city in the city* ", the Sadr City district of Baghdad, with the Mahdi army of Ayatollah Moqtada al-Sadr. The latter was isolated within his community, and so he had secretly organized his armed militia.

After he had killed and mutilated four American contractors — in a "famous" media-filmed-and-broadcasted sequence — the coalition's provisional authority decided to annihilate his militia.

Order had to be restored before the transfer of power to a new Iraqi government at the end of June 2004. During the Najaf battle, the Mahdi's army proved that its tactical know-how was basic. Thus, Marines were surprised to discover snipers in " too obvious " places, such as the minaret of a mosque, and stay there until they got killed. Similarly, their armament was old and badly maintained. However, insurgents demonstrated courage and cleverness several times. RPG shooters for example - a major element in this battle - had hand-changed the munitions security to make it explode within a 50 metre radius. They systematically fired on armoured vehicles from less than ten metres, aiming at the Bradley's vulnerable missile launcher pod. Obviously the odds to remain alive were few. Insurgents also used Dragunov SVD precise rifles to fire on vehicles' crews or hit American soldiers above or below their bullet-proof vests. Not only did these militia show courage and cleverness during the urban firefights like in Fallujah, but the way they used the terrain was also remarkable. Strong points were linked by an underground network between houses and placed against protected buildings, schools, public places and hospitals. In Fallujah, Marines faced the same methods of combat that the Japanese had used during the war in the Pacific: waiting for days hidden in cellars and other corners, insurgents let the enemy pass through, and then fired at them from behind before being killed themselves.

To stop the armoured advance in Fallujah, rebels massively used either IEDs (shells or mines) to make buildings fall when armoured vehicles went by, or suicide car bombs. ❑

planned. Many Americans were surprised at the Iraqi reactions after the military operations had ended: They thought the latter expected liberty only.

But after tens of years of war, embargo, and political repressive measures, the Iraqi population expected a minimum of physical and material security.

The gap between the deployed forces and the inability to provide security against the first weeks' lootings led to the incomprehension between the Iraqi people and the American soldiers which led to the guerrilla warfare.

Therefore, the USA were going to face " *the ever growing phenomenon of guerrilla* "with an army structured to wage a conventional war, in the words of a French military expert.

Instead of taking advantage of the first post-Saddam Hussein days to provide security and establish a policy radically different from the former dictator, Paul Bremer, the Ame-

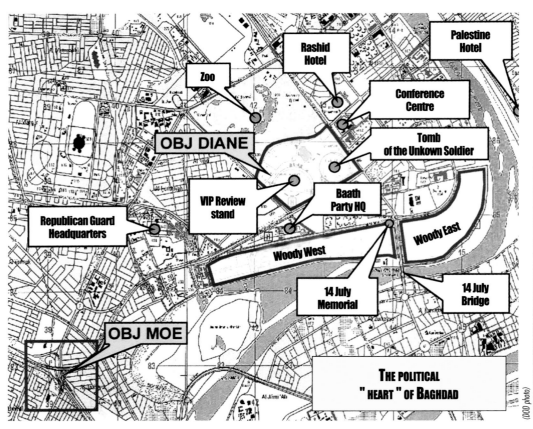

THE POLITICAL " HEART " OF BAGHDAD

Rashid Hotel

Palestine Hotel

Zoo

Conference Centre

OBJ DIANE

Tomb of the Unkown Soldier

VIP Review stand

Baath Party HQ

Republican Guard Headquarters

Woody East

Woody West

14 July Memorial

14 July Bridge

OBJ MOE

(DOD photo)

COIN OPERATIONS

Guerrilla was a real challenge for the high American hierarchy. It had trouble to evolve in the Iraqi conflict which was not regarded as a conventional war. At the beginning of 2004, the creation of a specialized cell within the Command and General Staff College (CGSC) allowes analysis of the current operations and progress proposals in terms of counter-insurgency operations or COIN. The first document this newly created cell issued was the Field Manual (FM) 3-07.22 about counter-insurgency. It consisted of two parts:

Part 1 deals with COIN operations whose aim is to directly attack the political cells and armed groups, and break their network and the conditions which favour their actions;

Part 2 gathers all aspects of violence containment and stabilization. These differentiated aspects allow maintaining the tasks performed by conventional forces separated from those carried out by units such as the Special Forces in charge of the most specific counter-guerrilla operations. ❑

Above. A PsyOps team integrated in a regular unit prepares for a mission in Baghdad. After the 2003 major ground operations, the Americans understood the vital need for recreating an Iraqi Army. They also played with the ethnic rivalries, using Kurd units in Sunnite regions for example. *(Photo SOCOM)*

Next page. When advancing towards Baghdad, the American units several times faced a strong resistance whether from the regular units or militiamen which led to personnel and equipment casualty. Here is a M1A1 tank destroyed by a highly explosive charge. *(Photo DOD)*

rican administrator made the huge error of suppressing all current security services leading the country to chaos.

Thus Security fell on the shoulders of the coalition's armies which were not enough to control all the official buildings and the hundreds of abandoned armaments depots, and of course, hadn't got enough time to patrol the thousands of kilometres of the borders.

During the first weeks of May 2003, combat units were unable to communicate with the people. Interpreters were

AMERICAN FORCES IN " INDIAN TERRITORY "

The American HQ first reacted by protecting its forces in " Indian territory ", nickname of the Sunnit triangle. Units settled in fourteen major bases: the Forward Operating Bases or FOB, nicknamed " forts ". They were located on the outskirts of the cities, away from the many urban-imbedded positions, away from suicide bombings and mortar fires.

However, rebuilding the infrastructure and protecting the logistics convoys required a more offensive attitude. To protect those who were no longer in the " rear ", soldiers were equipped with more effective bullet-proof vests, the IBAS (Individual Body Armor Systems) and heavier armament, and vehicles got more armoured.

Special Forces units worked with the Rapid Equipping Force (REF) personnel, an organization established in 2002 to provide a fast answer to real problems that units met in the field. Together with the Centre for Army Lessons Learned (CALL) which gathers all the information from the theatre of operations, and with the Training and Doctrine Command (TRADOC), REF personnel looked for solutions that could be implemented in less than three months (it is known that traditional procedures require an average seven years per programme...). As of June 2003, REF focussed on urban intelligence, information circulation, fire precision, non-lethal armaments and better adapted training programmes.

Within a month, to counter balance the lack of strength, a dynamic dividing up system was set up. It included mobile and permanent check points, patrols, screening of areas, searches and the establishment of Quick Reaction Forces.

However, " immersion within the population " was totally artificial. Not speaking the local language was a strong reason for it, but patrols attitude that systematically aimed at the passers by, or soldiers not removing their sun glasses when speaking to people chocked the Iraqi population...

Not to mention the civilian collateral damages which remained significant, even though urban clashes with rebels always turned in favour of the Americans. ❏

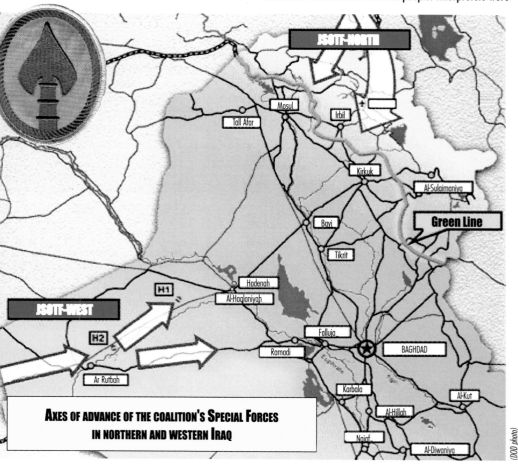

JSOTF-NORTH

Mosul
Tall Afar
Irbil
Al-Sulaimaniya

Kirkuk

Bayi
Green Line

Tikrit

Hadenah
Al-Haglaniyah

JSOTF-WEST
H1
H2
Falluja
Ramadi
BAGHDAD

Ar Rutbah
Karbala
Al-Kut

Al-Hillah

AXES OF ADVANCE OF THE COALITION'S SPECIAL FORCES IN NORTHERN AND WESTERN IRAQ

Najaf
Al-Diwaniya

(DOD photo)

THE " BODY COUNT " POLICY

The high American Command strongly thought that the capture of any hiding former regime's dignitaries would seriously affect the guerrilla, and they also had to kill a maximum of rebels (where is the link?). It was the return of the " Body Count " policy already applied in Vietnam. To set up the assessments, Americans looked at the ratio friendly and enemy losses to the number of attacks. Every patrol provided a "lessons learnt" report which fed the information network called BOLO (Be-on-the-look-out) which allowed refining the modes of operation. With each new tactic the rebels implemented a BALO report was written.

During the second half of 2003, the two major units located north of Baghdad, the 4th Infantry Division and the 101st Airborne Division had totally opposite policies. The first one copied an Israeli policy. It isolated the guerrilla by answering with artillery fires to mortar attacks, thus destroying the rebels houses and arresting their families. The second one followed the British " velvet glove " method which aims at gaining the population's trust. ❏

Patrol on foot for this AFSOC PJ
in the Sunnite region near Baghdad in 2004.
During the months which followed the major operations,
experts explain the coalition's success by the incompetence
and the lower level of the Iraqi forces. It's partly true.
However, reality is that coalition's soldiers,
airmen and sailors proved they were better trained
and adapted faster than their opponents to the situation.
(Photo USAF)

Above.
Special Forces dismount to counter enemy fire
in a "movie directed type " image. However, this 2005
photo is a typical one of the today's combats, with an evolution
of both the BDU and the additional protections
affixed on the Humvee.
The fact is that enemy attacks come from IED in majority,
without a front attack as it used to be in 2003.
(RR)

so few that they accounted for only one per battalion.

Translation was still the Special Forces domain, especially the PsyOps', who were also only a few and they couldn't be everywhere.

Anti-American attacks multiplied by the end of May which shut any door that would have led to closing the combat phase. The war against the Iraqi guerrilla began. ❐

SOLDIERS' MORALE REMAINED STABLE.

In 2004, there were two deaths per day on average, which did not compare to Vietnam (twenty deaths a day between 1965 and 1972) or what the French suffered in Algeria (ten deaths per day between 1955 and 1962).

The death/wounded ratio of one to ten in Iraq (against one to five in Vietnam), was the lowest ever recorded. Moreover, mobile surgery teams were capable of setting up a field hospital in sixty minutes. ❐

THE GREEN BERETS AHEAD
OF THE OPERATIONS

On 14 February 2003, there were about 800 green berets from the 5th Special Forces Group (SFG) of Fort Campbell (Kentucky) discreetly deployed over several bases in Djibouti. With them were helicopters of the 3rd Battalion of the 160th SOAR. Colonel John Mulholland, who headed the 5th SFG, became the SOF Task Force-West boss in deed though not in name. And his unit, normally comprising 1 400 people, jumped to 3 500 personnel during the operation.

The various SFG[1] units arrived in Kuwait and in Saudi Arabia fifteen days before the military operations began. Some liaison detachments were also discreetly sent to Jordan in order to not bother the Arabian policy of Amman. But the first personnel of the Special Forces did not arrive in Kurdistan, north of Iraq, until 23 March.

IN WESTERN IRAQ

The hunt for the Scud

Night had almost come when the first soldiers of the B Company[2], 1st Battalion of the famous 5th Special Forces Group, supported by soldiers of the Florida National Guard dug soft-

ly, with napkins, a breach in the huge earth and sand levee which made up the Iraq-Kuwait border. Major Jim Gavrilis, B Company leader was anxious while watching his men digging the sand to make the vehicles cross the obstacle. When at last the first Humvee entered Iraq, Florida National guardsmen formed a guard of honour at the foot of the Stars and Stripes and the Florida State flag poles, waving good luck to their Special Forces comrades.

Some hours later, farther south, ODA 531 (Operational Detachment-Alpha), Charly Com-

---

1. American Special Forces are headed by Brigadier General Gary Harrell, Commander of the Middle-East Special Forces, stationed at the As Saliyah headquarter in Qatar.
2. B Company also has a three-man NRBC team, a four-man electronic warfare team, a mechanic and a USAF Tactical Air Control Personnel (TACP), a targeting and air-control specialist.

A Special Forces of the 5th Special Forces Group, in southern Iraq, end of March 2003.
This SF wears a Safariland ELCS vest on a Spear bullet-proof vest. The ELCS vest is a modular platform providing two different types of plates for pouches. The Spear bullet-proof vest has Kevlar inserts providing a class IIIA ballistic protection. The M4 remains the most found carbine in this theatre of operations. Since Afghanistan, the American Special Forces have often replaced the helmet with a baseball type cap when carrying out Search and Destroy missions.

Title.
In the turret of his Humvee, a Green Beret behind a 40 mm Mk 19 grenade launcher provides protection to a convoy. Special Forces casualty has been remarkably low compared to the number of men engaged during Iraqi Freedom. Only six SF were killed.

Left. For the first time during operation *Iraqi Freedom*, complete ODA units were used as liaison between the major units. Thus, three detachments of ODA 916 provided the liaisons for the 3rd Infantry Division command, the 3rd Brigade of the 3rd ID and the 3-7 Cav.
(Photo SOCOM)

Right.
Here in Fallujah a year later, Special Forces are still deployed in Iraq. In addition to the specific fleeing-Iraqi-leaders hunt missions, SF also worked with the regular units against the guerrilla. It is worth noticing that already in 2004, the " regular " soldiers' had almost the same equipment as the SF's one.
(Photo DOD)

Below
In central Iraq, one of the ODA of the 5th SFG waits for his orders. During *Iraqi Freedom*, all Army SF units had a heavily armed Humvee called GMV (Ground Mobility Vehicle).
(Photo SOCOM)

The Special Forces of the 5th SFG in contact. The Green Berets have just designated Iraqi vehicles, with militiamen aboard, as targets to the coalition's aviation. While the Special Forces make sure the targets have been hit, one of them, equipped with a 7.62 mm M 24 SWS precision rifle and a Leupold Ultra M3A scope, checks that the surviving Iraqis don't try to flee.
(Photo 5th SFG)

Below. One of the " heavy " vehicles of the 5th Special Forces Group during a mission in the southern, western and central Iraq, between March and April. It is a specially-modified Special Forces LMTV where the cabin roof has been replaced with two machine guns.
(Photo SOCOM)

pany, did not discreetly blow up obstacles built on the levee. After several days of study of the avenues of advance, missions, timing, and obstacles of the Iraqi forces, Lieutenant-colonel Chris Haas, 1st Battalion Commander, had decided his fif-

teen teams would break the levee at two breaches only. But teams had to scatter as fast as possible once they had crossed the breaches because the firing of a tactical missile was still a possible threat, all the more so as nobody knew whether all ground surveillance radars had been destroyed.

ODAs of the two companies of the 1st battalion, 5th SFG, were stationed for fifteen days hidden in several camps in the Kuwaiti desert.

Speed was the key to success since hostilities had been prompted earlier-than-planned, some hours before dawn, on 20 March 2003, after an F-117 stealth fighter struck against a building where Saddam Hussein and his sons were alleged to be. Fortunately, coalition's Special Forces teams were already in Iraq. The 1st Battalion's primary mission was to hunt Iraqi ballistic missile launchers, Scud in particular, to prevent Saddam from using them against his neighbours, especially Israel. At this

"IRAQI FREEDOM" HAS NOTHING TO DO WITH "DESERT STORM"

The Special Forces' success in Afghanistan proved that they had capabilities useful for the conventional forces. If their missions had been few during the first Gulf war in 1991, Central Command commander in chief decided that this time they would play a key role in Iraqi Freedom. A key factor was certainly that the Secretary of Defense Donald Rumsfeld was an enthusiastic Special Forces supporter.

The key to success in a desert resides in preparation. Thus, Special Forces Groups' members studied for weeks Desert Storm reports and tried not to repeat the same errors. The first Gulf war had under estimated the Scud threat, and methods to counter missiles launches (86 launches overall) had been inadequate. The coalition's aviation had not been able to find the launch pads; Patriot's counter-missile defence had not been able to intercept the missiles.

Lastly the " counter-Scud " teams consisting of American and British Special Forces, moving on foot most of the time, had been truly vulnerable because of their limited range of action (see the famous SAS mission *"Bravo Two Zero"*).

One lesson learnt from Desert Storm was, on the one hand, that the aviation could not spot the Iraqi missiles and, on the other hand, that forces in charge of hunting them had to be very mobile, stealthy and sufficiently powered to be able to fight more numerous enemies. ❐

time, the Pentagon estimate was that Iraq still had about thirty of them.

To this aim, several teams, including ODA 521, had to cross more than 300 kilometres as fast as possible in order to perform their marshalling before dawn around the city of Ramadi where ground-to-ground missiles were alleged to be. For months, Special Forces had trained in the desert, in California and in the Middle-East, to drive at more than 100 kilometres per hour, wearing night-vision goggles. However, even though they were equipped with the most precise maps, they couldn't avoid a not-indicated wadi (a crack)...

The Special Forces HQ had divided the west Iraqi desert into sectors. A team had been assigned to each sector and was in charge of searching from which site the alleged missiles could be fired. Thanks to satellite photographs everything had been identified: resupply areas and possible missile launch pads,

On 26 March 2003, during the sand storm which swept the south and centre of Iraq, the Coalition's troops take a rest, while the Special Forces have to wait the end of the storm. Here, a LMTV transport vehicle of the 1st Battalion, 5th SFG, equipped with a 40 mm Mk 19 grenade launcher. (Photo 55th SFG)

The battle of Ar Rutba

0 — 5
Kilometres

Wadi Hawran

Enemy reinforcements

Ar Rutba

ODA 523

ODA 524

ODA 521

ODA 525

See inset below

North

21 March 2003

AOB 520

Wadi Hawran

IRAQ

Area of main map

Special Forces
Combat
Trenches
Roads

Iraqui - Troops

Close Air support strike

525 Mounted Patrol

Special Reconnaissance team location

525 Initial contact

Close Air support strike

525 Ambush

0 — 2 km.

Source: U.S. Army Special Operations Command

routes, railroads, tanks. Thus, every square meter of the desert had been observed and each team had been given around a hundred priority targets to reconnoitre. For days, Special Forces had studied these photographs, checking bridges and routes to see where the missile-launchers could go. What had also been done was an assessment of the infiltration and extraction axes, as well as an estimate of the enemy forces in the various areas that included the local population, the tribal, political, and religious bounds.

The third part of the strategy the Special Forces had set up was to closely link their very mobile force to the USAF's aircraft, in the same way it had been implemented in the Afghan operations. A fleet of F-16, A-10 and B-52 would be in contact,

27/7, with the SF which would designate every target.

During the conflict's first night, the Charlie Company's seven ODA primary targets were the camps and air bases in the vicinities of the Habaniyah, Mudyasis and Nukhyab cities. Bravo

Special Forces of the 5th Special Forces Group, southern Iraq, end of March 2003. Besides the ever found M4 SOPMOD carbine, the Beretta M9 pistol fielded in the 80's, is often replaced with the old "immortal" Colt 1911 .45 calibre. The MBITR (Multiband Inter/Intra Team Radio) radio remains the most found equipment. Motorola SABER radios may also be found. They are part of the PRC-68 family as are the PRC 126 and 128. Several helmets have been developed such as the Peltor Comtac which provides both an active electronic protection against the explosions and an amplification of the ambient sounds.

Above.
During Iraqi Freedom, every 5th SFG's battalion
had thirty five modified Humvee they called Ground Mobility
Vehicle, and that the Green Berets nicknamed " War Pig ".
(Photo 5th SFG)

"SPECIAL FORCES GROUPS" VEHICLES

Mid-1990, 5th SFG HQ decided to put " on wheels " the whole Charlie Company.

Therefore, in addition to the 4 x 4 vehicle such as the *"modified-for Special-Forces "* Humvee, SF ordered a light 2.5 ton truck — something SF had never done so far.

Several NCO then worked on the project: they modified a vehicle nicknamed *" War Pig "* by cutting the cabin to reduce its height, install a M240 machine gun in the front, an automatic Mk19 grenade launcher at the rear, a series of external compartments for supplementary wheels, diesel, water, ammunitions and food.

Without forgetting radio and satellite communication aerials.

Below.
Like the SAS who used French ACMAT VLRA transport vehicles,
the Special Forces modified some LMTV by themselves.
(Photo 5th SFG)

War Pigs were tested for the first time in 2000 at the National Training Centre. Soon after, to carry even more equipment, SF chose to have a more than 5-ton vehicle, to be used as_*" forward rear base "*.

1st Battalion's Company C had such good results that Bravo Company was " motorized " as of July 2002.

Bravo Company went to the Jordan desert to train with its new vehicles, including the Humvee, for the unit had been "on foot" and had had no experience of a " motorized " war so far.

The two 1st Battalion's companies had a total of 35 vehicles within seven ODA just before Iraqi operations began.   ❑

Company primary target was the city of Ar Rutbah and the so called H3 air base, west of Iraq. Major Gavrilis launched his ODA against the first objectives after the war pigs had been left in a wadi, south of Ar Rutbah. ODA 521 and 525 reconnoitered the two airfields. They were empty. Then ODA 525 reconnoitered Ar Rutbah vicinities where they found the communications centre had not been bombed. They immediately reported to an AWACS hovering above, which in turn, informed an F-16 patrol. Minutes later, the first guided weapons blew the buildings up into pieces. Farther west, ODA 523 and 524 found two empty sites that would have possibly been caches for missiles. After these first searches, Major Gavrilis gave his ODA the order to " hole up " and to observe Iraqi movements and reactions. Consisting of Special Forces divers nicknamed " the sharks ", ODA 525 split into two three-man teams per Humvee to watch the two roads of Ar Rutbah. At day break, an observation team saw a group of Beduins. Sergeant First Class Andy B reported: *" It was unavoidable. As friends involved in Desert Storm in 1991 had told us, in its emptiness the desert is never still. I would even say it is full of people moving! Also, I was not surprised when I saw in my field glasses a blue pick-up leaving the Beduins' camp and drive toward Ar Rutbah ".*

" Hi guys! How long will it take these Beduins to gather their friends and come around here? " Thirty minutes later the answer was given when a white "technicals" (Since Somalia, the American name for a civilian truck outfitted with weaponry) followed by four armed pickups got out of the city. From the roof of the truck the Iraqi militia leader had spotted the FS vehicles. ODA 525 was immediately on the move: in less than a minute the Humvees were loaded and left in a hurry. After a race, first eastward, then towards the south, FS stopped at an overlooking the-zone site. That's an ideal location for an ambush. Weapons in hands they waited for their followers. Soon the militia four pickups arrived.

From safe distance,.50 machine guns (12.7 mm) burst. Iraqi drivers got immediately nervous, and panic arose within the passengers as one fired an untargeted RPG-7 rocket... Two ODA 525 supporting vehicles also started firing at the Iraqis with their 12.7 machine guns and MK 19 grenade launchers. But the danger was still real: although the pickups had been destroyed, several "technicals" full of soldiers got off Ar Rutbah to fight with the Americans.

" It's about time to react ", thought Sergeant First Class B., who took the satellite link telephone to call for a close air support via the *" liaison Scud "* channel.

" - If you don't send close air support immediately, Americans will die!

" - Will you repeat? " answered an air-controller from an AWACS.

Then B. repeated the code three times: *" Sprint. Sprint. Sprint. "* And he added: *" Do you have an aircraft around? "* The air-controller confirmed: *" Roger! "*

The closest team, ODA 521 was also called in support. *" Come here fast! "* yelled B. in the radio.

On 21 March 2003, the Ar Rutbah battle began as the first F-16 fired a series of guided-weapons at the approaching Iraqis. Soon after, four coalition's aircraft fired at all the enemy vehicles getting out of the city.

And for two hours the aerial ballet went on. Aircraft crews were guided onto the targets by radio and by the FS laser targeting devices. While the directly assaulted ODA 521 and 525 defended themselves, ODA 524 arrived and took position on a hill, supporting the northern flank of the two other teams. In less than three hours, the 524 FS team beat off three assaults carried out by more than 70 Iraqis and half a dozen light vehicles. Farther west, ODA 522 and 523 fought with enemy reinforcements sent toward Ar Rutbah, with their 12.7, 7.62, 5.56 machine guns and their 40 mm grenade launchers. *"Attack! "*

Right. In the suburbs of Najaf, beginning of April 2003, an ODA 544 Special Forces watches the Iraqi civilian's movements while his buddies talk to the local authorities. All around pro-Saddam militia are still active and continue to fight with the coalition's forces.
(Photo US Army)

Below.
An excellent photo of a " War Pig " or GMV, a modified Humvee the Special Forces used in Iraq. Here is one of the 5th Special Forces Group in central Iraq.
(Photo 5th SFG)

yelled Chief Sergeant P., driving his Humvee full speed. He stopped in front of a vehicle full of soldiers, including some lying down wounded or dead, and yelled: " Arif adik! " (Hands up!). SF blocked Ar Rutbah accesses. Under such a hail of fire, the Iraqi soldiers preferred to hold their attack and *" wait and see "*... Major Gavrilis primary objective was not to seize Ar Rutbah, for his company still had hundreds of site to recon-noitre. His mission was to cut routes, search airfield facilities and the ammunition depots in the zone, then to reconnoitre the H3 air base and the surrounding desert. As Gavrilis would say it later on, *" we had to persuade the Iraqis they hadn't got a chance sending people to fire a ballistic missile without being killed "*.

H3 air base was watched by ODA 522, 523 and 581. It was a huge air base protected by numerous blockhouses. Although many of the 500 defenders had fled, a hundred well armed with 23 mm and 57 mm ZSU air defence guns were still the-re. During the night of 23 March, while they observed the air base non-stop, SF saw Iraqis fire at an imaginary target with all their artillery.

That's why the next day Lieutenant-colonel Haas gave the aviation the approval to strike at the base. The embedded into the ODAs Air Force Combat Controllers made a series of hit thanks to SOFLAM (Special Operations Forces Laser Marker) laser designators. After twenty four hours of such a tempo, Ira-qis began digging fox holes outside the buildings for they had so many casualties. Then a sand storm arrived, hiding all the targets. *" Impossible to guide an aircraft, assured Team Ser-geant V., until I saw in my field glasses, tens of vehicles lea-ving the base. Iraqis were fleeing with all that had wheels, civi-*

lian or military vehicles. *"* A convoy consisting of 54 vehicles and another one of 30 armoured vehicles drove in parallel on the Baghdad motorway.

It was 1700 when ODA 521 received the order to stop the convoy at all means, as it could have been hiding a missile launcher. The heading vehicle was stopped dead by a 12.7 mm machine gun burst into the engine, while the truck following blew up hit by a Javelin missile (it was the first time Green Berets fired a true Javelin).

Coming across were ODA 525 Special Forces, prepared to open fire when a fighter-bomber which had spotted the Iraqi convoy arrived and announced: *" Back-of! It's going to burn... "*

Iraqis aboard all sorts of vehicles had also understood the dan-ger for many of them scattered in the desert, abandoning their weapons. Destroyed one after the other, the Iraqi vehicles did-n't go any further.

The night had come, as did the cold temperature and icy rain which penetrated the BDUs (Battle Dress Uniform) of the SF of Bravo Company. The following day, on 27 March, although the sand storm was still heavily blowing, SF began to recon-noitre the H3 base, captured some Iraqis and seized numerous weaponries (50 pieces of 23 mm, 30 of 57 mm, a hundred SA-7 missile launchers, thousands of light weapons, and an unbe-lievable stock of ammunitions of various calibres).

SF'S RESERVES IN COMBAT

The 19th Special Operations Group, a reserve component, was activated because of the important deployment of the Special Forces active units.

Thus, during the 2002 Desert Spring operation in Kuwait, 19th SFG together with Special Forces Command and Control Element — Kuwait (SOCCE-Kuwait) closely worked with the 3rd Infantry Division. Almost one year later, 19th SFG was still in the region. Within JSOTF-West, it provided the V Corps and I MEF with tactical support.

For the first time a Special Forces' reserve unit was to carry out recon and combat missions, a first since Vietnam. Thus, 19th SFG's teams would support Task Force Tarawa during the Nassiriya combats. ❐

A pair of Chinook of the 160th SOAR took the chance to resupply the teams in water, gasoline, food and ammunitions.

On 28 March, ODA 581 captured a Lieutenant General who wore civilian clothes and tried to flee the H3 base in a taxi. Morale was high in the Special Forces, all the more so as ODA 523 personnel had found biological weapon samples in

Special Forces of the 3rd SFG, Kurdistan, April 2003.
This sniper holds a .308 calibre M24 SWS precision rifle equipped with day sighting scope with variable magnifier and a removable foldable Versapod bipod.
He has an Eagle A III Large Pack Airborne allowing carrying transmission equipment and his individual materiel for a several day mission.

Above.
On 18 April 2003, while some of them talk to the local authorities in a city west of Baghdad, these Special Forces protect their buddies and control the road traffic in this "governmentless" region.
(Photo DOD)

H3. Of course they were not weapons of mass destruction (WMD) but SF thought Iraqi soldiers had been trained to use such weapons.

As operations moved forward, the 1st Battalion HQ understood that the Iraqis had probably less Scud missiles than expected. However, he requested his SF to continue searching the desert.

The first days of April, Bravo Company came back to Ar Rutbah, because if most of the regime's officials had fled, the city was still held by Saddam's fedayeens. Special Forces made the decision to carry out a more conventional operation, with all their fire power, and together with the PsyOps teams whose mission was to convey the following message: " Americans have nothing against the civil population, only against the men of the regime. " On 8 April, Major Gavrilis decided to enter Ar Rutbah with his nine ODAs and the supporting units. He first surrounded the city, and then bombed the sites where the militia

40

5th SPECIAL FORCE GROUP (AIRBORNE)

5th Special Forces Group is stationed at Fort Campbell, Kentucky. It consists of a HHC, three battalions (1st, 2nd and 3rd Battalions) and a support company. The air support unit is the 19th Air Special Operation Squadron. ❑

was supposed to be according to intelligence. Some hours later, a delegation came out of the city and asked Gavrilis to stop firing, which he *accepted: "It is a move of goodwill on our side. We fight Saddam's regime, not the Iraqi people!"*

The following morning, at 0600 sharp, several Humvee columns entered in Ar Rutbah, while a B-52 bomber, then a pair of F-16 flew low over it. A-10s flew over the vicinities letting off decoy flares. The Americans' entry didn't go unnoticed. Special Forces settled in the police station and Major Gavri-

Above.
On 25 March 2003, Green Berets of one of the ODA of the 5th SFG take a photo for posterity in the Iraqi desert. During the last twenty years' seven major operations, while they represented less than 3% of the armed forces, the American Special Forces have had a casualty rate thirteen times higher than the conventional forces.

Below.
This Green Beret, armed with a M24 precision rifle equipped with an AN/PAQ 10 day/night scope, tries to localize and neutralize an Iraqi rebellion's sniper who has just been spotted.

SERGEANT-MAJOR MICHAEL B. STACK

On 30 April 2004, Sergeant-Major Michael B. Stack of C Company, 2nd Battalion of the 5th Special Forces Group was posthumously awarded the Silver Star for his *"bravery and personal sacrifice"* during his convoy's attack on 11 April of the same year. As a matter of fact, despite several combined assaults, Stack succeeded in taking back his twelve-element unit. That day he led the convoy on the Baghdad to Al-Hillah road when his vehicle came under small arms fire. The Green Berets, using all arms, got through the adverse fire, but several vehicles were stopped and some men wounded. Once the danger was over, Stack called for the closest friendly units and immediately went back to the combat zone. After he retrieved the wounded, Sergeant-Major Stack led the counter attack to eliminate the remaining insurgents. He fired on the entrenched rebels with his .50 machine gun.

Fortunately, SFs got a new vehicle from the Green Berets and were able to resume towards the Forward Operation Base 52, the closest support base to get ammunitions resupply. But taking advantage of the night, the insurgents had fled. That is why Stack's vehicles went to Al-Hillah. En route, Green Berets came under AK-47 and PKM fire of rebels hidden on both sides of the road. Stack began to fire back so that others could escape from the kill zone. But the enemy concentrated fire on his vehicle. Less than two minutes later a first rocket missed his Humvee, but the second one killed him instantly. ❑

---

lis summoned the local authorities immediately. *" I want you to designate a mayor and a city council within an hour,* he ordered. *Everybody must go back to work and all the weapons must be collected in. From now on, we are in charge of security. "*

Once Ar Rutbah security was assured, water and power back to normal, ODA 521 and 525 were dispatched along the Syrian border to try to control the frontier posts. Since the Iraqi border guards had disappeared, all sorts of smuggling had developed.

Beginning of May 2003, the 3rd Armoured Cavalry Regiment relieved in line the Special Forces companies. Even though the Special Forces of the B and C Company, 1st Battalion, 5th SFG had not found any Scud, the fact is that no Iraqi missile had been launched. Thus, the aim of their mission had been fully fulfilled.

IN SOUTHERN IRAQ
The " Special Forces " between the Tigris and the Euphrates rivers

While the various 5th SFG, 1st Battalion's ODAs of Lieutenant-colonel Chris Haas were in the Iraqi west desert, Lieutenant-colonel Chris Conner's 2nd Battalion was in southern Iraq.

This unit was responsible for a zone ranging from Basrah, the most southern city of the country, up to Karbala, in the centre of the country, less than 200 kilometres south of Baghdad. The 2nd Battalion's two companies had to operate between the Tigris and the Euphrates rivers, the less populated region of Iraq.

Major Jonathan Burns was Charlie Company's Commanding Officer (CO). C Company had to drive along the main road from Kuwait to Basrah, the second largest city of Iraq. Its task was to collect information for the benefit of the British forces and Marine units.

On its side, Bravo Company was to move up to the centre of Iraq and operate in the Najaf region. Lastly, Alpha Compa-

ny HQ was attached to the Army V Corps HQ to act as the liaison between the conventional forces and the Special Forces' teams ahead of the layout.

During Iraqi Freedom, it's the 2nd Battalion personnel which worked the most closely with the conventional forces. They tried to minimize the traditional differences between the Special Forces and the Army's regular units - an old antagonism made up of disdain or ignorance between those wearing baseball caps and the " grunts ".

The presence of Saddam's best units, the specific " between-cities-and-desert " environment, as well as one of the most complex political situations, was what the Special Forces had to be prepared to face. In summary, a battle field "suiting" the Special Forces!

To avoid Saddam Hussein burning the oil fields in the Basrah region - as he did it in 1991 during *Desert Storm* -, Special Forces command proposed an ambitious plan to secure the Rumaila's oil field, pumping stations and oil terminals during the first hours of the conflict.

Before night fall, on 21 March 2003, Marine bulldozers opened seven gaps in the huge, four-meters on height and width, earth and sand wall, covered with electrified wire netting. Once the openings were complete, parts of the ODA 554 Humvees ran first, supported by some Marine Recon's light vehicles. These SFs' mission was to reach the Basrah suburbs and to meet with four Iraqi technicians whose task was to guide the Special Forces within the oil field infrastructure and to designate which valves had to be shut to minimize possible sabotages. It took three hours for the ODA 554 Green Berets to reach Safwan and find the Iraqis.

It was longer than expected, as the column now had to come backwards and go through the friendly forces firing at the Iraqi positions and vehicles. The leading vehicle was equipped with a Blue Force Tracker system allowing the Battalion Commander to know where each team was. However, this technique has its limits when hundreds of armoured vehicles fight while moving and that you are in the middle of the night... That's why the SF decided to wait until the Marines came to them, and not the other way round. Everything went well despite the Iraqi fedayeens who fought to defend the motorway. ODA 554 SF were very happy to hand over the Iraqi technicians to the Marines and to rejoin their Charlie Company for a new mission more in the north: support the British units to find the enemy forces in the vicinities of Basrah.

On their side, Major Jonathan Burns Charlie Company's vehicles were following the British First Armoured Division, before setting up in a chosen site. However, British forces were heavily fighting, supported by some Marine AH-1W Super Cobras. The enemy resistance hardened before Basrah. When he entered Az-Zubayr, a city near Basrah airport, Major Burns thought it was an excellent location for an ambush, when at the same time many Iraqis armed with assault rifles and light machine guns appeared on the road in the midst of the night. As they saw them with their night goggles one of the SF personnel told them in Arabic: *" hand over your weapons! "* Nobody moved. A shooter in the turret of a Humvee fired a burst of tracing

Special Forces of the 3rd SFG, Kurdistan, April 2003.
An AN/PRC-113 radio provides the link to the battalion and the other members of ODA and USAF SF.
The sniper is also equipped with a MBITR radio to communicate within the group. GPS is used for navigation.

Above and right.
The US Army Special Forces first *"get accustomed "* to the conquest of a territory during the *Joint Gardian* operation, while they trained the liberation army of Kosovo in Albania; Then, they got experience in Afghanistan with the North Alliances forces during Enduring Freedom; lastly they fought the Iraqi army with the Peshmergas of Kurdistan during operation Iraqi Freedom.
(Photos SOCOM)

bullets before them. Iraqis looked frozen. Then Captain W. of the Civil Affairs who was in the column and spoke Arabic yelled again: *" hand over your weapons or we will shoot off your heads! And go away! "* Iraqis complied and ran in the night.

During these first hours of the war, the Special Forces didn't know the Iraqis' level of combat power. *"To disarm them was better than to kill them! "* reported a SF member.

ODA 554 had reached its safe house. It

was the house of a tribe chief, a prior-the-war CIA recruit. This man was ready to help the coalition and to give information about the enemy targets around Az-Zubayr, where the British had to face a strong resistance. As communications were not possible, Special Forces provided intelligence to the closest British forces instead of the Company command. For three days, ODA 554 carried out patrols in the area. Soon it looked like the Iraqi resistance was stronger than expected. Iraqi soldiers had taken off their uniforms, were disappearing into the population, while still infiltrating into the coalition's lines and mounting ambushes.

For the C Company's other elements, things were not changing, as the British had stopped their forward movement before Basrah. Obviously, they were waiting for the Iraqi defences to fall by themselves. Moreover, American Special Forces couldn't enter in the city without the Brits. That is why they focused on Zubayr and collected

Left. Some Special Forces of the 10th Special Forces Group carry out a patrol in a building that the April 2003 bombardments destroyed. This action took place during the hunt for the Iraqi rebels in the " Sunnite triangle ", one year after the ground operations. *(Photo 10th SFG)*

Below. By mid-April 2003, victory is real for this ODA team (almost all the members are on the photo) of the 5th SFG. In less than a week, the Special Forces Group teams seized more than 20% of the Iraqi territory, and without any casualty. *(Photo SOCOM)*

as much intelligence as possible from the allied tribes. For the first time, Special Forces used a Pointer mini-UAV (Unmanned Aerial Vehicle), and got positive results.

Along with the Special Forces were elements of the 4th Psychological Operations Group who every night, broadcasted messages of rendition toward the Iraqi defenders of Basrah.

In the morning, the British command informed the American Special Forces that Iraqi civilians had left Basrah by one of the bridges. They requested their support to control the inhabitants. For hours, Charlie Company's men questioned dozens of people to get a precise idea of who were the last defenders of the city. *" Because of the endless growing flow of Iraqis we were obliged to withdraw to the Basrah airport. Operations were finished for us. "* R said later on. And the fact is that Iraq's second city fell some hours later.

Urban Operations for Special Forces

During this time, the Bravo Company's ODA 551 succeeded in crossing the famous Karbala gap which controls the roads to Baghdad.

As far as possible, conventional forces avoided the most inhabited zones. However, Army units

10th Special Forces Group (Airborne)
ODA 086

had to cross the city of Najaf to reach Karbala, while the Marine had to go via Diwaniya to head north. The various ODA had to provide intelligence on the probable threats on each side of the coalition's columns, and to support the units, should any combat occur in and around these cities.

ODA 551's only mission was to find and count the Iraqi forces laid along the Karbala gap where the Iraqi Freedom planners thought Saddam had packed all his troops to stop the Americans forces there. After an exercise in Jordan end of 2002, the 2nd Battalion had been dispatched to the Ali al-Salem air base in Kuwait on 15 March 2003. During the night of 20 March, Humvees, heavy transport vehicles, and motorbikes were loaded in the SOCOM's (Special Operations Command) MC-130 Combat Talon and MH-53 J Pave Low, which flew them up to the Karbala southwest desert around 0400.

The "American spooks" hunt

In the field, ODA 551 had to hurry, for the 3rd Infantry Division would reach the gap within less

2nd BATTALION, 10TH SFG

March 2005, elements of the 2nd Battalion, 10th SFG, were deployed in Iraq. One month later as they were searching an anti-Iraqi training camp in Jazeera region, they eliminated several tens of insurgents.

For their action Master Sergeant Robert Collins, Sergeant 1st Class Danny Hall and 1st Sergeant Cornelius Clark have been awarded the Silver Star. Collins and Hall faced a hundred or so rebels entrenched in buildings and armed with mortars, rocket-propelled grenades, machine guns and grenades. After Collins directed close air support from F-16 aircraft with 500-pound bombs, he then led his elements to engage on the enemy, personally killing three insurgents and captured one of the enemy positions.

Collins, also Medical Sergeant, found a helicopter landing zone to medevac his wounded troops. Collins and Hall risked their lives several times while pinned down by enemy fire to recover a wounded soldier. Once in safety, they began medical care and saved his life. ❐

than thirty six hours and it needed to know what its opposing forces would be. After they raced through several inhabited areas, SFs found a discreet spot where to set up and carry out their recce. They had to build a very precise inventory, including the weather conditions, temperature, wind, roads quality, and so on. Overall, all types of details that satellite images, air recons, Iraqi deserters' report, or intelligence analysts were able to provide.

Above and below. ODA 563 at Diwaniya and ODA 544 at Najaf succeeded in organizing the only two Iraqi uprisings against Saddam's government, and seizing a city, at least for the former ODA. ODA 563 passed from a counter guerrilla mission to the neutralisation of Iraqi targets, while taking on the administrative management of a city. On its side, ODA 544 carried out its target acquisition and designation missions for the conventional forces, opened discussion with the Shi'ite clergy, and also performs commando raids against the Saddam's militiamen.

THE FREE IRAQI FORCES (FIF)

In June 2002, the US Army was given the mission to train 5000 Iraqi citizens to form a " liberation force " to take part in a possible future operation against Iraq. By the end of 2002, instructors from several official Army education and training units - as well as CIA and American Special Forces elements - were ready in a Hungarian camp, not far from Tazar.

On 17 February 2003, the first 55 FIF began training, soon followed by 23 additional Iraqi. Mid-March, they were deployed to Kuwait and integrated within the US Army V Corps, USMC I MEF and 352nd Civil Affairs Command. During the operations, FIF carried out negotiation actions with Iraqi units and facilitated communication between coalition forces and local populations. FIF also took part in searches and seized-documents assessments to capture fleeing Baath party leaders. ❏

days. Water was rationed, and only one meal per day was provided. Moreover — as to multiply the difficulties - men had to keep their NBC protection gears on as intelligence reports had mentioned chemical weapons in the zone.

SF discovered tens of conventional or militia units deployed along the gap, as well as light vehicles going in all ways as if they were in search of something. The answer came later on: on the operations' first day, the Iraqi radio had broadcast that American commandos were operating in Iraq; thus, numerous searches had been launched. However, the fact is that ODA 551 teams stayed in the same zone without guessing the presence[3] of the Iraqi positions, though they were less than 400 metres apart.

Following page.
Before operation Iraqi Freedom, the 10th SFG, as well as the 5th SFG, performed several high intensity exercises to prepare their teams for an operation in Iraq. During these trainings, lessons learnt from Enduring Freedom in Afghanistan were implemented. Thus, in August 2002, the 3rd Battalion of the 10th SFG ran an exercise whose aim was to train a significant guerrilla force and to fight against a conventional army. The five active duty Special Forces and the two reserve SFG studied the lessons learnt from Enduring Freedom, performed a series of exercises, modifying tactics and improving techniques and procedures. *(Photos SOCOM)*

Above. During the March and April 2003 major ground operations, SFG detachments work together with PsyOps teams to talk to the local population and collect information. *(Photos SOCOM)*

Right. The fall of the Iraqi government made the missions of the Special Forces evolve from the collection of information for the regular forces to hunting the fleeing leaders and the elimination of the insurgent groups. *(Photo 5th SFG)*

However, as early as the first day, the team faced unfortunate trouble: satellite communications didn't work. Several times SF disassembled and reassembled their equipment until they understood their location was too steep-sided to receive satellite signals. They had to move on a hillock to solve the problem. However, the next day they had to face a sandstorm. The wind blew at more than eighty kilometres per hour, and visibility was very low.

Despite the dust, the teams took three-hour duties to carry out patrols to localize the Iraqi positions. This sandstorm also slowed down the coalition's forces, and therefore, the 3rd Infantry Division decided to hold its forward movement. SF had then to adapt their mission originally planned to last three to five

---

3. Later on, ODA 551 SF learnt from prisoners that the location was a former firing range where Iraqis had fired ammunitions, shells and missiles for years. All in all, the best location to watch without being disturbed... but also the most dangerous!

Above
On 21 April 2003, ground operations of *Iraqi Freedom* have jus[t]
ended, and two ODA of the 5th SFG, almost with all their men[?]
take a photo to celebrate the victory in central Iraq. One can notic[e]
the LMTV vehicles, true " beast of burden " of the Special Forces[.]
(Photo 5th SFG[)]

SOCCENT IN ACTION

Special Operations Command Central (SOCCENT), stationed at MacDill in Florida, is a unified command subordinated to central command (CENTCOM). SOCCENT is responsible for planning Special Operations in all CENTCOM's area of responsibility.

During operations such as those carried out in Afghanistan or Iraq, SOCCENT was the core of the Joint Special Operations Task Force.

Thus, Special Forces deployed in Afghanistan were a Combined Joint Special Operations Task Force's component (CJSOTF), whose headquarter was at Bagram air base and had forward bases at Kandahar and Khost, southern and eastern Afghanistan. CJSOTF comprised Green Berets, Delta Force, Navy SEAL units, Australian and New-Zealand Special Forces, a unit of the French Special Operations Command, as well as Danish and Norwegian Special Forces.

Special Forces were in direct support of the conventional forces during Iraqi Freedom, but also carried out their own missions. They were headed by Brigadier General Gary Harrell, SOCCENT Commander in Chief. ❑

ten days in the desert, around 2200, SF rejoined the 3rd ID's first columns to deliver their intelligence report in details.

While ODA 551 extracted from the Karbala gap, other teams of Major Lohman's Company worked for the 3rd ID benefit before Najaf, 75 kilometres south of Karbala. The pilot team, ODA 544, entered first in Najaf to gather information about the Iraqi forces and their relative strength. ODA 554's two Humvees and two civilian pick-ups had been flown to an abandoned Iraqi air base by two MC-130 Combat Talons the night the coalition troops crossed the border

Then, SF drove for some hours up to the gates of the city. After they had hidden their vehicles

During the night of the sixth day, helicopters of the 11th Attack Helicopter Regiment (AHR) carried out recon patrols without knowing where the eleven SF were. Captain F., ODA 551's leader, succeeded in informing the liaison officer to warn the helicopters of their presence. The next day an 11th AHR's aircraft was downed. The crew had to be rescued rapidly. Unfortunately, the Apache had crashed on the other side of Karbala, and unless fighting eleven of them against the city's whole defence, it was impossible to rescue the pilots.

Extraction without casualty

On day 8, SF saw the first 3rd Infantry Division recon vehicles. Now the hardest had to be done: to extract without casualty! ODA 551 had to leave its camp without attracting the Iraqis' attention... and avoiding firing of their friendlies. After

Special Forces of the 3rd SFG, Kurdistan, April 2003.
The Eagle A III Large Pack Airborne is often used as a stable support for rifle fire. SF snipers had an important role on the front line in Kurdistan. As a matter of fact, employed in small groups with mid to long range 7.62 mm to 12.7 mm calibre precision rifles, snipers dealt with any type of objective of Iraqi troop.

Above and right. The 3rd and 10th SFG main mission in Kurdistan consisted in keeping twelve Iraqi divisions busy in northern Iraq in order to prevent them from being committed while the coalition's forces were advancing north towards Baghdad. Then, Special Forces mission was to seize Mosul and Kirkuk.
(Photos 3rd SFG) `

Below right. Night operation for this Army and SEAL combined Special Forces team in August 2004 when tracking the insurgents. SF will deploy near a main road and try to neutralize rebels setting up IEDs. *(Photo SOCOM)*

under camouflage nets, the men rested during the day. After night fall, ODA 544 reached Najaf. However, things accelerated since the 3rd Infantry Division was advancing faster than expected which left SF with less than twenty four hours to gather intelligence. That's why ODA 544 teams set up check points on the various routes and stopped civilian vehicles at random to know what the city defenders' intentions were. Several drivers had heard that the military command had ordered the fedayeens to attack the *"American commandos"*.

The next day, SF set up check points again and understood that more and more civilians were leaving the city. Thanks to satellite images they had studied for weeks, Special Forces knew Najaf well. They knew where the Army, the Fedayeens, and the Baath party HQs were. Americans were convinced the Iraqi officials were going to fight and would try to cut their supply lines.

A handful of Special Forces to seize Diwaniya

The US Command decided to seize Najaf, but without urban combat as it was the 101st Air Assault which was in charge of the operation. The SF mission was then to make the Fedayeens get out of the city to avoid urban combat, on the one hand, (the Mogadishu example is still in minds) and, on the other hand, to select the major targets for the aviation. That's why aviation was called to strike as soon as an Iraqi mortar position was located. Overall, out of the 30 selected targets, 20 were hit within forty eight hours. However, it was only when questioning prisoners and people in the vehicles that the SF knew what damages had been really done.

The assault against Diwaniya was decided on 29 March. ODA 544 was with a battalion of the 101st and called for close air support (CAS) whenever the Iraqi artillery was firing. On its side, together with another 101st unit, ODA 556 entered in the city through the north gate. Within a couple of hours, Najaf fell and ODA 544 was able to settle in it. However, Najaf's battle was not complete as the Fedayeens' harassment against the Americans continued. SF decided to "*hire*" the services of a Chiit militia. As a matter of fact, because of what they had suffered under the Saddam's regime, Chiits had a revenge to take over the Sunnits. To prove its loyalty, the Chiit militia captured tens of Baathist officials, Fedayeens, and candidates for suicide, in just a couple of days. On 7 April, thanks to intelligence tips the militia gathered, SF succeeded in capturing a regional Baath party leader after a heavy fight[4]. On 11 April, Najaf resistance is considered as broken. The Green Berets paid themselves the luxury of designating a mayor and restoring the whole city administration in power.

On its side, ODA 563 had moved east of Diwaniya, near the motorway # 8. It had contacted five tribe chiefs. Because they feared the within-range Navy artillery could destroy their village, the tribe chiefs made the proposal to seize al-Hamza on their own. No sooner said than done! A few hours later, they announced through the satellite telephone: "*We have seized it! The city*

On 6 April 2003, The Debecka pass battle, near Mosul and Kirkuk, was decisive. SF succeeded in stopping an Infantry brigade with T-55 and armoured personnel carrier vehicles. Iraqis tried to bypass the American position four times in a row. Thanks to the aviation support and to the Javelin anti-tank missile launchers, the Iraqis had to withdraw and left eight of their tanks as well as sixteen APC vehicles after four hours of combat. Thus, thirty one members of the American Special Forces and eighty Peshmergas supported by CCT-guided Air Force fighter-bombers stopped several thousand of Iraqi soldiers.

is ours! " ODA 563 entered into al-Hamza and asked the Iraqis to continue in the same way and to now seize Diwaniya, a more important and better defended city. "Protected" by a series of air raids on 21 pre assigned targets, American Special Forces together with fifteen armed Iraqis seized the city, aided by a PsyOps team and a handful of Marine Recons. True is the fact the Marine aviation had done a good job, striking the designated targets without collateral damages and killing more than 200 militia and people closely linked to Saddam's regime.

But only when the city was seized did the Special Forces true work begin. But now the city had to be secured and the population to be protected from uncontrolled pro-Saddam militia and bands of thieves that take advantage of the situation to rob banks and public buildings. That is why a vehicle of four SF kept watch around the "*base camp*" (a medical school at the time), another patrolled in the city, and the last Humvee was on alert as "*rapid reaction force*". Within days, under the command of an inflexible tribe chief, a police was re-established, and power restored to 80% of the city.

---

2. SF fired several thousands of 5.56 mm rounds with their M-4, 200 rounds of 12.7 mm machine gun and nine 40 mm grenades.

Special Forces of the 10th Special Forces Group, Kurdistan, April 2003. His equipment is similar to his SFG comrade's in desert BDU in southern Iraq. But as Kurdistan is greener, the Woodland BDU was preferred. The RACK (Ranger Assault Carrying Kit) is over an IBA (Interceptor Body Armor), providing the same characteristics a Spear BALCS vest offers. It is worth noticing the M4 is equipped with a Knight Armament SIR Hand guard kit, a Sure fire M900 high-output lamp, and an Aimpoint M2 scope. We also see the Beretta M9 pistol in a Safariland 6004 holder. A civilian telemeter fieldglasses is used to spot and designate a target to the group's sniper.

As of 7 April, Special Forces handed over to the regular units, their mission fulfilled.

As of the first week of April 2003, the Green Berets of the 10th SFG began to advance along the cease fire line, and thanks to the aviation support, overthrew the Iraqi defences. Here, a Special Forces set up a 81 mm mortar on a position overlooking the enemy.
(Photo 10th SFG)

IN CENTRAL AND WESTERN IRAQ

Two days before the ground operations began, one of the Special Forces'MJ-53J Pave Low helicopter transported ODA 553 for a recon mission of Nassiriya outskirts. But the Pave Low crashed down during its flight. Three men were injured, crushed in one of the vehicles carried aboard. They were quickly rescued by another SF helicopter. The mission could resume. Soon ODA 553 men understood they were too far from the objectives they had to recon. Yet, after a fight with paramilitaries, and while the Army units were advancing north, the team reached one of the strategic bridges and provided the required information.

SF crossed the famous bridge in question with the conventional units, and then began another intelligence mission within Nassiriya.

Training the "Free Iraqi"

While ODAs were deployed in centre Iraq, Major Burns of Charly Company was given a new mission. Its aim was to pick up a detachment of " free Iraqi " of the Free Iraqi Force (FIF), due to land at a recently captured airfield in Talil, south of Nassiriya, and to set up a camp there.

This anti-Saddam Iraqi group was headed by the controversial (especially because of the US intelligence community) Iraqi National Congress leader Ahmed Chalabi. ODA 542, 543, 546 and 565 had only four days to train the " free Iraqi ". That is why each ODA took responsibility of a group of men to create platoons of combat groups. Major Burns said: *"Iraqis came with so many armaments that they could have equipped a whole division"*. However, they were first equipped with small armaments: *" mortars, recoilless rifles, antitank and air defence howitzers would come later…"* However, ODA 543 had fetched 200 Milan and as many other antitank missiles that the Iraqi Infantry had abandoned. Therefore, they decided to train the Free Iraqi with these weapons. Once training was complete, each ODA was given another mission, with the exception of ODA 565 which escorted Chalabi towards Baghdad with a FIF platoon. ODA 542, with 158 FIF, went toward Kut, the only major city closed to the Iranian border. Once at Kut, the mission was to control the city's situation where anarchy had taken place in these first days of April. After they eliminated looters, SF and FIF split into three groups, each responsible for one of the following three missions: security, civil administration, and search for abandoned armament. Moreover, Special Forces carried out patrols along the Iranian border. During all of April, ODA 542 acted in and around Kut. FIF had also to be disarmed (which was a White House order, but not an easy task) for they now had to *"return to the civil life"*. Then ODA returned to Talil.

On its side, ODA 553 was still in Nassiriya and fed intelligence to the Marine units fighting the various militias in the inner city. The network of informants increased along with the decreasing of the Fedayeens threat. Thus, end of March, an Iraqi came to the SF building and said that a young blond lady from the American Army was under care at a city's hospital. This was the first reliable information about where Pfc Jessica Lynch was. This informant came back later with a video showing the building, accesses and the room where she was. It was from the ODA 553 various

Photo of ODA 086 of the 10th SFG during its second tour in Iraq in 2004. At this time all operations are exclusively targeted at the guerrilla, in particular in the " Sunnite Triangle ".
(Photo ODA 086/10th SFG)

reports, plans and photographs that the Rangers, SEAL and Air Force SF operation was carried out on 1 April 2003, with the success that we know.

In Kurdistan

In February 2003, a part of Colonel Charlie Cleveland's 10th Special Forces Group arrived at the Constanza air base, in Romania. Task Force " Viking " became the unit's name. It didn't move from Romania for days: for political reasons Turkey did not agree with American troops using its territory. The new plan was named Operation Ugly Baby which made a SF man say: "Damn! That's an ugly baby! " On 22 March, the green light came and Colonel Cleveland eventually took off toward Kurdistan with 280 SF operators aboard six Combat Talon aircraft. Above Iraq, one of the Combat Talon was hit by an Iraqi antiaircraft battery and had to make an emergency landing in Turkey. The five other planes landed at night at Bashur airfield, just outside Irbil. The next day, Ankara agreed over flight rights: the rest of the Task Force " Viking " flew directly from Romania into Kurdistan.

Colonel Cleveland understood his 5,200 men and about twenty thousand Kurd combatants had to take on thirteen Iraqi divisions, more than 100,000 soldiers, along a 350 kilometre front! Special Forces had never before attempted something like this by themselves.

Originally the 4th Infantry Division had to take position in Kur-distan, but the Turkish political position prevented it. (At this time 4th ID was steaming around the Arabic peninsula).

The " rules of the game "

Task Force " Viking " had three Special Forces battalions, about 50 ODA, supported by several AC-130 Spectre gunships, as well as intelligence, signals, PsyOps, Civil Affairs and support staff detachments. The " front " was divided into two zones: 10 SFG's 2nd Battalion headed by Lieutenant-colonel Bob Waltemeyer in the north, and 10 SFG's 3rd Battalion headed by Lieutenant-colonel Ken Tovo in the south. 3rd Battalion's task was to capture the oil-rich Kirkuk area with the help of the militia of the Patriotic Union of Kurdistan (PUK); while 2nd Battalion's task was to capture the Mosul area with the help of the militia of the Kurdish Democratic Party (KDP).

Right from the beginning, the Americans explained the rules of the game to the Kurds: don't provoke the Turks; Kurds units had not to enter into Mosul and Kirkuk without an order; the highest priority was to push the Iraqi divisions back in order to prevent them from firing chemical ammunitions onto the Kurd villages. SF had also to manage serious logistical problems, and transport was one of the most serious. The Quad-cab Defender pick-up vehicle fleet they had bought in Turkey was locked in a warehouse there. Therefore, Special Forces borrowed or bought vehicles from the Kurds — most of them smuggled from Baghdad! Each ODA broke down in split teams pairing up with 150 to 1,500 Kurdish militiamen! Many "veterans" of the first Gulf War were among the 10th SFG's SFs; some of them had already served during the Kurdish refugee crisis after Desert Storm. Actually, after the coali-

tion's victory, Saddam's troops had threatened to attack the Kurd region, which had led thousands of Kurds to flee toward Turkey.

However, Lieutenant-colonel Tovo of the 3rd Battalion had to attack and destroy Ansar al-Islam terrorist group before the main assault on the thirteen Iraqi division which was along the Iranian border. ODA 081 was chosen to conduct reconnaissance and note all coordinates of the targets (camps, trenches, artillery positions) to allow the aviation to strike them before and during the attack.

At midnight on 21 March, waves of 64 Tomahawk cruise missiles slammed down onto the Ansar al-Islam positions. Lieutenant-colonel Tovo's original plan was to attack two hours after the last air strike. But he was lacking ammunitions and equipment which were still on the runway in Romania. Thus, against his will, he just conducted air strikes to prevent Islamic combatants from fleeing.

The operation was to be followed at high levels of the government

Special Forces felt Ansar al-Islam would not be easy prey: every time the former carried out reconnaissance, the latter fought them with mortars. It was not going to be a pleasant walk; so much as Ansar al-Islam fighters were well equipped, trained and entrenched in positions where they intended to stay.

Special Forces were also very nervous, for they knew operation Viking Hammer would be followed at high levels of the government, all the way to the White House in particular...

It was only on 28 March at dawn (at 0430), that the nine Special Forces teams of ODA 081 and several hundreds of Kurdish combatants arrived in tens of trucks, personal cars and taxis.

" Heavy " armament consisted of 12.7 mm M2 and 7.62 mm

Bottom. Since March 2003, Special Forces units consisting of reservists have been continuously rotating in Iraq and Afghanistan. Here, Green Berets of the National Guard take a photo before a night operation. *(Photo 10th SFG)*

M 240 machine guns, 40 mm Mk 19 grenade-launchers, 60 mm mortars and sniper rifles… At 0600, the two columns of Special Forces moved forward into the Sargat valley. The objective was to capture Gulp and Sargat villages where there were various buildings of the terrorist movement. While ODA 091 and 300 Kurds captured Gulp (around 0900) and then entered the adjacent valley to the Iranian border, six soldiers of ODA 081 and 700 Kurds continued in the valley leading to Sargat. They moved quickly at first, but they were vulnerable because Ansar al-Islam combatants still held the valley sides.

Suddenly they were pinned down by several posts of machine guns. SF immediately called for an air strike. Two Navy F/A-18 answered the call and dropped laser-guided bombs (JDAM: Joint Direct Attack Munition). Less than two kilometres from Sargat, Americans found two heavily defended positions on their right. They shot back with M240 and Mk 19, and thanks to the PKM and DShK machine guns of the Kurds, they rooted their attackers in less than thirty minutes. Everyone re-boarded the vehicles of the not too much military convoy. But the bulk of the Ansar al-Islam fighters were entrenched around Sargat: "*The most difficult part has still to come* ", thought the SFs.

The first assault ODA 081 leader mounted with 40 Turkish combatants received an onslaught of 122 mm rockets, RPG-7 rockets and 14.5 mm bullets. The SF leader thought about calling an air strike but the enemy positions were too close to his, where hundreds of Kurds had gathered. The air strike could have hit as much friendlies as the enemy. Captain F. understood that he had no option than to fight the way through. "*It would be an Infantry battle from start to finish*", he said later on.

The Kurds' artillery finally arrived and began blasting the Ansar al-Islam strong point. The heavy fighting paid off three hours later when the Islamic fighters gave up their positions and withdrew into caves and the mountains behind Sargat. SF asked the Kurds to not enter into the city not to destroy evidences of chemical armaments or of documents proving links with Al-Qaeda existed. While the few wounded Kurds were taken care of by the ODA 081 medic, Americans saw a surreal truck full of hot food arrive. "*If the Kurds had not been able to bring their artillery in the front line in less than an hour before Sargat during a life-and-death battle, on the other hand a hot meal had shown up at1pm on the dot!* " said Captain F later on.

Call for " cavalry "

Some Kurds were assigned to keep the deserted village of Sargat, while SF and the other Kurds set off again in the afternoon to pursue and try to capture those Ansar al-Islam fighters who were fleeing toward the Iranian border.

SF climbed into the high grounds of the mountain pass behind Sargat, where intelligence sources had said were numerous caves hiding Ansar al-Islam Islamic Kurds and Arabs. The caves were searched one by one and destroyed with AT-4 rocket launchers. "*Sir would you like a Coca and some cookies?* " the American Captain was asked by one Kurd of the escort who thought it was time for an afternoon break…

As they moved higher up, a machine gun fire ranged in on

Above. Exercise of forward movement in Iraq during a reconnaissance of a building. Regularly, the Special Forces carry out real operations, tracking insurgents and freeing foreign hostages, or most of the time nationals, high jacked for a ransom by criminal groups.
(Photo SOCOM)

the Special Forces from above. *"We absolutely need close air support to get off this situation "*, said the SF Captain who immediately called the " cavalry ". SF waited under enemy fire for twenty long minutes for a pair of fighter bombers which blasted the enemy position with six precision-guided JDAMs.

As it was getting dark, there was no question of pursuing the hunt. Moreover the Kurds had no NVGs. At 1700, everybody returned to Sargat for the night.

Overall, 23 Kurds had been wounded and three killed, compared to 70 enemy killed in the positions around Sargat (but 300 bodies would be discovered later on). Passports and identity cards found on the bodies proved that half the deaths were foreigners from Yemen, Sudan, Saudi Arabia, Oman, Qatar, Tunisia, Morocco and Iran.

On 29 March, a CIA team arrived at Sargat searching for a chemical weapons facility. It rapidly found traces of potassium chlorine and ricin, as well as NBC gears, atropine injector's bags and documents in Arabic on how to make chemical munitions. Reports concluded Sargat was an international terrorist training camp, much like those Al-Qaeda had run in Afghanistan.

The Captain, Team Sergeant and Sergeant responsible for the communications would receive the Silver Star for *" their exceptional courage and bravery "* during operation Viking Hammer.

After they had cleared the Ansar al-Islam region, Task Force " Viking " could switch its efforts toward the " Green Line " (the cease fire line the coalition established to separate Kurds and Iraqi troops, and create a *" de fait "* autonomous Kurd region). Lieutenant-colonel Tovo sent Charly Company to the southern part of Tuz. SF called for air raids on Chamchamal hilltops, east of Kirkuk. The American plan was to isolate Kirkuk on three sides until it fell. But the air strikes were so precise that the Iraqi troops decided to withdraw into Kirkuk.

On the " Green Line "

During the night of 9 April, the day when Baghdad fell, a hundred Iraqi vehicles fled south as they were facing about a hundred SF and the nine ODA plus a thousand Pesh mergas. All went fast as Americans did not want the Kurds to capture Kirkuk before the regular units arrived from the south. Bravo Company then captured a hill overlooking the city, while Alpha Company seized a hilltop after a series of seventy-two-hour non-stop combats. Then Lieutenant-colonel Tovo decided to fast pace to Kirkuk with his staff cell. In front of a presidential palace abandoned just a few hours ago, he ordered his men to shave and wear clean combat fatigues and to patrol the city streets: Alpha Company on one side of the river, and Bravo Company on the other side.

The city's occupation was made under exclusive SF control, which restored water and power as early as 13 April. A sort of civilian peace settled even though tensions between Kurds and Arabs could burst into flames at any time. With cleverness LTC Tovo signed a cease-fire with a group of exiled Iranian of the Mujahideen e Khalq, whose aim was to take the power in Iran and not to fight Americans. A SF team went to secure a bridge north of Kirkuk to allow the 173rd Airborne Brigade to secure the oil-rich zones around and to patrol within the big city.

On their side, and having fought since 30 March, Lieutenant-colonel Bob Waltemayer's 2nd Battalion teams secured Irbil's airport and outskirts. They marched toward Mosul. The plan was to assault the city from three sides. But on the " Green Line ", Iraqi didn't look ready to move, despite the repeated air strikes. Thus, both sides watched each other through field glasses and sent messages. *"We do not intend to surrender to a bunch of guys riding simple pick-ups! "* said the Iraqi for instance. Mosul, where numerous Officers resided was one of the political strongholds of the regime.

On 2 April, the situation suddenly changed, combats burst and lasted for seven days. ODA 065 and its Kurdish allies faced two Iraqi brigades along the Zab River. While they had thrown the Iraqi out of the hills, it was now the American turn to entrench there

for three days. Iraqi blasted the hilltops with their artillery while Americans lessened their assailants' zeal with air strikes. However, Americans gathered two additional ODA, 100 Kurdish combatants, the 173rd Airborne Brigade artillery, as well as all the Kurdish artillery howitzers they were able to find, which eventually led them to have the last word: they seized 23 kilometres of road, killed 257 Iraqi soldiers, took 15 bunkers, 34 vehicles, a dozen artillery howitzers, and destroyed two T-55 tanks. Two Silver Stars were awarded for the Aski Kalak battle. An ODA 065 Team Sergeant who had stopped four mechanized counter-attacks, killed 40 enemies, destroyed two tanks, four mortar positions and four bunkers, was awarded one of them!

The battle of the Debecka pass

Teams north of Mosul had " inherited " the most difficult terrain that could be. A first three-ODA detachment took more than twenty four hours to seize Ain Sifni, capturing 240 Iraqi soldiers, while preserving the city. Another two-ODA detachment plus 350 Peshmergas fought for three days to sever the main road south of Mosul. Lastly, a third six-ODA and more than 9000 Kurdish combatant detachment assaulted three enemy divisions on a 40-kilometre front. Supported by air raids and the 173rd artillery, American forces were less than 20 kilometres from Mosul.

On 6 April 2003, the battle for the Debecka pass, south of Mosul was decisive; it would become famous in the history of the Special Forces.

The Task Force in charge of attacking Mosul from the south consisted of Alpha Company, 2nd Battalion and Alpha Company, 3rd Battalion of the 3rd Special Forces Group. It then faced two mechanized brigades entrenched on the Debecka plateau. It is a rocky ridgeline along the road between Kirkuk and Mosul. SF had to cross it at any price.

SF and Kurds had M2 machine guns, Mk19 grenade launchers, and most certainly Javelin anti-tank missiles to face the Iraqi armoured vehicles.

"We succeeded in stopping a T-55 and APC brigade", explai-

ned Sgt 1st Class Frank Antenori of the 3rd SFG. *"Three times Iraqi forces tried to break through our lines and to by-pass the positions. Thanks to the aviation support and to the Javelin (whose ad-hoc training we had some months before, in Kuwait), Iraqi withdrew and left eight tanks and sixteen APC in the field after four-and-a-half-hour fire fight"*. Thus, 31 SF members and 80 Peshmergas, supported by CCT guiding Air Force fighter-bombers stopped several thousands of Iraqi soldiers. A Staff Sergeant of 3rd SFG squatted and fired shoulder-launched javelin anti-tank missiles to take out four armoured vehicles. But at a key moment of the combats, an F-14 mistakenly dropped a bomb on a friendly column and killed twelve Kurdish combatants, high ranking ones for the most.

Taking advantage of the Iraqi defeat, Alpha companies by-passed the strategic pass, captured two cities and seized tens of anti-aircraft howitzers and Frog-7 missile launchers. On 10 April, the third company captured the mountain overlooking Mosul.

Fast pace to Mosul

At dawn on 11 April, while Lieutenant-colonel Waltemayer told the Kurds not to enter into the city before his troops, V Iraqi Corps representatives announced they were ready to surrender.

Below.
Army Special Forces deployed both in Afghanistan and in Iraq within the Task Forces in charge of capturing or neutralizing insurgent groups and armed religious formations. Within these Task Forces Groups there were also Delta Force, SEAL and 160th SOAR helicopters.
(Photo SOCOM)

WARFARE AGAINST IRAQI COMMUNICATIONS AND COUNTER-MEASURES

During the nine months prior to the attack against Iraq, American specialists did everything they could to know about the Iraqi's communications or counter-measures systems. By the beginning of 2003, the Iraqi army purchased several GPS jammers, as well as INMARSAT and Thuraya telephones for the Republican Guard regiments.

US Army counter-measures units seized an org. Chart showing the basic Iraqi army's communications structures. From then on, electronic warfare specialists built a network capable of jamming all enemy communications. 3rd Infantry Division succeeded in breaking more than 300 communications. ❑

Waltemayer thought the situation was unsettled. He decided to fast pace toward Mosul with only 30 men packed up in six vehicles to capture a city of 1.7 million inhabitants!

SF arrived in a city of total anarchy. Militiamen were firing every minute or so, but against looters. Streets were full of armoured, APC, artillery guns, but there was nobody around. Iraqi soldiers had all fled! To re-establish peace in the big city, Waltemayer (who had only 200 men) opted for a public relations policy: he asked various Sheiks to disband the armed militia and he made a statement on the local TV to make sure a regional government be set up and weapons be given back.

Forty eight hours later, elements of the 26th Marine Expeditionary Unit joined the coalition's forces in Mosul. But the city was still unstable, various communities (Kurds, Sunnits, Chiits, Turks, Assyrians and Chaleans) fired at each other to settle their problems. The situation remained chaotic until 22 April 2003 when the 101st Air Assault Division arrived and, thanks to its strength, imposed peace.

Hunt the Baath party leaders!

By 15 April 2003, as soon as the situation began to stabilize in Kurdistan, V Corps conventional forces moved north and relieved C/JSOTF-North Special Forces. The latter redeployed in the Sunnit zones with some units of Peshmergas. Then the hunt for the fleeing Iraqi leaders began and became the main mission. Each battalion split into various companies (under the name of Advanced Operational Bases or AOB) and was given a zone of action. On the other hand, JSOTF-North's HQ, as well as JSOTF-West's, set up in Baghdad. The newly formed command became C/JSOTF-Arabian Peninsula (CJSOTF-AP) and headed all operations in Iraq from that date.

During those months, SF teams built data bases about all suspect or influent persons of the zones where they operated. To do so, they used a targeting methodology called Joint Combined Observer that Colonel Charlie Cleveland had established in Bosnia. Thanks to these continuously enriched data bases, Special Forces carried out autonomous operations to capture, for a first time, Baath party leaders and regional cadres. Quickly, searches and operations targeted rebel organizations and their leaders. ❑

Previous pages.
Patrol in a semi-desert zone of western Iraq for Rangers of the 1st Rangers Battalion. During *Enduring Freedom*, Rangers were systematically deployed, and without any interruption, in the major operations in Iraq and in Afghanistan, thanks to the rotations of the three battalions of the 75th Rangers Regiment. It is worth noticing that despite the trend of over armoured vehicles, American Special Forces prefer working, with rare exception, with light non-armoured vehicles. *(SOCOM Photo)*

On 24 March 2003 at precisely 1830, 3rd Battalion's C Company's RSOV (Ranger Special Operations Vehicle) and GMV (Ground Mobility Vehicle) as well as a detachment of the HHC Company entered into western Iraq and began their recon mission not far from the city of Al-Qaim, near the Syrian border.

Left, from top to bottom.
End of 2004, in the" Sunnit triangle ", seen as the most dangerous region of Iraq, a DMV (Desert Mobility Vehicle) of the 1st Ranger Battalion patrols searching indications of rebels in the sector. DMV is one of the Humvee many versions specially built for the Special Forces. This vehicle is also known as GMV (Ground Mobility Vehicle) which is a modified M1097A2 Humvee, with a more powerful engine and heavier armament. *(SOCOM Photo)*

When patrolling in the " Sunnit triangle " in 2004, Rangers of the 2nd Battalion provide fire support to their comrades moving on both sides. Unlike Special Forces, they are more or less equipped as the soldiers of the " regular " units are, with the exception of the Woodland colour rigging over the desert camo BDU. *(SOCOM Photo)*

Ranger from 75th Rangers Regiment.
In theatres of operations such as Iraq, the pump-action short-barrel Remington 870 is often used in "door breaching " urban operations. The BDU, the Ranger Assault Carrying Kit (RACK), and the MICH TC-2000 helmet are characteristic elements of a 75th Rangers Ranger's gear. If the US DOD well equips its soldiers in electronic and optical devices, the US GI often chooses some more personal materiel such as the Sure fire lamps or even a third weapon such as an automatic pistol for example.

Rangers of the 2nd Battalion disembark from a Bradley M2 armoured vehicle after a patrol in enemy territory.
After the " hit and run " operations in the western Iraqi desert in March-April 2003, Rangers had to abandon their DMV (Desert Mobility Vehicle) and GMV (Ground Mobility Vehicle) for heavy armoured vehicles better protected against IED.
(SOCOM Photo)

Below.
Despite IEDs along the communication routes, Rangers still used DMV (Desert Mobility Vehicle) in some operations, because of their speed and fire power.
(SOCOM Photo)

Above.
Patrol at night in Tikrit, former home city of Saddam Hussein, at the heart
of the rebellion. When rotating in Iraq, Rangers worked with the Army major units,
particularly in the " hottest " zones.
(75th Rangers Regiment Photo)

Below.
During Iraqi Freedom ground operations in March and April 2003, Rangers closely
worked with the 160th Special Operations Aviation Regiment (Task Force 160)
aircraft. Here, Rangers screen a zone in central Iraq during the fall of 2004.
(75th Rangers Regiment Photo)

Left.
During an operation at night, a Rangers team of the 2nd Battalion uses an AN/PEQ-2 infra-red target pointer/illuminator/ aiming laser to designate enemy targets. Rangers are equipped with AN/PVS-14 NVG. *(Photo SOCOM)*

3rd Ranger Battalion A Company's Rangers began Operation Iraqi Freedom on 27 March, while they fast paced in the night to the "nicknamed" H1 airfield, located 80 kilometres south-west of Hadithah. A Company's Rangers were followed by B Company's[1] who arrived during the night of Saturday 29 March. H1 airfield, located in the middle of a desert, was to be used as a rear base for the 3rd Battalion which was to launch recon operations in the region and seize the Iraqi capital's communications routes.

The next day, B Company moved northeast to link with a C Company's platoon. At dusk, it stopped 35 kilometres of the rear base. At this time things speeded

---

1. The Company moved toward the H1 airfield from the Jordanian border with the HHC's second detachment of the 3rd Battalion at 1835 local time.

Gunner from 75th Rangers Regiment.
Two different gears for his 75th Rangers gunner. The Woodland and desert camo BDU is typical of the beginning of the conflict.
Under the RACK is always a ballistic protection against the assault rifle fires. It's either a RBA, or an IBA SPEAR vest with the Small Arms Protection Inserts (SAPI) and ceramic plates to enhance the protection. The M249 light machine gun is in wide service in various versions.
Here is a specifically developed ELCAN M145 optical sight with a M249 reticule.

up, for intelligence reports said Iraqi were mining the Hadithah dam on the Euphrates River. This was very worrying: the dam's destruction could lead to a major human disaster on the one hand, and to considerably slow down the 3rd Infantry Division advance, on the other hand.

Seize the dam at any price

As a result, B Company was given the mission to seize the dam in order to prevent the Iraqis from sabotaging it and allow the coalition's forces to continue its advance. According to the latest intelligence, 200 soldiers, ten or so armoured and about fifty pieces of air defence artillery defended the dam. In less than two hours, a plan was worked out: 1st Platoon would secure the western flank to allow the 2nd Platoon to enter within the infrastructures, while engineer teams would verify that the dam was not mined.

Night had begun to fall on 31 March when a Rangers vehicles column moved ahead toward objective Lynx, 31 kilometres from the dam. *"After a mechanical incident of one of our APC,* said Platoon Sergeant D. of B Company, *and despite the NVGs and a relatively clear sky, we realized we had already made one third of the distance. That is why, while C Company's 3rd Platoon was screening the zone to find the road leading to the base of the dam, I walked on a small hill with my combat team from where I realized how complex it was to fulfil the mission.* "The dam was huge: There were several buildings, not only one! While the 3rd Squad began searching the constructions, C Company's 3rd Platoon reached the power station where it faced some guards which were eliminated with 12.7 mm machine gun fires.

" Suddenly, things became mad continued to say Platoon Sergeant D. *Within seconds we were under fire of tens of assault rifles, machine guns, RPG, and ten mortars at least. Surprisingly, nobody was wounded, despite the heavy fire. "*

Rangers counter-fired and radioed aviation to blast every mortar position. For four hours, American fires responded to Iraqi fires. But at dawn, American commandoes saw that the

Below.
February 2004 at Fort Campbell, Sergeant Jason Parsons pins medals on the chest of Rangers of the 2nd Battalion, 75th Rangers, for their participation in various operations in Afghanistan and in Iraq. That day, 200 Rangers were rewarded.
(Photo SOCOM)

desert before them was full of bunkers and trenches, as far as they could see! To prevent the Iraqi from moving, the Platoon Sergeant asked for more than ten air bombings. Yet, the enemy was able to regroup in 50 to 100 element formations, about 7 kilometres from the Rangers. Another solution was to fire 120 mm mortars to beat them off.

Artillery, the major Iraqi threat

In the meantime, mid-afternoon, B Company's 2nd Platoon had finished securing the dam and its facilities.

During the whole second day, the Iraqis tried to regain the dam and advanced toward the American positions, but without assaulting them.

The third day, the Iraqi artillery started to fire 155 mm howitzer rounds. Fortunately, an Air Force Combat Controller attached to the B Company for the operation called Air Force fighter-bombers to blast the artillery guns. Twenty hours later the east-of-the-dam Iraqi artillery threat was over. But the Rangers counted more than 350 shells fired around the dam. However, southern howitzers continued firing intermittently.

Said Platoon Sgt. D: *" The fourth day, their artillery had been able to fire several shells just some meters from our mortar positions, and I clearly remember an artillery man flying in the air and falling behind a wall. The other men were frenziedly radioing, and I was expecting the worse when I arrived with the medics. Iraqi observers who had spotted us " happily " fired on our position. The seriously wounded and unconscious Ranger was cared of between fires, and then transported back to the rear.*

But at the time we moved to care for this Ranger, a 155 mm shell crashed on the Platoon's position, next to a protection where a Humvee and three Rangers were. The three men were thrown against the walls and the Humvee lifted out of its place by the explosion! Eventually, my Rangers were only concussed… and deaf for the remains of the day! "

To hold until a relieve came

At last, on day five, the Iraqi artillery ceased firing. Everybody thought the aviation had killed it. Platoons were given

Next page
Under protection of Rangers of the 2nd Battalion, two 448th Civil Affairs Battalion elements cover leaflets of the Iraq rebellion in the Avgani region in December 2004.
(SOCOM Photo)

TOWARDS " HEAVY ARMOURED "

During the fall of 2005, 75th Rangers' 2nd Battalion received sixteen Stryker armoured vehicles to use in Afghanistan.

According to General Bryan Brown, the initiative to purchase these armoured vehicles did not reflect a larger shift toward armoured vehicle operations on the part of the Rangers. Yet, we now see in Iraq that Rangers units operate almost only with M-113 or Humvee armoured vehicles. ❑

me order to reconnoitre the buildings. Armaments and ammu-
itions were so numerous that they could clean two buildings
nly that day!

The day after, enemy artillery resumed firing. Between the
ain of shells during the day and digging shelters over night,
angers began to look tired. However, by the end of the after-
oon two M-1 Abrams tanks arrived and moved north. At the
ame time, B Company's 3rd Platoon relieved the 2nd Pla-

Ranger from 75th Rangers Regiment.
Combat at night makes every Infantry man more vulnerable.
The US DOD has well understood the lessons learnt from the previous conflicts.
Each soldier is equipped with a low-light intensification device. In order to ease American soldiers'
identification, infantry men have an IFF (Identification Friend or Foe) marking device
under the form of a reflective-to-IR square of glint tape on their helmet top
or a US flag on their left sleeve.

As early as 19 March evening, 160th SOAR helicopters, (here is a MH-47D Chinook), took off from Jordan toward the Iraqi desert, with Rangers and their light vehicles aboard. A few hours later, Rangers captured an airfield to be used as an air base during the operations in the heart of Iraq. *(SOCOM Photo)*

oon which went back to the airfield they had left seven days earlier.

Overall, within one week of combat, B Company of the 3rd Battalion, with its heavy weapons, mortars and coalition's aviation only, was able to kill or capture more than 230 Iraqi soldiers, 29 T-55 tanks, 28 155 mm howitzers, 22 82 mm mortars, 6 60 mm mortars, 9 S-60, 4 ZSU-23/2 and 14 14.5 mm heavy machine guns.

On 3 April 2003, Sergeants Nino Livaudais and Ryan P. Long, as well as CPT Russell Rippetoe of A Company, 3rd Battalion, were killed by a suicide bombing.

On their side, C Company Rangers carried out many reconnaissances along the Iraqi border to prevent Iraqi leaders from fleeing to Damascus on the one hand, and to avoid Islamic volunteers entering into Iraq on the other hand. These missions, performed with British and Australian SAS, moved them closer to the heart of Iraq day after day. On July 2003, Rangers of the 3rd Battalion returned home. They were replaced by soldiers of the 2nd Battalion from Fort Lewis.

On 12 February 2004, at Fort Lewis, more than 200 Rangers of the 2nd Battalion, 75th Ranger Regiment, were awarded various medals and badges, from the Bronze Star to the Combat Field Medical Badge, for their actions in Afghanistan and in Iraq. ❏

Rangers of the 2nd Battalion, 75th Rangers Regiment, April 2003, Iraq.
The M4 SOPMOD assault rifle accessory kit allows the weapon to be mission customizable. The kit includes the Crane buttstock with additional batteries for a tactical lamp, the Aimpoint sight.
The 40 mm M203 grenade launcher provides this 75th Rangers Ranger with a significant fire power for urban combat.
The Gallet MICH helmet swing arm allows mounting night vision goggle and ESS/NVG protecting lens.
The Ranger Assault Carrying Kit allows carrying a wide modular set of equipment and ammunitions.
Lastly, the pump-action Remington M870 rifle allows door-breaching actions.

Psychological Operations units had been carrying out actions in Iraq well before 2003. One can say they never stopped since the end of the first Gulf War in 1991!

Thus, during operation Desert Storm, PsyOps units were employed only at the tactical level to convince the Iraqi army to surrender. In the following years, they tried to persuade the Iraqi population to overthrow Saddam Hussein through the "*Voice of America*" radio.

Put the Iraqi leaders under pressure

In 1998, before and during operation *Desert Fox*, PsyOps encouraged Iraqi units to remain in their barracks and to disobey to orders they were given about raids on Kuwait. During the fall of 2001, American armed forces tried to defuse the tensions in the Iraqi-aviation-no-fly zones, by dropping thousands of leaflets on the Iraqi air defence positions telling them not to fire on the American and British aircraft.

Members of 9th PsyOps Battalion place antiterrorist flyers over graffiti during a patrol in Mosul, Iraq, Aug. 16, 2004.
(US Army Photo)

THE 4th PSYCHOLOGICAL OPERATIONS GROUP (AIRBORNE)

4th Psychological Operations Group (Airborne) (PsyOps), based at Fort Bragg, North Carolina, is the only active Army psychological operations unit.

Its 1,145 military and 57 civilian personnel constitute 26% of all US Army Psychological Operations; the remaining 74% are reservists. The 4th PsyOps consists of six battalions (1st, 3rd, 5th, 6th, 8th and 9th PsyOps Bn.), of which four are regionally oriented.

The 4th PsyOps can be deployed anywhere in the world in a very short time. Its mission is to conduct PsyOps activities, but also CIMIC operations for a unified command, or a department or an agency, but also for the National Command Authority. ❑

In 2003, PsyOps units were at the heart of action during the combat operations trying to make the Iraqi armies surrender.
But after spring, their mission was to broadcast messages targeting the civilian population.
(USASOC Photo)

However, it was only after 2002 the Pentagon employed all the PsyOps' so-far-under-employed[1] capabilities against Iraq. The first step was at strategic level. The goal was to explain the American policy on Iraq to the Arabic countries and to avoid anti-American reactions. The next step was at the tactical and operational level.

The objective was to try to convince the Iraqi people and armed forces not to move in case of conflict. Thus, security forces and their leaders "*were put under pressure* "to ignore orders they would be given to use WMD or to sabotage the national infrastructure.

_____

1. In February 2002, the department of State approved a new directive named "Information Operations", in which it deeply reviewed the missions of the PsyOps units, allowing them to operate against the leaders, their population, whether they were friend, neutral or enemy. Moreover, these could be clandestine operations.

PSYOPS
ASSAULTS THE IRAQI HEARTS AND MINDS

At the same time, support was provided to the Iraqi opposition which had to organize *coups d'état* with the help of military leaders which were promised high responsibilities after the fall of Saddam Hussein. To persuade the Iraqi military leaders not to do anything in case of conflict, PsyOps focussed on the new communication capabilities: cellular telephones and fax of the high ranking militaries. Moreover, subliminal images were inserted in the Iraqi television broadcasts.

As of the end of 1991, the Department of State and the CIA, both in favour of a non-military overthrowing of Saddam Hussein, set up twenty or so radio stations in Amman, Cairo, Kuwait and of course in the Kurdistan. Most of the broadcasts were made with the help of either the American PsyOps units, or the Jordanian or Saudi intelligence services. Between September 1996 and the end of 1998, these broadcastings were transmitted by EC-130E Commando Solo aircraft of the Special Operations.

As the Civil Affairs teams, PsyOps units carry out public relations operations with the local population. The message is clear: " Coalition's troops are in Iraq to bring democracy ". (DOD Photo)

67

Previous page and above.
Win the Iraqi "hearts and minds" is the PsyOps' mission since spring 2003. Distribution of flyers, newspapers, radio and television broadcasts, a range of vectors to gain the Iraqi's trust. However, it is a risky bet as rebellion is still imposing terror.
(USASOC and US Army photos)

Right.
During operation *Iraqi Freedom*, PsyOps of the 3rd Infantry Division were part of the As Samawah battle. However, high winds and sandstorms notably reduced the speakerphones range, means 500 to 1000 metres. First messages targeted the civilian population to tell them to stay home, and not to stay on the roads.
(USASOC Photo)

As of end of December 2002, a Commando Solo of the 193rd Special Operations Wing, with Kuwait-based operators, continuously flew over Iraq. Many messages were broadcasted to Iraqi soldiers only to encourage them " *to overthrow the regime* ". At the time, all the messages were produced by Fort Bragg 4th PsyOps Group's elements, and approved by the Department of State before being broadcasted.

To go into the " next gear "

Two months before operation Iraqi Freedom began in March 2003, the PsyOps campaign became less informative and persuasive to move into the "next gear". Iraqi soldiers and civilians were warned to stay far from the military facilities, some strategic centres and the American and British forces. Between October and November 2002, 600,000 flyers were sprinkled on the Iraqi air defence in the south of the country.

This number increased in January and February 2003 to reach 1 million copies. By mid-April about 32 million leaflets

were dropped [2] and 108 messages radio broadcasted by the radios of the region as well as by the 193rd Special Operations Wing aircraft.

During the ground operations, PsyOps teams were included in the combat units and participated in the psychological actions in the combat zones.

Thus, they participated in the broadcast of messages by speakerphones - read by American-uniform-dressed Iraqi translators that the CIA had chosen - to invite Iraqi soldiers to surrender, and distributed flyers to the Iraqi population in the captured cities.

As soon as Baghdad was captured, PsyOps teams began to repair the radio and television networks to allow the broadcasting of allied-controlled messages.

On 12 April 2003, the Iraqi television resumed broadcasting [3].

2. *In 1991, more than 29 million leaflets had been dropped over Iraq, and 2.4 millions in 1998 during operation Desert Fox.*
3. *Because Americans had the capability to interrupt Saddam Hussein's broadcasts as early as the first air strikes, Specialists of the PsyOps units wondered why it had not been done that early.*

Gaining the " hearts and minds "

The end of the ground campaign did not stop the psychological actions. On the contrary, PsyOps teams remained in Iraq and were given zones under the responsibility of major units. The PsyOps action resumed for good as of the fall of 2003 when the coalition forces had to recapture cities, and even regions, the rebellion ruled.

In the designated friendly zones, the units' attitude was totally different and more of a stabilisation phase type. Soldiers participated in the conquest of *the "hearts and minds "*.

During the combats, negotiations were conducted with local authorities, the central government and even the insurgents, sometimes simultaneously! These discussions allowed the local authorities not to loose face. The principle was clear: *"They needed to get the feelings they did not give up because of us, but because of the general interest. It offered an alternative to a hopeless resistance. "*

At Najaf, First Cav' soldiers distributed meals presented in Arabic language and prepared in the local tradition, and medically treated civilians in mobile first-aid posts.

Moreover, to demonstrate reconciliation and show condolences, American troops gave $ 1.9 million to the 2,600 inhabitants.

And in October 2004 at Sadr City, " peace " was gained thanks to the promise of a huge $ 500 million aid.

Previous page, top.
A 9th PsyOps Battalion element walks with newspaper to be handed out at the outskirts of a city. A way to disseminate information in support of the coalition's work and the Iraqi government.
(US Army Photo)

Left.
A 9th PsyOps Battalion Humvee equipped with a speakerphone and since 2004, two roof-mounted machine guns to support Special Forces when they distribute flyers.
(USASOC Photo)

Top right.
A 9th PsyOps Battalion element writes a message to be published. PsyOps have studios to record audio and video messages, but also have printing facilities to produce leaflets, flyers and newspapers.
(USASOC Photo)

PSYOPS MISSIONS

4th PsyOps Group mission is to conduct psychological actions thanks to the production and distribution of leaflets, flyers and objects, as well as radio and video broadcasts, in order to disseminate information either at the tactical or strategic level.

To disseminate information, 4th PsyOps has light and heavy printing equipment, audio and video production studios, AW, FW and SW radio stations, and vehicle or aircraft-mounted speakerphones. ❐

To show a positive vision of the coalition

In February 2004, some weeks before the first elections, Civil Affairs units were involved in operation *Rock the Vote*. Their goal was to convince electors to trust the government that would be elected after the former leaders and rebellion chiefs had been captured on the one hand, and to show a positive vision of the coalition's forces in Iraq on the other hand. In the Ramadi region, Civil Affairs of the 346th PsyOps Company worked along with the 1st Brigade Combat Team of the 1st

Next page top.
Within the framework of counter-terrorist actions,
Sergeant Bill Whittaker of the 361st Psychological Operations Company,
a reserve unit, writes a message targeting the Mosul population.
(USASOC Photo)

PURPLE HEART
FOR BRAVERY

April 2004, a PsyOps team of the 17th PsyOps Battalion, atta-ched to Company B of the 3rd PsyOps Battalion of Fort Bragg, patrolled in the market of Fallujah trying to determine the effect of radio broadcasts on the local population.

"Throughout the day we had heard sporadic small arms fire said Sgt. 1st Class John Fisher, 3rd PSYOP Bn. It had been a very tense morning. On our return to our base west of the city, we encountered an IED that detonated not more than 20 feet from our vehicle.

Selby, who was driving the second vehicle, received the majo-rity of the blast, sustaining lacerations to the face, a concussion and a ruptured eardrum. Yet, he managed to maintain control of the Humvee and get us out of the area, without further inci-dent until our home base "

Selby was medically evacuated to Baghdad for treatment of his injuries, and then on to Germany and to Washington, D.C. On 21 May, Staff Sgt. Scott Selby received the Purple Heart for bravery. ❒

Infantry Division. "We wanted to give the local people a better understanding of democracy and explained that everyone would have an equal voice in the new government", explained Spe-cialist Jason K. Secrist of the 346th PsyOps Company.

The psychological operations unit's job was to become invol-ved in meetings between commanders and key leaders in the community, such as sheiks, imams or other religious leaders, tea-chers and council members. "After establishing relationships with key community leaders, continued Specialist Secrist, we went on to conduct a door-to-door campaign to saturate the city and sur-rounding area with information concerning the government, a timeline to sovereignty, a tip line to report suspicious activity, how to react to and understand traffic-control points and curfew information.

And another reason to establish a relationship with the lea-ders of the community was to answer questions from local peo-ple directly! " ❒

Above.
Staff Sergeant Scott Selby, B Company 17th PsyOps Battalion,
a reserve unit of Chicago, receives the Purple Heart
from Major General Herbert Altshuler, Commander,
US Army Civil Affairs and Psychological Operations Command.
(USASOC Photo)

Opposite, bottom.
A PsyOps team participates in a hit and run operation on a road
to Caldia. Here, Sergeant Joseph Rossi, 9th Psychological Operations
Battalion, mans a .50 machine gun in support of his team mates.
(USMC Photo)

THE CIVIL AFFAIRS
MISSIONS WAS TO "WIN THE IRAQI'S HEARTS AND MINDS"

When the Iraqi Freedom operation began, the enlisted or reserve personnel of the Civil Affairs (CA) teams were at last embedded in the combat units. The American Command had finally understood that taking care of the population had to be as soon as possible. It was no longer acceptable to leave a "gap" between the combat units and the arrival of the Civil Affairs.

CAs mission consists to quickly identify the population's requirements

All the more so, as the Civil Affairs teams were supporting the various commands in the field to tentatively gain a fast adhesion amongst the local. They were also supporting both the so called classical units and the Special Forces, and were also capable of supporting the civil administration in the operation areas.

On April 2004, in Dibbis, a team of C Company of the 96th Civil Affairs Battalion (Airborne), Fort Bragg, carries out an inspection of an abandoned barracks of the former Iraqi army. These buildings had to be rebuilt and then handed over to the new Iraqi National Guard. (Photo USASOC)

If in the past the American military command gave little importance to the Civil Affairs units, things have seriously changed as it is not currently possible to design a military operation without Civil Affairs teams. Thus, during operations Enduring Freedom and Iraqi Freedom, 96th Civil Affairs Battalion (Airborne), was and is still engaged in Iraq and Afghanistan with almost all its personnel. (USASOC Photo)

CAs are drilled to quickly identify the local population's requirements during a war or when a natural disaster occurs. They can also find the local resources available to work for the benefit of the military operations, plan and execute civilian evacuations, and then establish and maintain a liaison or a dialogue with NGOs and the private or state-owned trade companies.

To this aim, they speak the local language or hire translators and interpreters, and work with the local authorities and civilian organizations to rebuild the infrastructures and to restore stability.

After the collapse of Saddam Hussein's regime, all American soldiers, American and local civil authorities then turned to the Civil Affairs units to restore " the Iraqi machine ". As the demands were huge, so did the task for the hundreds of Civil Affairs personnel spread all over the country. First power and gasoline had to be provided to everyone. Then they had to reorganize the public services and to convince the Iraqi civil authorities to cooperate. All of this with war in the background as insurgents were numerous and did everything they could to prevent a return to a normal life in Iraq.

Because of the rebels' threats and repeated attacks, Civil Affairs elements made significant efforts towards the local population.

For example, the 96th teams deployed in pre-selected villages, listened to the local demands for a start, then establis-

Several elements of Team 5 of the Detachment 2 of the 5th Civil Affaire Group (a unit of the 445th Civil Affairs Battalion) meet the population in the southern suburbs of Fallujah in June 2005. A Civil Affairs team usually consists of ten personnel. (US Army Photo)

hed priorities, and when funding had been obtained they made sure the requested equipment was delivered.

Thousands of projects

On the surface, some might not see the military implications, but they were considerable. Thus, sergeant 1st class Keith Ducote, team sergeant of the battalion's B Company, reports an example of an end to end action he carried out: " *Shortly after the ground war kicked off in Iraq, troops were getting "sniped at" in a village outside Baghdad. Ducote's team started handing out toys to children in the village to begin forming bonds with the people. But what really made the difference, he said, was when the team sponsored a dental hygiene class to teach about 300 local children how to brush and floss their teeth, then handed out dental kits. One week later, people of the village approached us to report where insurgents had hidden weapons. They didn't want to be in trouble any longer.* "

Everywhere in the country, Civil Affairs teams started working on hundred of projects. Thus, elements of the 432nd Civil Affairs Battalion worked with 504th Parachute Infantry Regiment paratroopers in the city of Al Karma to train the local police, to equip them with arms and equipment, and to carry out common patrols.

On their side, in Mosul, north of Iraq (at Ankawa exact-

THE CIVILS AFFAIRS

Civil Affairs units had provided the American Command with a tactical support during operations *Just Cause* in Panama, *Desert Shield* and *Desert Storm* in the Middle-East, *Promote Liberty* to establish the Panama's government, *Restore Hope* in Somalia, *Uphold Democracy* to the Haitian government, as well as in the peace keeping operations in Bosnia-Herzegovina and in Kosovo, and recently *Enduring Freedom* in Afghanistan as well as *Iraqi Freedom* in Iraq. ❐

ly), only twenty personnel of the 416th Civil Affairs Battalion replaced two hundred comrades of the 404th CA to perform the same work! That meant building new schools, providing medical aid, restoring the water purification and sewage treatment systems, resurfacing roads and improving public security.

Captain Mike Carson *(left)* of the 451st Civil Affairs Battalion briefs his squad before driving for a mission to evaluate the progress of construction work at the Mishkub Police Station located near Najaf *(US Navy Photo)*

As matter of fact a brigade normally supports a Civil Affairs battalion. It provides food, cleaning and transport. But in this case the 416th CA operated as an independent unit.

Another CA mission: In August 2004, during Iron Fury operation, teams of the 478th Civil Affairs Battalion worked along with soldiers of the "First Cav" in Sadr City, one of Baghdad's quarters. At the time, this true city was ruled by the Mahdi's army. Methodically, First Cav's elements beat off or eliminated all militias showing resistance, while Civil Affairs personnel aimed at reassuring the population and explaining

Above and following page, top to bottom.
Civil Affairs teams support US Command when they work with the civilian authorities and local population in the war zones to rebuild civilian infrastructures. Extension of the battle field during operation Iraqi Freedom led to a " total battle space" where all units were on the front line.
Thus, there was no "rear zone" anymore, and every soldier might have to fight at any time.
(DOD Photos)

OPERATIONS *HEARTS AND MINDS*

During the summer 2003, the 101st Airborne was the first American major unit to try to win the *" battle of the hearts and minds "*.

All 101st' companies and battalions, with first the PsyOps and Civil Affairs units, were involved in multiple projects for the benefit of the population.

Within a few months, these methods were going to pay off and to bring a lot of information. Officers would understand they had to meet Sheiks, tribe chiefs, Imams and demonstrate respect and sympathy. ❑

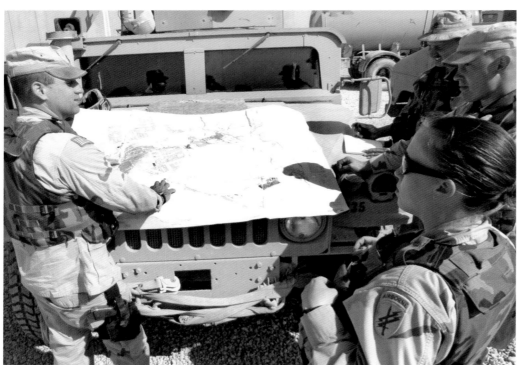

the reasons for this operation [1]. Within five days, the Mahdi's army had almost vanished. During these operations, Civils Affairs personnel had worked under rocket fires and explosions of IEDs (Improvised Explosive Devices) set up by militias.

In October 2004, replacing the 425th CA Bn, the 414th Civil Affairs Battalion which had just been deployed in Iraq was given the mission to train the Iraqi police officers at camp

---

1 However, one has not to forget that the help of the coalition is counterbalanced by similar actions the insurgents organize with the financial means they are not lacking.

WATER FOR EVERYONE

431st Civil Affairs Battalion Master Sergeant Bill McGuckin (originally of the 416th Civil Affairs Bn.) didn't know what was in store when he arrived in Iraq in March 2003. He was with the 101st Airborne up north of Mosul during the conquest of Iraq, the country being still in a sort of "end of reign" where anarchy was combined with joy of freedom after the fall of Saddam Hussein.

He previously had crossed into Iraq from Afghanistan and moved to Mosul after a month in Baghdad working with the Public Health Care.

At this time Mosul was in a state of disrepair. The city had been damaged from years of neglect because it was considered as a pro-Kurd city. Not to mention recent fighting in order to liberate the city had not made things any better. In a first step, Master Sgt. McGuckin worked with the civil engineering team to repair the power plant and the water purification centre which served a city of almost two million people. "After water had been restored to everyone, the second thing was to convince the people to go back to work, begins McGuckin. The biggest project was to repair the dam, a vital source of electricity for the people of Mosul.

"After his "tour of duty" and two weeks spent in the USA, Master Sgt. rejoined his original unit, gave a series of classes at Fort Bragg to prepare the deployment of the 416th CA Bn. elements in Iraq, and went back to Mosul again as expert for the missions already launched during his first tour. ❏

(USASOC Photo)

Hawk, near Baghdad. They ran language tests and physical exams before they performed the first screening of the applicant candidates of which 40% would be sent to the training schools in Jordan. *"Of course in Iraq it's a difficult task* said Staff Sgt. Patrick Cummings, a team Sergeant in the 414th CA Bn., *but most all of my team had already been deployed in Afghanistan. And we tried to identify the good elements among the recruits."*

THE "HUMAN TARGETING"

CIMICs are often embedded in the "human targeting" scheme which integrates all operations according to several objectives: win over the enemy, then secure the area, finally improve the infrastructures. In this combined-arms manoeuvre Civil Affairs are associated to the contact capabilities of the combat units on the one hand, which means gathering the population's requirements and being able to dialogue daily, as well as on the other hand to the technical competence of the combat support branches. ❏

Above.
In January 2004, 304th Civil Affairs Brigade's elements return to Champion base after the launch of a construction project at Ar Ramadi, whose aim was to restore several infrastructures destroyed during the 2003 offensive. *(USASOC Photo)*

Left. In southern Iraq, jointly with British Civil Affairs officers, a 455th Civil Affairs Battalion' member and an American contractor study the capabilities of a new civilian back up equipment the US gave to Iraq. *(MOD Photo)*

Below.
October 2003, a team of 4th Civil Affairs Group attached to 5th Marine Regiment has just been attacked by an Iraqi rebel group in the outskirts of Fallujah. They watch the buildings under USAF aircraft strike. Civil Affairs were part of a security and stabilization operation in the Al Anbar province. *(USMC Photo)*

In addition, during their " tour of duty ", the 425th CA Battalion teams, whose missions area was the Iraqi North-West zone, rebuilt fifty primary schools, recruited two hundred and fifty police officers, vaccinated three hundred goats and sheep's, and provided a job to several hundreds of Iraqis to clean out streets and ditches, and help to launch a local radio sta-

2. *It is worth noticing that it represents 4% of the civil affairs forces, the remaining 96 percent of the Army's civil affairs forces are found in four Civil Affairs Commands, subordinate brigades and battalions in the Army Reserve*

tion. In May 2005, A company, 403rd Civil Affairs Battalion of New York, deployed in Baghdad vicinities, had three women as Humvee gunners.

Paradoxically, this had a calming effect on the population, and the unit was able to work in forty three villages within the Al-Rashid area. On its side, still deployed in Baghdad's vicinity since May 2005, the 443rd Civil Affairs Bn. worked upon 162 projects and provided some jobs to more than three thousand Iraqis. The first project run in the 3rd ID's area of responsibility aimed at first installing, a water purification unit, then at distributing water to each house in Jueba village. In the long run, economic projects were pre-launched according to the local authorities' level of cooperation.

The required presence of Civil Affairs

If in the past, the importance the military command gave the Civil Affairs was relative, things have really changed over time as it is currently not possible to design a military operation without embedding CIMIC teams.

A ROUTINE MISSION

91st Engineer Battalion, 2nd Brigade Combat Team of the 1st Cavalry Division returned from Iraq after nine months of duty. This battalion was reorganized in five teams of eight elements each, each team attached to a 1st Cavalry Unit. The battalion had one month of training in Missouri before its deployment to Iraq. The training had been on how to fight when embarked in a vehicle, to learn medical first aid, close combat, and a " refresh " on combat methods: firing when moving, moving in an opponent's area and gestures to communicate. These methods would prove useful as Captain Marc Chung, Team Leader, 425th CA Bn., reported " *On 19 August 2004, with three men of the Alpha Team, an Iraqi interpreter and I, we headed about twenty kilometres east of Baghdad in a convoy consisting of five vehicles. The weather was sunny and warm and we already knew this road. It was a routine day as many others. After a last briefing we joined the two Bradley's in charge of the escort. The Humvee had all been equipped with additional armours on both sides and on the doors. Moreover, metal plates protected the bodies of the vehicles. I was confident in the men and in the vehicles that carried us.* "

Captain Chung well remembered the cows grazing on the sides of the road as his view was drawn toward some garbage on the right which looked new. *"For any reason, I thought there was something different on this road, but I was not able to identify what it was really.* "

A few seconds later Chung, who was in the front passenger seat, was flooded with a wave of heat which came from the floor and pushed him against the body of the Humvee. An IED hidden in the garbage had just exploded near the right wheel. While he felt his arms and legs to see whether he had been wounded, Chung realised the air vents had literally melted and the passenger compartment was flooded with a thick black smoke. *"The engine is going to break! Go on! "*shouted Chung to Sergeant Sandra Lee, the driver. And it was driving crabwise, the engine roaring, the windshield covered with oil and coolant, that the Civil Affairs Humvee ran another hundred meters before it definitely " died ".

Chung and Lee got off the wreck and ran for safety. In the mean time the Bradley's had come back and fired their 30 mm guns toward the ditches where the insurgents might have been hiding. Then, Chung realised this attack had not affected his people's morale. Less than an hour later, after a short break at the base camp to eat and drink, the mission was resumed. ❏

Since April 2004, the 96th Civil Affairs Battalion (Airborne), headquartered at Fort Bragg, is the only active Army Civil Affairs unit [2]. It is committed in Iraq and Afghanistan with almost all its personnel. There is a plan to double its strength from two hundred to four hundred elements by 2006. ❏

79

The 160th SOAR 's "Night Stalkers"

"FOR EVER FURTHER, FOR EVER LOWER"

Mid-February 2003, 3rd Battalion [1] of the 160th Special Operations Army Regiment (Airborne) helicopters were already deployed in the Saudi and Jordanian deserts. Overall, more than a hundred personnel and 40 aircraft had been airborne from Fort Campbell. They supported 5th Special Forces Group's elements, whose major part was still in Djibouti.

During the night of 19 March, three MH-47 E carried out the first heliborne operation of the coalition's troops. They dropped a hundred Rangers and their fast vehicles in the Iraqi desert, west of the country.

In the heart of the Iraqi desert

The mission was to capture an air base. Wearing AN/AVS 6V3 NVGs, pilots were quiet in their Chinooks, flying low-level in a dark night. Any error would lead to a crash. Less than an hour later, helicopters landed in the dust and unloaded the Rangers and their Desert Mobility Vehicles.

1. 3rd Battalion, stationed in Savannah, Georgia, comprises a staff, an HHC and three combat companies (A, B and C), and has 20 MH-60L (including 1 modified as AH-60L) and 8 MH-47D.

MH-60 and OH-58 pilots have lighter overalls than the MH-57 helicopter pilots. Generally, they use Infantry-man rather than air crew-man BDU.

160th SOAR combat commander.
160th SOAR crew BDUs may differ.
If the basic BDU often remains the same,
a CWU-27P overalls or an Aircrew BDU in Nomex,
the vests may vary.
This MH-47D crew chief wears an AWS vest
with an integrated harness for extraction. It replaces
the CWU-33 Air Save, of the SARVIP or OH-1 vests
which are also often used. The bullet-proof vest
and SAPI protection shingles provide
the personal ballistics protection.

Above.
In a MH-47 E, a machine gun operator behind a door-mounted 7.62 mm M134 Minigun. Another identical machine gun is affixed on the other side.
(160th SOAR Photo)

With eleven MH-47 D, twenty five MH-47 E, and now the brand new MH-47 G, 160th SOAR (A) has the world's most extraordinary special-operations fleet of helicopters. These aircraft's capabilities are unmatched, whether it is for electronic systems aboard or the quality and experience of the crews which have been continuously deployed in combat operations since 2002.
(USASOC Photo)

Air refuelling operation for a MH-47 E and MH-60 taking gasoline from a MH-130 P Combat Shadow of AFSOC. During *Iraqi Freedom*, this type of operation was performed several times in the hostile Iraqi sky. *(USASOC Photo)*

Left.
Chief Warrant Officer Michael Weddington served as an AH-6J Little Bird flight lead pilot in several missions during the night of 11 June 2003, flying low-level (less than 3 meters) at more than 100 km/h; 200 to 400 meter gap between the recce element and the support element equipped with guns or rocket launchers pods. *(USASOC Photo)*

The 160th SOAR

The 160th Special Operations Aviation Regiment (Airborne) provides aviation support to US Army Special Operations forces. It consists of four battalions: 1st, 2nd and 4th Battalions, based at Fort Campbell, Kentucky, and 3rd Battalion at Hunter Army Field, Georgia. In 2003 the 160th SOAR had 1,400 men and 104 helicopters, including 30 AH-6 and OH-6 Little Bird, 50 MH-60 Pave Hawk and 24 MH-47 E Chinook. The organisational structure of the 160th SOAR (A) allows the Regiment to quickly tailor its unique assets to meet the mission requirements of special operations forces. ❏

MH-47 E was specifically intended for Special Forces. It has several specific systems: long-range communications and advanced avionics, electronic counter-measures with decoy flares and infra-red captors.
(SOCOM Photo)

off the MH-47 E within two minutes. At dawn they were back at one of the bases in Saudi Arabia, where a new mission was just up.

160th SOAR (A) helicopters have been continuously engaged in Iraq, flying more than 4 500 hours since spring 2003.

The most well-known media-covered operation was the rescue of Private Jessica Lynch, captured by the Iraqi on 23 March

and detained in a Nassiriya hospital. It was carried out during the night of 1 April. American command decided to set up a joint rescue operation with Rangers, SEAL, Combat Controllers, 160th SOAR helicopters and US Air Force Special Operations Command aircraft. While AC-130 Gunships flew over in the sky ready to blast any Iraqi action, MH-60 of the Night Stalkers landed in front of the hospital.

Rangers disembarked first to set up a security perimeter around the buildings, and SEAL climbed up the floors to rescue Jessica Lynch. Once the prisoner was identified and rescued, they all ran back to the rotary-wing aircraft. Overall the operation lasted twenty five minutes.

160th SOAR crew chief.
160th SOAR helicopters often fly during the night. Crews are trained to fly with AN/AVS-6 and AN/AVS-9 night visions goggles. " ANVIS " are equipped with third generation low-light scope.
The lowest residual light is electronically amplified and allows a stereoscopic vision. Power is provided by batteries or by a power link to the helicopter. 160th SOAR also tested the new AN/PVS-21 which should replace the ANVIS system in Iraq.

Close-up on a MH-60 L DAP (Direct-Action Penetrator) door-mounted armament, where the 30 mm M230 gun and the 7.62 mm M134 Minigun can be seen. This armament provides a heavy fire power with the M230 4 000 metres maximum range.
(160th SOAR Photo)

The 160th SOAR helicopters' main missions are infiltration and extraction, close air support and medical support for SOF.

160th SOAR has three types of MH-60 Blackhawk: models L, K and the DAP (Direct-Action Penetrator) version. (USASOC Photo)

Until the end of the ground operations, Night Stalkers carried out about thirty major night operations involving more than a dozen helicopters, from MH-6 to MH-47 E, and several times under heavy Iraqi soldiers' fire.

Overall, 160th SOAR deployed 6 AH-6, 7 MH-6 Little Bird, 18 MH-60 Blackhawk and 14 MH-47 E during operation Iraqi Freedom.

Against terrorism

Two months after the fall of Saddam Hussein's regime, counter-terrorism operations were still going on for the 3rd Battalion's crews.

On 11 June 2003, Chief Warrant Officer Michael Weddington's AH-6J Little Bird flew over a combat zone supporting a commando drop. He was delivering precision aerials fires on three targets when his aircraft took heavy enemy

fire, from machine guns to rocket-propelled grenades. Weddington immediately left the targets to engage the shooters. " I turned right and saw Iraqi firing continuously on my 2 o'clock. I fired all I had: machine guns and rockets. My right wing man did the same to protect my flank. Enemy positions went silent at the third pass. "

During this time Army commandoes were safely dropped; they could begin the mission. In less than thirty minutes, Weddington and his wing men flew back to a forward base to resupply in gasoline and ammunitions. They were given a new mission: they had to carry out a recon mission forward of the ground troops.

Some minutes later, they were called to eliminate an Iraqi position. During the four hours of this ground troops support mission, Weddington returned twice to different Forward Arming and Refuelling Points (FARP). " We have been well trained said Chief Warrant Officer Weddington. Always first on the zone and last to quit when the last commando has left the zone. That's our difference! ". Weddington

Crewman of the 160th SOAR.
GU-56/P helmet is now more used than the former SPH-4. With a better ergonomics, it has an air-conditioned system and a standard clear/tinted dual visor. The helmet shell is constructed of advanced graphite and polyethylene.

The helmet shell protects the head from impact and sharp objects. The equipment has been designed to optimize crew survival whatever the crash conditions may be.
Survival equipment is dispatched in the numerous pockets of the vests; survival knife, first-aid kit, food for twenty

and his team mates flew from dusk to dawn, meaning eight hours overall, resupplying at a FARP several times. In May 2004, he was awarded the *"American Legion Aviator's Valor"* Award for *"courage and selfless under fire"*.

Companies of the four battalions of the 160th SOAR are currently deployed in Iraq, Afghanistan and the Philippines. ❑

Top. During night, at a forward operating base in Iraq, a 2nd Battalion B Company's MH-47 E crew combat commander performs the last inspection before take off. *(Photo 160th SOAR)*

Right. On 28 April 2005, 80 awards were presented to 66 soldiers of the 160th SOAR (A). It included 7 Distinguished Flying Crosses (DFC) and 70 Air Medals, for valour in war zone during operations Enduring Freedom and Iraqi Freedom. Overall, soldiers of F and D Companies of the 1st Battalion and 2nd Battalion have been awarded 140 DFC since October 2001. *(USASOC Photo)*

Below. Several helicopters of the 160th SOAR were assigned to Task Force 121 between 2003 and 2004, to hunt fleeing Iraqi leaders and rebels. They were part of Saddam Hussein's capture and his transfer to his detention location in December. *(160th SOAR Photo)*

ur hours and
en an HABD,
me sort of small
er bottle providing
ough autonomy to get off
ould the helicopter sink
deep waters.

(Photo 160th SOAR)

"TASK FORCE 121"
MANHUNTS
THE 55 MOST WANTED IRAQIS

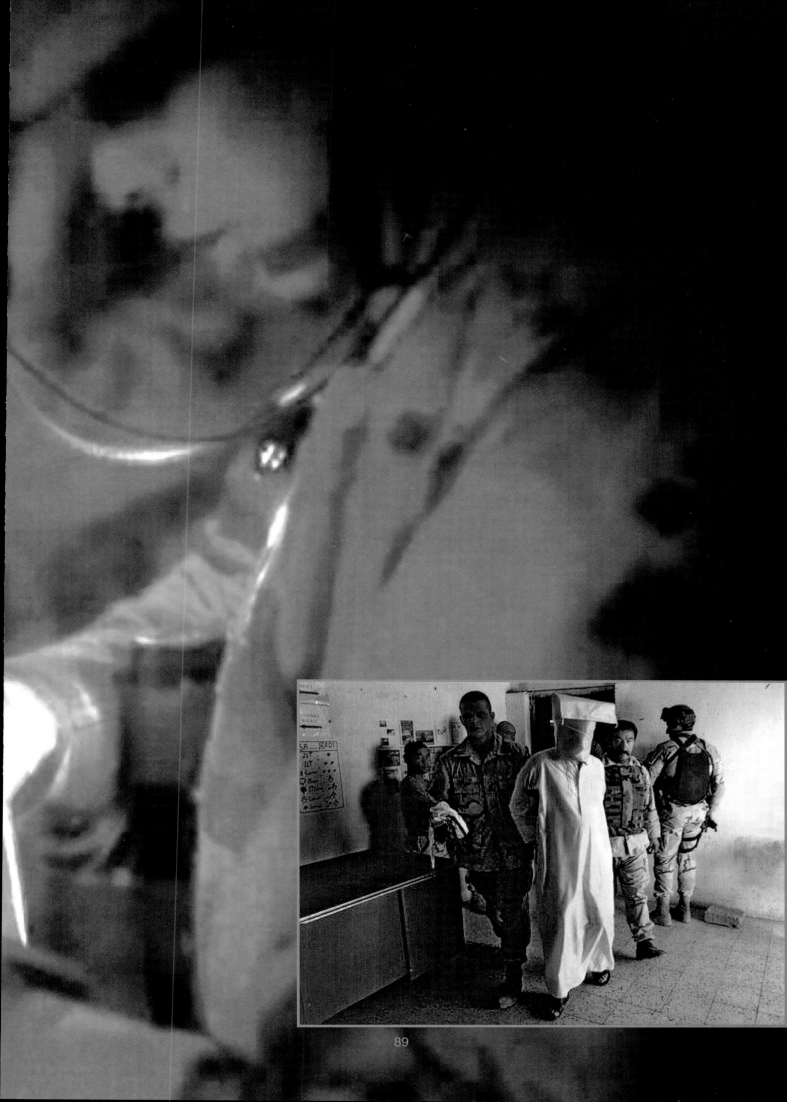

In summer 2003, Central Command (CENTCOM) secretly decided
to create a new clandestine unit in charge of capturing Saddam Hussein,
Osama bin Laden and the other main terrorists of the Middle-East.
The creation of this unit was an answer to both the White House's
and the Pentagon's frustrations to see neither bin Laden nor Saddam
Hussein captured despite the deployment of the coalition's troops
in Afghanistan and Iraq.

Page 88, bottom left.
Mid-2003, Coalition's American Command in
Baghdad ensures that " Saddam Hussein's
hunt is a 24/7 job " for Task Force 121.
(DOD Photo)

Page 89, bottom right.
A suspect is arrested in Baghdad by elements
of Task Force 121. The creation
of the TF also reflected a desire by senior
administration officials and top military officers
to ensure the American commitment
in Iraq did not detract from the hunt
of fleeing Iraqi and Taliban leaders.
(DOD Photo)

Top.
At night, on the roof of a building in Samarra
where they are stationed, Army Special
Forces are under attack by a team
of insurgents. Task Force 121 was considered
as the worst enemy by the Iraqi rebellion
which fought it using all means.
(US Army Photo)

SAW Gunner, Delta Force
of the 1st SFOD-D, member of TF-121.
This SAW Gunner of TF-121 is a Delta Force of the 1st SFOD-D.
The light BDU allows ample and quick movements unlike
a more ballistics-protection oriented BDU. As a matter of fact,
TF-121 elements must be very mobile to immediately intervene
on terrain information.
The Minimi M249 light machine gun provides a fire-cover thanks
to its important fire power. It is fed either
by 100 or 200 round belts, or by standard M16 belts.
Every SF is radio linked, here a MBITR, a TASC-II helmet
equipped with a NVG.

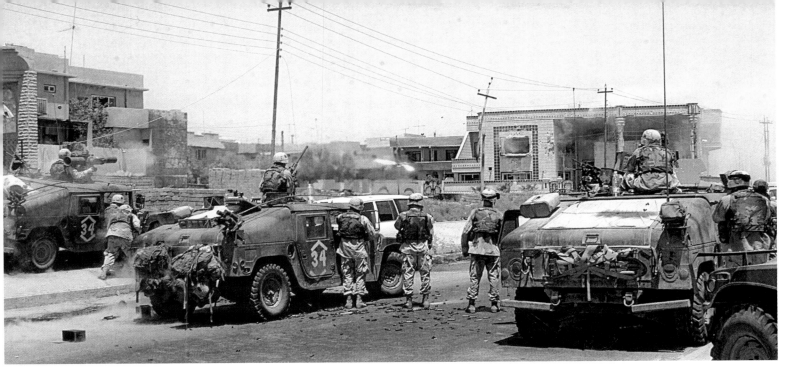

At this time, the American Secretary of Defense, Ronald Rumsfeld, said almost every day: "*Capturing Saddam Hussein, or killing him, would be very important. So, we need to catch him and we will!*" A senior officer of the American-led coalition in Baghdad echoed on its side: "*Saddam Hussein's hunt is a 24/7 job.*"

Left. A SEAL Team 8 SEAL with a suspect that a TF 121 team has just arrested.
(DOD Photo)

" Jump " across borders

The mission of this newly created very special unit, headed by Rear-Admiral Bill McRaven (see inset), was to work as fast as possible on information that intelligence services and information gathering units collected in the field. This unit's force was that it had no obligation to operate in Iraq or in Afghanistan only; they could cross borders to hunt their targets in neighbourhood countries, mainly Pakistan, Iran, Uzbekistan, Tajikistan, Jordan, Turkey and Syria, with or without the agreement of the respective governments.

After Task Force 5 (TF) which operated in Afghanistan, and TF 20 and 21 which worked in Iraq were disbanded at the end of spring 2003, this unit was designated Task Force 121. TF 121 was more flexible and less numerous (see inset on Task Force 20) than the former ones - according to General

Above and below.
Well known images taken on 21 July 2003 in Mosul, during the hunt and the killing of Saddam's sons, Uday and Qusay. The official documents related the units in the foreground, 101st Airborne Division (Air Assault) soldiers firing a TOW missile launcher against the house where the two brothers took refuge. However, TF 121 elements around the building and which spotted them were not mentioned.
(DOD Photo)

John P. Abizaid, who commanded all American troops from the Red Sea to the Indian Ocean -, and since that date operated throughout the entire region. In fact, the Special Forces command had realized it was useless to have two TFs on alert 24/7 when one was sufficient.

Whether it was to manhunt or to capture either Al-Qaeda leaders or fleeing former Iraqi leaders, the work was the same. As long as TF 121 teams were able to be airborne from

(continued on page 92)

TASK FORCE 20

Some days after the fall of Saddam Hussein, the Special Forces command in Iraq was given the mission to assemble a new unit in charge of, on the one hand, searching proof of weapons of mass destruction, and on the other hand, capturing terrorists and arresting Baath party leaders.

This is how Task Force 20 was born, consisting of more than one thousand personnel from the 5th and 19th Special Forces Groups (green berets), 75th Rangers Regiment, Delta Force operators and of the CIA.

This secret unit's commanding officer set up assault teams of twelve members each. TF 20 missions were obviously covert operations and carried out in full autonomy, without any consultation with the American units in the field, which several times led to clashes with other coalition's units, especially at night. Task Force 20 only reported to the American forces Commander in Chief in Iraq or even directly to Washington.

Less than one year later a similar unit was also created: Task Force 21. However, because TF 20 and TF 21 had few results, the Pentagon decided to disband them and assemble a " more flexible and lighter " unit: Task Force 121. ❐

Left.
TF 121 consisted of teams from the Green Berets, SEAL, elements from the Air Force military intelligence units, as well as aircraft from 160th Special Operation Army Regiment and Air Force Special Operation Command.

THE "TASK FORCE 121" COMMANDER

Young Lieutenant on the famous and very secret SEAL Team 6 when the legendary Dick Marcinko was Commanding Officer (CO), Rear Admiral Bill McRaven was now head of Task Force 121 in charge of hunting and capturing Al-Qaeda leaders. This unit, which captured Saddam Hussein in December 2003, remained secret until 2005. Actually, his CO's name was not revealed until recently.

Before he worked at the National Security Council after the 9/11 attacks, Bill McRaven was SEAL Team 6 Commanding Officer. He was one of the authors of the White House strategy for combating terrorism.

Assigned as Task Force 121 CO, McRaven had a free hand to organize this new unit. Previously founded and manned with military personnel only, TF 5, TF 20 and TF 21 had not proved effective. Therefore, McRaven decided " *to bridge civilian and military worlds* "by assembling teams of green berets and SEAL with CIA agents and NSA analysts. Saddam's capture proved the rightness of his decision. What is true is that TF 121 would have all the " powers " and many assets — which would lead to a certain jealousy. ❑

92

Previous page.
Task Force 121 had an important ground
and air " fire power ", for it could align significant
means in a short time, having every approval
and power needed to carry out its operations,
whether it was in Iraq or Afghanistan.
Here, an operation
with 10th Mountain Division
elements in the Sunnit
region of Iraq.
(USSOCOM
Photo)

**SAW Gunner, Delta Force
of the 1st SFOD-D, member of TF-121.**
See caption page 90.

Task Force 121 men surround a building, and arrest a suspect thanks
to the intelligence network the American Special Forces set up. (USOCOM Photo)

OPERATION "RED DAWN"
THE HUNT AND CAPTURE OF SADDAM HUSSEIN

For months, teams of TF 121 and the CIA made pressure on the Baath party leaders, of which some were in prison, and on Saddam Hussein's family to know where his hideout was.

Intelligence had led to think Saddam was near Tikrit, his home city, where he had tribal and family ties for protection. TF 121 knew that the arrest of every Baath dignitary brought them closer to the number one target. In December 2003, after months of painful searching and hunting, one of Saddam's bodyguards, Omar al-Musslit, was captured. Known as "the fat man", he was one of the rare peo-

ple to know Saddam's whereabouts. The fat man was then directed to one of the former President's palaces and questioned non-stop by Kurdish specialists. *"At first he lied, but he did not hold out for long"*, said Samir[1]. *"He started crying and said, 'Don't kill me, I will take you to Saddam before it gets too late. Saddam's going to know I've been captured. Let's go now'."* On a map of Tikrit area he pointed out the small town of Ad Dawr where, *he claimed, Saddam was hiding on a farmland belonging to a family of loyalists."*

No sign of Saddam

On 13 December 2003, the night fell when members of Task Force 121 took Al-Musslit in a window-tinted Iraqi vehicle so that he

Top
Famous image of Samir, the Iraqi translator with Task Force 121, who is "literally on" Saddam Hussein for the shot. The photo was taken on 14 December 2003 after Saddam's capture. *(USASOC Photo)*

Bottom, left.
In a few moments, Task Force 121 Special Forces will open the cache where Saddam hides. At this time, nobody thought the former dictator was there, less than two metres under ground.
(USASOC Photo)

could not be recognized. They went for a reconnaissance of the location hoping Al-Musslit would precisely tell us where Saddam was hiding. To avoid Al-Musslit's escape, Task Force 121 Commander called some 4th Infantry Division units to cordon off a two kilometre security perimeter around a village designated as Wolverine 2 objective. Within a closer perimeter, American Special Forces and their Kurdish " assistants " took position to intercept any Iraqis.

At 8 pm, two teams of twenty Special Forces raided two buildings designated by the former bodyguard. Wolverine 1 was the codename of this objective. There was nobody around and the buildings were likely to have been inhabited for several days. Doubt settled. The question was: had Al-Musslit just lied in order to get the Americans out of the way? Al-Musslit turned pale under his warders' accusing looks. *"Not far from here there is a more or less dilapidated farm with a hideout dug in the garden. It's over there! "* he said. Americans followed him, but in the night Al-Musslit could not find his way (and they couldn't switch a light on). *"This one. No, no, the other one. No, this one, the other one "*, less convinced time after time.

Eventually, after about fifteen minutes of hesitation, with nightvision goggles lent to him by a Special Forces member, he said. *It's here! "*. And he showed a series of one-story buildings surrounded by orange groves on the bank of the Tigris River. An Apache helicopter which hovered above the area covered the assault team's progression noises. As the Americans swept through the site, they captured two young farmers, but there was still no sign of Saddam.

Inside the house there was a small bedroom and a lean-to kitchen. In the bedroom, clothes and shoes were strewn about; the kitchen contained food, including a box of Mars bars. Washing hanged from a clothes line crudely strung between two palm trees in the courtyard. Dried fruit and meat were hanging from a nearby tree. But there was no sign of Saddam. Even a dog of the Task Force failed to find a scent.

"We know Saddam is here ", translated Samir. *"Ask the two farmers where the hidden location is! "* Captain B. of Task Force 121 ordered. Of course the Iraqis kept silent, but Samir knew they were lying and felt *" some pressure might help "*. Thus, the two brothers were separated: one was kept outside; the other was dragged into the house to be interrogated. *" We started by scaring him with the dog.* "Talk!" *But he didn't, I punched him in the face, I was shaking him up and down telling him, 'we're gonna find Saddam, and if you lie to us we're gonna put you in jail for a long time. You're not going to see your family again'. "* It was no use. Either fear or devotion prevented the farmer from giving up Saddam.

As time went, the Task Force members knew every minute counted. The most hunted man in Iraq could disappear at any time. Finally, the Task Force Commander ordered Al-Musslit into the house.

" Shit! The fat man is lying. If you don't tell us where the hideout is, we kill you! Translate, Samir " Samir translated: *"You told us Saddam is here. You told us there is a bunker in the ground. Tell us now! Show us where the bunker is!"*

"Don't kill me! "

Al-Musslit knew the Kurds and Americans around him weren't playing game. The dice was cast now. The only thing to do was to save his life which was more important than his former master's one. Looking defeated, hands still in handcuffs, he slowly raised his arms and nodded to a rug at the edge of the compound area, less than ten meters from where he stood. One of the Special Forces soldiers was standing on the rug, and looked down at his feet in slow surprise. *" It's there, says the fat man tapping with his foot. Dig in here! "*

Pulling the rug aside, one of the soldiers began digging at the soft earth. About fifty centimetres down he stopped abruptly. There, amidst the dirt and sand, were two rope handles. The soldier gently cleared the earth around the handles and tugged. A large Styrofoam block came away revealing the entrance to a hole barely large enough for a man. *"We used to see Saddam on TV, the hero, the powerful man, the scary man. Just no way I believe he's in that hole - a small, dirty hole."* Samir would confide later when talking about this unforgettable episode. The hole was less than a meter deep. At the bottom of it was a narrow entrance into a tunnel. Squeezing into it would have been no mean feat for a 66-year-old such as Saddam. A Task Force soldier directed a burst of gunfire of his M-4 into the hole and there was a scream of terror from inside. "Samir, tell him to come out before he gets killed."

Samir moved to the edge of the hole surrounded by the men of Task Force 121 who aimed their weapons into the darkness, the lights on the guns offering some illumination. *"I want to see your hands up! Put your hands up!"* Samir yelled. From within the hole, a voice responded in Arabic: *"Don't kill me! Don't kill me!"*

Saddam could not understand the order to put his hands up, said Samir. *"First he put up his right hand and they told me to tell him we want to see the other hand up. When I told him I wanted to see the other hand up for some reason he thought we wanted his left hand. He put his right hand down and he just put the left hand up. And I told him, 'No, both hands up'."*

Finally two shaky hands emerged. All men leaning over him thought he was going to shoot[2], or activate an IED, or commit suicide. But nothing. Soon he appeared. Then he was pulled by his clothes, his hair, and his beard. Thrown onto the ground. Saddam uttered only one phrase in English: *"America, why?"*

Old and dirty

His appearance was shocking. He was very dirty, had long hair and a long beard, he looked so old and was shaking. *"For his eight months on the run, when did he have his last shower? "* wondered Samir. As Saddam was searched and handcuffed by the soldiers, Samir snarled: *"You destroyed my country. Where were the promises you made on TV? You said you're gonna fight the coalition forces. You didn't do it. You are a coward man. Where is your army? Where are your bodyguards? Where are the people that are gonna*

Above.
After Red Dawn operation, a soldier of 4th ID shows the Styrofoam block which closed Saddam Hussein's hideout.
(4th ID Photo)

Right.
Under about fifty centimetres of earth, a Styrofoam block with two rope handles hides the entrance of the former Iraqi dictator's shelter.
(4th ID Photos)

Below.
Saddam Hussein still shaking after capture, scared that the American Special Forces team would kill him, waits for the helicopter to Baghdad.
(USASOC Photo)

---

1. Samir was a code-name of one of the translators of Task Force 121 who was present when Saddam Hussein was captured. He was 20 years old when he fled Iraq, as thousands of Kurds and Sunnis, to settle in the United States after three years in a refugee camp. In March 2003, in hope that he might see his family again, he offered his services to the US military and was quickly hired as a translator. As a convinced Anti-Saddam, he was assigned to the special unit in charge of hunting down the 55 most wanted members of Saddam's regime.
2. Special Forces would find a pistol, an AK-47 assault riffle and $ 750,000 in $ 100 bills.

Previous page, top.
In the courtyard of Wolverine 2 objective, soldiers of 4th Infantry Division look at the bag in which Saddam held his dollars.
(4th ID Photo)

Previous page, bottom.
At Ad Dawr near Tikrit, the house where Saddam Hussein hide consisted of a small untidy bedroom and a lean-to kitchen containing food and a box of Mars bars. In the courtyard there was a hideout hole especially for him.
(4th ID Photo)

Above. Before he was heliborne to Baghdad airport, in a highly-protected cell, Saddam was presented a last time to Task Force 121 men who had hunted him for months. In this night of 13 to 14 December 2003, Task Force 121 had achieved its greatest success.

Right. Image of Saddam Hussein less than an hour after his capture. His appearance was shocking, for he was very dirty, had long hair and a beard, looked old and was uncontrollably shaking.

fight for you? Nobody wants to fight for you. You are hiding in that hole like a rat!" Saddam Hussein's bewildered demeanour disappeared and he snarled back: *"I am Saddam Hussein! I am the President! You're a traitor, you're not an Iraqi!"*

Then Samir almost lost his mind. He grabbed Saddam by the beard with both hands, and violently shook him. But the Americans had to stop him before he broke one of Saddam's arms. *"You love America, you are a spy!"* This sentence upset Samir who started punching Saddam in the face until his mouth was bleeding.

Special Forces soldiers pulled Samir off. Then they took photographs with Saddam Hussein among them.

Half an hour later a Little Bird helicopter of the 160th SOAR landed in the neighbouring field to take the most wanted man of Iraq. But when the soldiers started to strap him, Saddam Hussein struggled. He was scared that the accompanying team would kill him and throw his body in the river. Quickly *"calmed down"*, Saddam was thrown up into the aircraft, before being flown toward Baghdad airport, in a highly-protected cell.

In the night of 13 December 2003, Task Force 121 has just achieved its greatest success. ❑

Left. A Green Beret of 19th Special Forces Group takes aim with his M-4 while patrolling in the Kandahar region, a pro-Taliban region. The Task Force was also in Afghanistan and carried out actions in the neighbouring countries. *(USSOCOM Photo)*

Below. January 2004, a Humvee of 3rd Special Forces Group patrols in the Daychopan region in Afghanistan to *" landmark the territory "*. In fact Taliban infiltrations from the tribal zone are very rare at this time of the year. *(US Army Photo)*

to send in Several Predator unmanned aerial vehicles (UAV), "screening " the sky of the region for several days.

At the same time, several thousands of Pakistani soldiers were deployed to divide up this same area. But bin Laden would narrowly escape and cross the Afghan border to find refuge in a region the Taliban controlled. According to some experts, he escaped within just a few hours.

Before this failure, Americans convinced the Pakistanis to launch an operation in the Waziristan to arrest several women married to Al-Qaeda fighters, and to destroy houses of tribesmen suspected of sheltering Al-Qaeda fugitives. ❑

THE HUNT FOR BIN LADEN

Beginning of 2004, after its success in Iraq, Task Force 121 shifted its forces to the Afghan region to try to capture Osama bin Laden. Then the classic cat and mouse game began. This hunt was a confrontation between XXIth century leading-edge technology and old-age guerrilla tactics. In spring 2004, NSA listening intercepted several bin Laden's cellular-phone conversations. A trail appeared.

However, analysts were sceptical, because it was known the al-Qaeda leader did no longer use electronic means of communication, with the exception of Internet. As a matter of fact, searches by heliborne teams dispatched as soon as information was known proved unsuccessful.

The TF 121 CO requested to concentrate on the mails exchanged on the Web in the region. Two months later, McRaven " hunters ", with the help of the Pakistani services, captured Hassan Ghul, an al-Qaeda operative in charge of carrying a message from bin Laden to the most wanted Abou Mussab Al-Zarqawi. Interrogated, Hassan Ghul yielded information on bin Laden's location.

Thanks to cross examinations with other information, TF 121 and the CIA succeeded in localizing bin Laden within a border zone between Pakistan and Afghanistan. Thus, they were able

Below, from left to right.
Still in Iraq, Task Force 121 teams now closely worked with several Iraqi special units they trained. Here in May 2003, SEAL Team 8 SEAL has just captured a series of suspects and taken them to interrogation.

And as a senior American official said, *" Iraq now becomes more a peacekeeping operation than a hunt for the former Iraqi leaders, and Task Force 121 place is more in Afghanistan where it can do a good job ".*
(DoD photos)

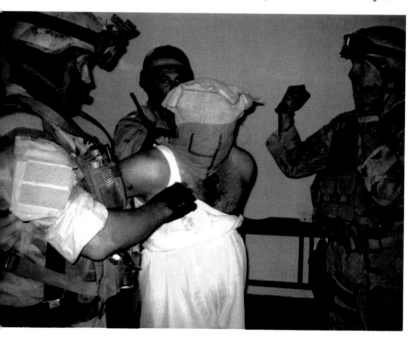

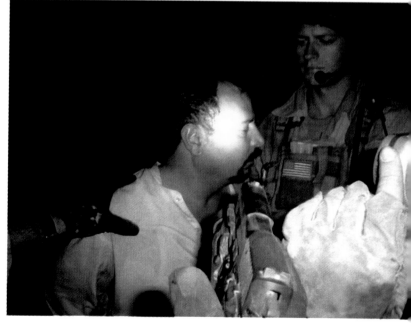

American senior official said: " *Iraq has become more of a policing problem than a hunt for high-value Iraqis. Afghanistan is the place where TF 121 can do more.* "However, this official omitted to say TF 121 teams were to operate mainly in Pakistan where most of the Taliban and Al Qaeda leaders had found refuge.

On 10 January 2004, an Iraqi tipster permitted TF 121 to locate one of the Baathist party leaders of the Anbar province, in the Fallujah, Khalidyia and Ramadi zone. It was Khamis Sirhan al-Muhammad, number 54 on the 55 most wanted Iraqis list.

American intelligence community considered him as leading a deadly and persistent guerrilla resistance. The day after, a TF 121 team, supported by pararescuemen of the 82nd Airborne captured Al-Muhammad at Fallujah. To encourage Iraqis to speak, the tipster received $ 1 million from the temporary authority just a few days later.

Still in Iraq, Task Force 121 teams now closely worked with several Iraqi special units that they helped training. This time the target was called Abu Mousab al-Zarqawi.

After Saddam Hussein's capture by Task Force 121 men in December 2003, the Pentagon decided to deploy numerous elements in Afghanistan and Pakistan to amplify the hunt for the Al-Qaeda leaders. For in Iraq, most of the 55 most wanted leaders had been captured or killed.

one zone to another, and therefore not be constrained within borders of a region, they could carry out both types of mission at the same time.

TF 121 firepower

TF 121 consisted of Army Delta Force, green berets, SEAL Team 6 (previously SEAL were not embedded into TF 20 and 21), Air Force military intelligence units, as well as the 160th Special Operation Army Regiment (SOAR) and the Air Force Special Operation Command (USAFSOC); without forgetting the traditional teams of the CIA's Special Operation Group (SOG).

Fire power was the number one asset of this unit: it could deploy significant means in a short time. Moreover, it had all required authorization and power to successfully carry out operations.

TF 121 got information from the whole intelligence community: intelligence units from the three services, NSA (Natio-

nal Security Agency), FBI and of course the CIA, which had assigned several personnel to the newly assembled unit. However, even though the *"TF 121 - CIA"* collaboration was complete, the famous organization still carried out terrorists' man hunting with its own SOG teams.

The creation of the task force also reflected a desire by senior administration officials and top military officers to ensure the American commitment in Iraq did not detract from the Al Qaeda and the Taliban leaders hunt in Afghanistan and in neighbourhood countries.

All the more so, as antiterrorist warfare experts thought attacks against American interests would only amplify in the Middle-East and the Horn of Africa.

Rotations between Iraq and Afghanistan

After TF 121 captured Saddam Hussein in December 2003 (see inset), the Pentagon decided to deploy numerous personnel in Afghanistan and in Pakistan to reinforce the man hunting against Al-Qaeda leaders.

While the most important Iraqi targets had been captured or killed, the intervention in Iraq moved to a new step as an

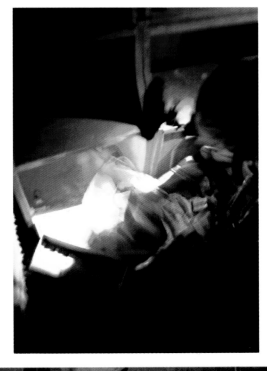

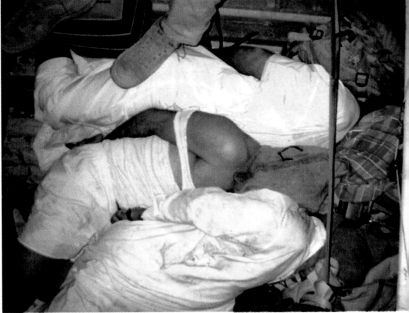

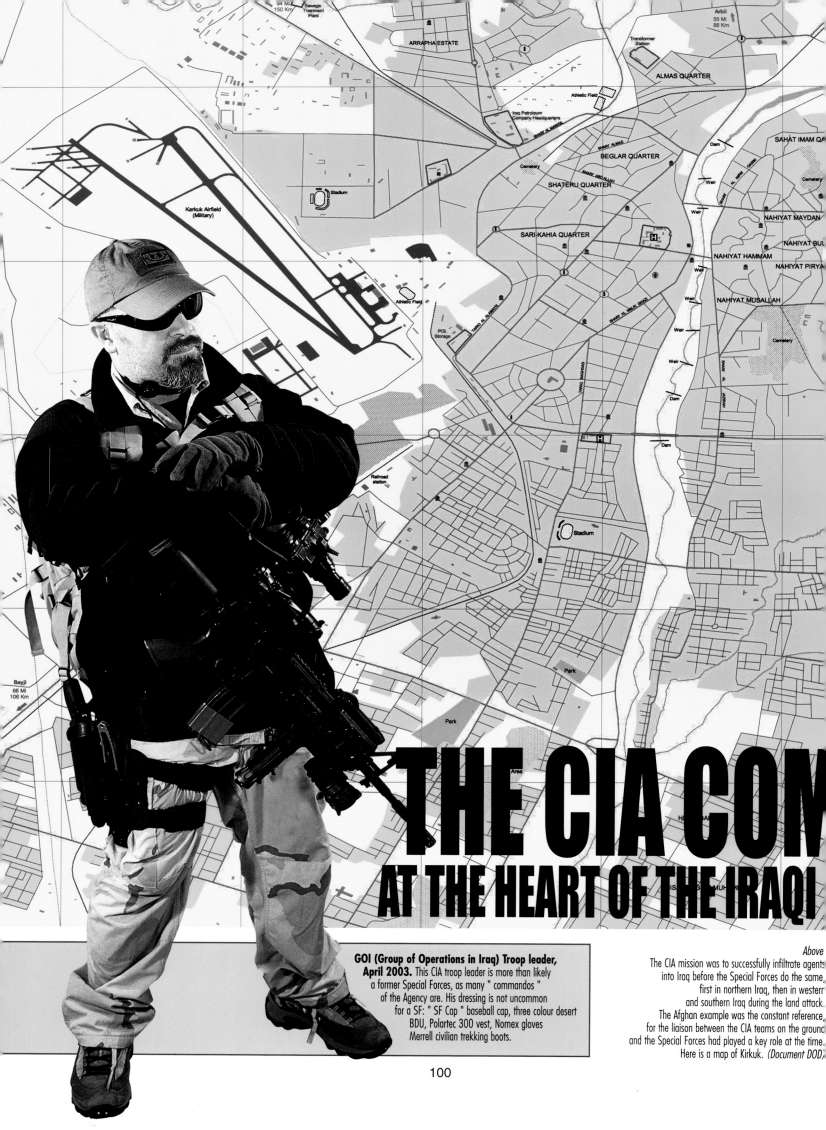

THE CIA COM
AT THE HEART OF THE IRAQI

GOI (Group of Operations in Iraq) Troop leader, April 2003. This CIA troop leader is more than likely a former Special Forces, as many " commandos " of the Agency are. His dressing is not uncommon for a SF: " SF Cap " baseball cap, three colour desert BDU, Polartec 300 vest, Nomex gloves Merrell civilian trekking boots.

Above
The CIA mission was to successfully infiltrate agents into Iraq before the Special Forces do the same, first in northern Iraq, then in western and southern Iraq during the land attack. The Afghan example was the constant reference, for the liaison between the CIA teams on the ground and the Special Forces had played a key role at the time. Here is a map of Kirkuk. *(Document DOD)*

On Wednesday 21 November 2001, at the end of the National Security Council meeting at the White House, President George W. Bush asked Donald H. Rumsfeld: *"By the way, Donald, what military plan do you have about Iraq? "* The Secretary of Defense had not a lot to propose, apart a *" desert storm 2 "* type of plan, a vaguely improved version of the 1991 Gulf War plan.

The White House was conscious the CIA was a key player for collecting intelligence and for any other secret activity in Iraq. The very recent war in Afghanistan had proved it. In that war, the intelligence agency had demonstrated its efficiency: thanks to the millions of dollars distributed and to the contacts established among the Afghan tribes, its undercover commandos associated to the Special Forces had won the war in a few weeks. On 27 September, only sixteen days after the New York and Washington attacks, a team of " operation " agents of the CIA entered in Afghanistan. It was only twenty two days later the first Special Forces member arrived in Afghanistan.

On 5 February 2002, Cheney, Powell and Rumsfeld met again. The deputy director of the CIA, John E. McLaughlin, was also attending, sitting for his boss, George Tenet. The meeting objective was to assess the American policy in Iraq and to define the respective status of the diplomatic, military and clandestine policies. Everybody wondered: *" Do we have to deal with the Iraqi opposing group, both inside and outside Iraq? When do we have to provide them with armaments and equipment?*

IA NDOS
ME

Who will be in charge? Will it be the CIA or the Department of Defense? " Since 1998, the Congress sanctioned the payment of 97 million dollars to the Iraqi opposing forces in military aid to overthrow Saddam Hussein.

In response, the CIA named the chief of the Group of Operations in Iraq (GOI), the key person who would carry out the clandestine actions against Saddam. Saul was already well known within the operations directorate, the CIA department in charge of the clandestine operations. He was the head of the CIA training centre, the famous " farm " in Virginia, then, in 2001, he was promoted deputy to the CIA deputy director, John McLaughlin. The GOI succeeded the Iraqi operations group,

1. On 17 September 2001, the President signed a top secret order authorizing the CIA and the armed forces to carry out counter terrorist operations across the world. At this time, Afghanistan was the number one priority.

2. The 1003 operations plan had more than 200 pages, plus about twenty appendices amounting for an additional 600 pages. According to this plan, the USA needed seven months to deploy a 500,000 man force before being able to begin the military operations.

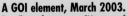

A GOI element, March 2003.
To collect information a CIA agent often becomes an amateur film maker. Equipped with small digital movie camera, they film the crowd in case of demonstrations or gatherings. Specialists then scrutinize the videos looking for *" known faces "*. This agent changed his M4 with a locally manufactured AKM which has a more effective calibre in urban area than the "lighter" M4's. The Point-blank bullet-proof vest he wears under his Goretex ECWCS is capable of stopping most of the bullets fired with the individual weapons found in today's battlefield, except the assault rifles.

MILITARY HEAVY
EQUIPMENT TRANSPORTER

MOSQUE

TOBER 2002

IRAQI DECLARED FOOD
STORAGE WAREHOUSE

MILITARY REVETMENT FIELD

Above, from left to right
Every time a DIA satellite spots locations where armaments could be
hidden (here around a Mosquee in Kut), the Agency is required to
confirm the information. *(Photo DIA)*

The information that considered this near-Baghdad food storage
as a " weapon of mass destruction " depot
was to be double-checked by the CIA
(Photo DIA)

ironically named
" the house of the
broken toys". Why
this   nickname?
According to some
people, " the list of
the actions the group
had carried out over
about ten years looked
like a manual of idiotic and
missed clandestine actions. It was
a series of failures: too few, too late, too unprepared, lack
of planning, lack of realism. Fun was next to fear ".

"The house of the broken toys "

As soon as he was promoted, Saul set up a well experienced group of agents and analysts coming from the intel-

A CIA " action " pair in Kurdistan, April 2003.
The right man uses a LASH throat micro headset equipped with a
transparent earmuff which is more discreet than the TASC headset
and can be more easily hidden under a turtle neck type of collar or a
Shemag.
The M4 assault rifle has a KAC SIR, a Trigicon ACOG sight for short
range sniping and a Sure Fire M910 lamp. He also has a Glock 17 side
arm in a Safariland SLS 6004 tactical thigh holster.
The AN/PVS-7D NVG has almost disappeared from the American armed
forces, replaced with the more "multipurpose" PVS-14, although the
former is one of the best NVG system, providing a high quality vision,
thanks to a third generation lens. The PVS-7 may be used as
handheld field glasses or worn with a facial mask.

Above, from left to right.
Here in Mosul, one of Saddam Hussein's residences. The American thought it hosted a command post. *(Photo DIA)*

Satellite image of a part of Al Musayyib chemical factory in the south of Baghdad. It was on the check list of the Pentagon. *(Photo DOD)*

CIA OBJECTIVES

CIA had the objective to target the various centres of gravity within Saddam's government.

— **The first target** was the leaders' inner circle, especially the first circle around Saddam and his two sons Uday and Qusay.

— **Next,** were the internal Security and the regime's intelligence organization.

— **Then,** was the C3 network (Command, Control and Communication),

— **The weapon** of mass destruction infrastructure,

— **The missiles** production, maintenance and launch pads centres,

— **The Republican Guard** divisions, in particular the specially dedicated Baghdad's ones,

— **The regions** and territories of the inner Iraq which already have a *"de facto"* autonomy such as Kurdistan,

— **The Iraqi regular army**,

— **The Iraqi economic** and trade infrastructure,

— **The diplomatic** structure abroad the country,

— **Lastly,** the civilian population.

ligence directorate. Several of these experts had worked for twelve to fifteen years on the Iraqi matters, while others had participated in clandestine operations in the Balkans.

After a careful study of the problem, the Agency made clear that the only way to succeed was to provide its support to a military invasion of Iraq, as it did it in Afghanistan. But the GOI boss was formal: *"A clandestine action was not enough to overthrow Saddam. Only a CIA-supported traditional invasion had a chance to overthrow the ruler of Iraq."*

The Agency proceeded with a drastic exam of the clandestine actions carried out in Iraq during the previous years. The result was not brilliant: the odds of a clandestine action only were 10 to 20%.

Saul met with Donald Rumsfeld on the 1st of February 2002, in order to draw up a clandestine action aiming at supporting the American armed forces during the operations to overthrow the Iraqi regime. By the beginning of February, the CIA's operations directorate held weekly meetings about Iraq. Saul dis-

covered the CIA information sources in Iraq were few: four in total, meaning two at the foreign ministry and another two at the ministry of oil! In fact, it was the British intelligence which provided the information about the armed forces and the secret services.

" This is serious "

On 20 February 2002, which was twenty days after the directive was signed, a CIA reconnaissance team secretly entered into the Kurd zone in northern Iraq in order to prepare the deployment of CIA " action " units, named NILE (Northern Iraq Liaison Elements). One month later, the CIA director met two key players of Kurdistan: Massoud Barzani and Jalal Talabani, the chiefs of the main Kurdish groups in northern Iraq. He told them the following: " *The President is decided to overthrow Saddam's regime. It's serious. The CIA will intervene, then the armed forces.* "

During the second week of July 2002, eight " action " agents headed by Tim (a fictive name) entered the Kurdistan aboard a Land Cruiser and a truck.

Deputy of the group's CO, Tim was later on given the responsibility of what was to become the CIA base at Sulaymaniya. Out of the eight agents four remained at the main base, while the other four set up in a camp near Turkey.

The Turks ignored that Tim's main mission was to set up an operational base of clandestine actions with some help from the Kurds in order to overthrow Saddam. But, by the end of August, Turkey had decided to expel all the CIA agents. They were back to square one. Eventually, the CIA put such a pressure on Ankara and promised so many guaranties that the Turks gave in, but on the condition that the escort be Turk.

Back to the USA, Tim chose a team of ten persons: six agents among the best Arab-

CIA Commando in Kurdistan, April 2003.
This agent's M4 has the most recent SOPMOD equipment: an Eotech holographic sight, an AN/PEQ-2 IR laser illuminator/designator, a V-Ltor MOD-stock buttstock battery compartment for the Sure Fire M900 lamp CR-123 additional batteries and a Knight's Armament QD silencer which allows to significantly reducing the noise of the weapon. The PVs-18 is a small monocular submersible NVG that the Navy SEAL and the USCG use.

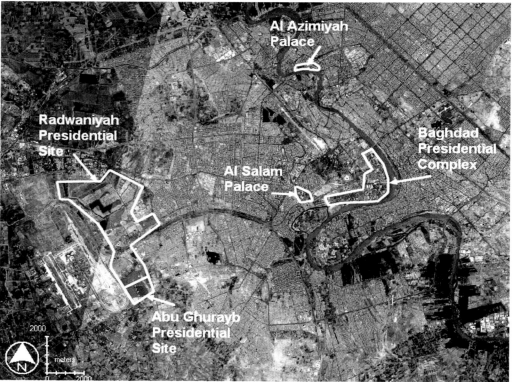

Above. This Agency's twin turboprop aircraft lands at Mosul airport. It's escorted by a Special Forces element. In Afghanistan, CIA's decisive operations were successful thanks to the relations established with the Afghan opposing leaders and groups, in particular with the "Alliance of the north". At the beginning, this war " requested " 115 CIA members and 300 Special Forces.

Left. The presidential complex and Saddam Hussein's various presidential sites are shown on a map of Baghdad. The hunt for the Iraqi dictator was permanent during the air operations.
(Photo DOD)

speaking people of the Agency, three experienced agents from the " action " services and one communications specialist. " *The cream of the cream* ", did he say later on. Three experienced NCOs of the 10th Special Forces Group of Fort Carson were also chosen to go with the NILE team which was to work with the PUK. The second team was to work with the PDK, the other Kurd group.

By mid-September, the CIA men had returned to Kurdistan, with the Turk agents still " on their back ". They carried tens of millions of dollars in 100 bills with them, set in black boxes. The CIA gave Tim some 32 millions of dollars — he had to provide a receipt for every amount disbursed! Rapidly a man showed up saying he wanted to help the United States. This tipster put Tim in relation with two men. The latter were brothers. They were immediately recruited. In turn they introduced Tim

Above.
A map of Mosul, one of the big " Kurd " cities in Iraq,
where the CIA successfully operated with ten or so local agents
who had infiltrated the various States' organizations.
(Photo CIA)

to a Brigadier General, the chief of staff of one of the major
Iraqi air base. The Americans studied this base for several hours.
Three nights later, the brothers brought the head of an air
defence Roland missiles battery assigned to the Republican
Guard. Then an officer arrived with a 300 page plan showing
the Republican Guard units deployment north of Baghdad in
case of war.

By the end of December, the CIA had about ten reliable
agents in Iraq. On its side, after waiting more than one month,
Saul succeeded in getting an approval from Washington to infiltrate one of the CIA agents into the heart of Iraq. It was an
American citizen who had not a "Yankee " face, but had a solid
operational experience in the most hostile countries of the pla-
net. Once infiltrated in Iraq, the man soon provided first hand

**CIA " action " team, Sulaymaniya air base, Kurdistan,
March 2003.** CIA agents are more often in civilian attire than in BDU.
The clothes are a combination of the famous R&R 5.11 trekking gears and parts
of BDU. Since Afghanistan, the Polartec polar vest has also often been worn
as a distinctive sign of the Special Forces units together with the " SF cap ".
Each agent bears a Raid Pack or 3D Pack style backpack in which are the radio,
photo and video equipment in order to collect and transmit any information
in real-time-satellite liaison.The armament varies but always offers a great fire power.
The mission of this troop is a night infiltration as all elements have a Sure Fire lamp
and an AN/PVS-14, AN/PVS-18 or AN/PVS-7 NVGs.

Air image of Saddam's residence at Radwaniya located south west of Baghdad international airport. The palace also served as a prison. Radwaniya is currently both a Special Forces camp, and also a camp for the CIA's and the FBI's agents. *(Photo DIA)*

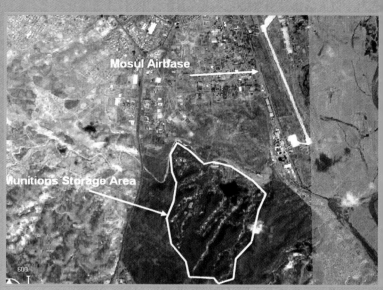

The CIA agents successfully implemented a network of intelligence agents just in a few weeks. These intelligence agents were people of key responsibilities and reported all the military movements in real time. Here is one of the big ammunition depots, south of Mosul. *(Photo DIA)*

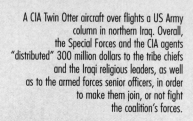

A CIA Twin Otter aircraft over flights a US Army column in northern Iraq. Overall, the Special Forces and the CIA agents "distributed" 300 million dollars to the tribe chiefs and the Iraqi religious leaders, as well as to the armed forces senior officers, in order to make them join, or not fight the coalition's forces.

Here is an exceptional image that a satellite took on 9 April 2003. It shows an explosion of an ammunition depot in the suburbs of Baghdad. At that time of the war, the CIA agents exploded charges against tactical or strategic targets. *(Photo CIA)*

Manufacture of mortar and medium size calibre ammunitions at Al Musayyib, 70 kilometres south of Baghdad. *(Photo DOD)*

The CIA was asked by the White House to provide detailed intelligence of the strategic missile engines test centre that is shown on this satellite image. *(Photo DOD)*

Kurdistan-based CIA teams had intelligence agents in most of the Iraqi army bases and camps. Here is the Mosul air base which was regularly bombed. *(Photo DIA)*

107

Above, from left to right.

Aerial view of Muthanna research centre watched by CIA agents. The Pentagon thought this centre was a " weapon of mass destruction manufacture ", in particular of chemical products.
(Photo DIA)

The Baghdad Abu Ghraib's presidential site. CIA declared straight forward before the second Gulf War that its agents had to be able to announce the USA was strongly determined and that the American army was going to intervene.
(Photo DIA)

information about the Iraqi air defences and on other strategic military installations. Overall, he sent some 130 intelligence reports. This mission in Iraq is one of the best protected secrets of the CIA.

35 millions of dollars in cash

Tim wanted to have all his agents deployed by the 10th of February as the war was planned to begin mid-February at the latest.

One of the two brothers handed a CD-ROM over to Tim and said: " *Here are the 6,000 files of the Iraqi secret services personnel, including names, complete CVs, missions and ID photos* ". This information was immediately sent to the United States. At last the CIA had high quality informers, nick-named the " DB/Rockstar " (DB being the Iraq's country code). Tim now paid a monthly one million dollars to the two brothers to collect information from the " Rockstar " agents. " In less than a week, the two brothers were able to spend the whole of it! " said Tim. One of the brothers explained: " *In Sulayma-niya we don't find anything for less than 100 dollars. But, Tim, I would prefer getting 1, 5 and 10 dollar bills.* " One has to remember that one million dollars in 100 dollar bills weighs about twenty kilos. In 10 dollar bills that would be 50 kg and in 1 dollar bills we could round it off at one metric ton! Thus, every week, the CIA agents crossed the border both ways, with bags full of dollars in the trunk of their car. Saul sent 35 millions of dollars in cash, meaning a good metric ton of 100 dollar bills! The CIA " action " agents required three trips to enter all that money in Iraq. The dollar bills were hidden in MRE cases (Meal Ready to Eat) and other equipment.

It is worth noticing that one of the " Rockstar " agents best

"coup" was the " high jacking " of the Foreign Affairs Minister's transmission system! Transmission specialist officers of the Iraqi secret services officers assigned to several leaders of the regime were recruited and joined the network. One of Qusay's (one of Saddam's sons) body guard was also recruited.

The " Rockstar's " intelligence became so important that at Langley, the CIA headquarters, all counter-intelligence specialists were required to match some information with the telephone tapping's, and the satellite and aerial images. Washington was pleased the quantity and the quality of the intelligence the CIA network were providing.

By the end of February, Tim's network amounted to almost 90 " Rockstar " agents in Iraq. To avoid debriefing them individually in Kurdistan — which could be dangerous for them —, Tim distributed Thuraya cellular phones to 87 " Rockstar " agents across the whole country. Thus, they were able to transmit their information in real time towards a telephone server directly managed by Tim's agents and the two brothers. It is worth knowing that the so-called Jamestown " communications centre " consisted of three old caravans hidden with plastic canvas, located in the mountains at 3,000 metre altitude. Three agents and two Special Forces were rotating to provide security. As soon as the translations had been done, the other CIA elements built reports out of all the " Rockstar " messages and sent them to the CIA HQ.

In Washington, the CIA HQ was flabbergasted by the success in Iraq. Never before had the Agency succeeded in a long-term cross-border operation, and never had it been able to infiltrate the Iraqi secret services and Saddam's Republican Guard.

One the " action " agents, a specialist in explosive, trained several Kurd teams in a few days. The teams infiltrated into Iraq to carry out attacks. The first target was the Mosul to Baghdad railway, a vital link for supply. After they exploded the railway, the Kurds called the railway company and told them:

GOI " action " agent in Kurdistan, April 2003.
This CIA commando wears civilian attire only, except the Belleville Desert Boots. The trousers are a Royal Robbins of the 5.11 company, a manufacturer of outfits which has developed a more tactical line of products that the SF and contractors have favoured since the war in Afghanistan. The flex-antenna we see in the backpack reveals the presence of a radio, likely an AN/PRC-113 allowing audio/data transmission. This radio uses the Havequick III standard which allows all American units communicating between themselves, whether they are aircraft, ships, vehicles or dismounted ground elements.

REGIME COMMAND AND CONTROL FACILITY SADDAM INTL., IRAQ
PRE STRIKE

Above.
One of the Iraqi armed forces command posts near Baghdad. CIA successfully recruited some 90 agents within the Iraqi government's military and police organizations. *(Photo DOD)*

Above, right. The Al Salam presidential palace in central Baghdad, and the Republican Guard General Headquarters. Along the years, CIA had set up links with the various opposing groups such as the Kurds in the north and the Chiits in the south. During Iraqi Freedom, the Kurds agents of the big Iraqi cities were infiltrated. *(Photo DIA)*

"We have destroyed the railway. Don't launch trains anymore!" A train of oil on the Baghdad to Syria line was shot with a RPG-7. It burned all night long. Tens of other attacks occurred, aiming at official vehicles, Baath party buildings and even the intelligence services offices.

A wonderful operation

Twenty or so tribes were " recruited " to ease the coalition's ground forces advance, the Agency was also able to successfully contact Iraqi engineers working at the oil fields. The latter agreed on providing real time information about any Saddam's regime attempt to sabotage the wells. In March, a CIA

commando team crossed the Kuwait-Iraq border together with some Special Forces elements. Their mission was to rescue the Iraqi engineers in their homes.

The CIA agents also participated in the Saddam Hussein hunt. When one of the Rockstar, someone by the name of Rokan, reported that the dictator was at Dora Farm, somewhere on the Tigris river south-east of Baghdad, Jamestown became excited.

However, it took the information almost an hour to reach Langley, in the United States. But this time the tipster was 99% sure. He said *"Saddam is due to come back at the site around 2: 30 in the morning, local time"*. The news was then forwarded to the oval office at the White House. *" Send the aviation! This bombardment may drastically change this war"*, said President Bush. At the same time, on 19 March, the first Special Forces of the coalition based in Kuwait and in Jordan crossed into Iraq.

Five days later, Tim set up a mission with his men and some reliable Kurds towards Dora Farm. Among craters and destroyed vehicles they found neither the bunker the tipster had signalled, nor Saddam's body (he was captured one year later).

Bagdad had not totally fallen yet when the CIA " action " agents began to search the official buildings and secured whatever they could.

Some weeks later, after the collapse of the Iraqi regime, Tim gathered several " Rockstar " who would help hunt the fleeing leaders. Besides, these Iraqis continued working for the Agency.

Iraqi Freedom was more than likely one of the best operations the CIA commandos have carried out. ❐

CIA OBJECTIVES

On 16 February, President Bush signed a secret document requesting the CIA to help the American armed forces to overthrow. The document included seven clear recommendations:

1. To support the opposing individual and groups whose aim was to overthrow Saddam.

2. To carry out sabotage actions in Iraq.

3. To work with tier countries like Jordan or Saudi Arabia, and to support their intelligence clandestine operations.

4. To carry out operations aiming at broadcasting true information about the regime.

5. To Launch counter information operations whose aim was to deceive Saddam and the political, intelligence, armed forces and security services leaders of the regime.

6. To attack and disorganize the banking system, the revenues and the finances of the regime.

7. To disorganize the rings allowing the regime to illicitly obtain equipment for its military machine, in particular for its WMD programs. ❐

CIA Sniper in Kurdistan, April 2003.
The M14 remains an effective mid-range sniper weapon. Updated with a synthetic buttstock and a Rail Interface System, it is in service in all US Army units. This CIA sniper is ready to fire at night. A monocular AN/PVS-14 is mounted on the rifle with an AN/PAQ-4C IR laser designator which allows acquiring, designating and neutralizing a target during the night or in low visibility. A MBITR radio with a TASC-1 helmet provides the inter-agent radio liaison. The SF well used this radio system in Iraq.

Above.
In southern Iraq, SEAL training in " operational zone " in 2004. Since 1990, SEAL have always been present in this region, from Kuwait to the United Arab Emirates, and as of March 2003 in Iraq.
(DOD Photo)

Below.
In the Khawr Abd Allah waterway, on 23 March 2003, one of the SEAL craft has just been launched from *USS Chinook*. She is a Class *Cyclone* ship of the Naval Special Warfare Command, deployed during Iraqi Freedom. Its mission was to intercept Iraqi ships which wanted to attack the coalition's fleet along the coasts. It also served as floating base for the high-speed crafts of the Special Boat Team 20 and the SEAL. *(US Navy Photo)*

Following page, from top to bottom.
In an Iraqi army ammunition depot, a SEAL team and navy EOD (Explosive Ordnance Disposal) examine abandoned ammunitions of all types of calibre. Within a few days, during the ground offensive in March-April 2003, American Special Forces seized thousands of tons of armaments, which had to be destroyed before they were recovered by pro-Saddam militia.
(US Navy Photo)

Above. During the first hours of Operation Iraqi Freedom, SEAL teams and Polish GROM carried out several simultaneous off-shore actions to capture oil terminals, vital for the Iraqi economy. Here in the Persian Gulf, a rappelling exercise is performed one month after the operations.
(US Navy Photo)

SEAL COME FROM THE SEA

very discreet. And when they flew over hundreds of armoured and vehicles, and thousands of the coalition's soldiers the latter immediately understood a special operation wa: to come.

About twenty minutes after, the Pave Low landed. Navy commandoes ran off the aircraft through the rear door and fast paced toward their objectives they knew by heart. A least they knew them "on paper", as they had studied fo days numerous aerial photos, plans set up since 1991 and hundreds of Iraqi witnesses who worked for the CIA. The mission was to seize oil-rich infrastructure on the Faw peninsula, closed to Kuwait, in order to prevent Saddam's people from sabotaging or setting them alight.

During the night they rendezvoused with pro-Iraqi engineers and technicians who led them to the strategic buildings and equipment. Quickly the few watch-men were captured Installations were gigantic, but soon they were screened and protected.

SEAL had now to wait for the arrival of the British Royal Marines of 40 Commando, which had more strength for the surveillance of the infrastructure.

A vital action for the Iraqi economy

At dawn the day before, 35 SEAL and 24 elements of the Polish GROM, led by ten sailors of SBT 12, on ten fast boats,

Although little information has been provided about the SEAL teams operations, it is more than likely they played a key role in the major actions of the first days of the war.

For *Iraqi Freedom*, the Navy Special Forces HQ decided to deploy some 250 SEAL of the SEAL Team 8 and Team 10 aboard the various ships cruising in the Persian Gulf and the Indian Ocean, or on the light boats ported in Kuwait and in the United Arab Emirates as of January 2003. There was also an additional 500 personnel or so from the various Special Boat Teams (SBT), as well as from intelligence and communications command of the Navy Special Operations.

These elements formed the most important deployment of " Navy Special Forces " since the Vietnam War.

At the heart of the Iraqi oil

Everything began during the night of 21 March 2003 when two pairs of USAFSOC Pave Low helicopters took off from a Kuwaiti base with seven teams of five SEAL each. Even though these aircraft flew blackout they were not

From top to bottom.
On the pier of the Iraqi harbour of Umm Qasr, on 28 March 2003, SEAL teams and Polish GROM seized the port infrastructures without major resistance. The Iraqis did not explode equipment and ships at port.
(US Navy Photo)

SEAL member of SEAL Team 10, Persian Gulf, 2003
This Navy SEAL is ready to board a suspect ship within the framework of a maritime counter-terrorist mission. The light BDU allows him easy movements in the narrow passageways. Usually a simple bullet-proof vest or sometimes an Armor Plate Carrier is used with a vest to carry ammunitions. Although it does not provide ballistic protection, the Protec helmet is preferred to the heavier MICH one for this type of mission. The SEAL is armed with a M4 CQBR (Close Quater Battle RAS). The Beretta M9, the SIG P226 (Mk24) and the HK Mk23 pistols are the most used side arms.

...ff the Iraqi coast, a SEAL behind his M60A3,
...bserves the high-speed advance of a Marine LRAC.
...s of April 2003, SEAL missions included patrols
... the Persian Gulf waters and interception
... any suspect ship.
...SOCOM Photo)

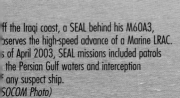

...ight. In January 2003 SEAL teams were already deployed, and trained
to maritime interceptions from helicopters; here from a CH-46
Sea Knight, on *USS Mount Whitney.* That ship hosted a part
of the American Special Forces HQ at that time.
(US Navy Photo)

Right below.
...A combined "SEAL/Navy investigation team" team ready to board and
search a vessel in the Oman Sea. Despite thousands
of vessel searches in these waters, counter-terrorism results were
minimum, at least compared to the efforts made.
(US Navy Photo)

...nder the command of Chief Warrant Officer David Wylie
...who, in August 2005, was awarded the bronze Star for that
action), assaulted two oil off-shore terminals, not far
from Faw peninsula.

Again, it was vital for the Iraqi economy to take
control of the terminals before the Iraqi soldiers
were given the order to sabotage them. The operation was carried out in less than fifteen minutes. One hour later, Royal Marines had both
debarked from the sea and had also been heli-
...orne on Bubiyan Island. At 0600 sharp, Australian HMAS
...nzac fired more than 70 127 mm shells on precise targets.

Once the Faw oil infrastructures and off-shore terminals
...ere seized, SEAL teams gathered on the fast boats of SBT
...2. They now had to secure the western waters of Faw, befo-
...e the Oum Qasr harbour, which commanded the biggest
...umping station of the terminal.

Carrying reconnaissance in often mined waters, SEAL were
...ble to intercept and capture all the ships and vessels which
...ere able to lay moored mines. In fact, the Iraqi Navy had
...isappeared since 1991, sank by the coalition's aviation
...uring the various raids.

Above, from left to right and left.
Within the framework of operation *Iraqi Freedom* in the Persian Gulf, this SEAL group is carrying out a heliborne exercise, including vessel search, on HSV X1 ship.
They are on HH-60H Sea Hawk helicopters from the Helicopter Anti-Submarine Squadron Six (HS-6).
After the March-April 2003 major operations, a SEAL Team detachment was permanently deployed in southern Iraq, either on ground or ashore.
(US Navy Photo)

Below.
In July 2004 at Virginia Beach, a combat group of SEAL Team 4 before its deployment to operation Iraqi Freedom. In 2002, two additional SEAL Team were created, SEAL Team 7 and 10, the former on the west coast, the latter on the east coast. However, increased number of Teams did not mean additional SEAL, for Platoons downsized to six from eight per Team.
(SOCOM Photo)

Subsequently they made their latest ships able to discreetly lay sea mines in their national waters — and even those of their Iranian or Kuwaiti neighbours.

For eight days, SBT's Mark V and RHIB (Rigid Hull Inflatable Boat) sailed Khor AZ Zubayr waterway, the channel which links Oum Qasr harbour to the Persian Gulf. Men were still looking for high-speed crafts capable of transporting sea mines; according to intelligence reports which proved to be true, Iraqis had many almost undetectable old and modern mines, such as the Italian Manta.

Navy SEAL Team MBSS (Maritime Ballistic Survivor System)

The MBSS gear is exclusively manufactured for the SEAL units for the ship or oil platforms boarding missions. This element is equipped with a CWU-27/P flight suit coverall and a MBSS Armor Plate Carrier vest. We can see on the LC-2 belt, a double magazine holder for the P226 (Mk24) pistol, which is in a Safariland SLS 6004 tactical thigh holster.

The M4 CQB-R rifle is the main weapon. It is equipped with an Eotech 552 A65F holographic weapon sight-NVG capable.

An AN/PEQ 2 infrared laser pointer is also mounted on the hand guard kit as well as a Sure Fire M900 high-output lamp. On the MBSS backpack is a Remington 870 pump-action shotgun for overwhelming fire in a passageway or a quick door opening.

In addition to the light crafts, Naval Special Warfare Command also deployed *USS Chinook* (PC 9) and *USS Firebolt* (PC 10) patrol vessels in the Kuwaiti and Iraqi waters. The latter, a class Cyclone, made a series of raids a few days before the beginning of the operations, boarded and inspected two ships and a barge carrying 86 sea mines to be moored before the coalition's ships.

Securing the Mukarayin dam

Another important five-day long operation performed by SEAL and Polish GROM was to seize and hold Mukarayin dam, less than 80 kilometres from Baghdad. It was again to keep the dam from being destroyed by Saddam's militia.

SEAL and Polish GROM, plus USAFSOC Combat Controllers boarded USAFSOC Pave Low helicopters in Kuwait. After a nap on the earth flight of more than four hours over the desert, inclu-

Above.
Since the beginning of Operation Iraqi Freedom in March 2003, SEAL teams have been permanently deployed in Iraq. They were part of Task Force 121 counter-terrorism operations, or used as a maritime counter-terrorism force in the Persian Gulf or the Indian Ocean.
(NAVSPECWARCOM Photo)

Left.
SEAL of SEAL Team 7 have just captured an Iraqi, alleged to be a member of the guerrilla. They are heliborne with their prisoner who will be interrogated. SEAL with Delta Force are the " spear head " of Task Force 121, the anti-Al-Qaeda unit.
(DOD Photo)

Below.
M2 12.7 mm calibre machine gun fire exercise in the Kuwaiti desert. SEAL presence in Kuwait has been almost permanent since 1991. During the March April 2003 operations, while SEAL of Team 7 and 8 were in Iraq, a detachment of Team 4 and 6 elements was deployed in Afghanistan.
(US Navy Photo)

ding air refuelling with HC-130P/N Combat Shadow, SEAL rappelled to the ground on the dam. They secured it and the adjacent power station which were not well defended.

It took hours to search the massive structure for explosives and potential saboteurs, and all in vain, the dam was not mined as the captured Iraqi confirmed. SEAL concluded Bagdad had not judged good to mine this yet strategic dam.

Special Forces joint operation

SEAL also took part in the rescue of a soon famous American military woman: Private Jessica Lynch who was detained in a hospital of Nassiriya, in the heart if Iraq. Everything began in the last days of March, when Special Forces of Charlie Company's ODA 553 of the 5th SFG heard from an Iraqi source that an American woman was in the city where they patrolled. Nassiriya was still partly under Saddam's regular units and militiamen rule.

Special Forces were able to quickly gather precise information and a video of the location where she was detained. They set up a mission proposal immediately sent to Central Command in Tampa. A very clear order directly came back from the top: *"you must save this military woman!"*

Right.
The SEAL Team 8 has certainly been one of the most remarkable Navy units during the beginning of the Iraqi conflict. In fact, a series of published photos show a SEAL Team 8 team climbing down on fast rope from a HH-60H Seahawk. One may notice the patch Navy SEAL wore for the first time in Iraq: the Calico Jack pirate patch.

The local Special Operation Command formed an intervention unit within hours. It consisted of 160th SOAR helicopters, USAFSO-C's Pararescuemen, Rangers and SEAL of Team 8. It was too late to rehearse the mission several times. And so they just used maps, aerial photos and the video they had. It was all up to them!

Helicopters took off from Kuwait and, two hours later, after a nap on the earth flight, landed in the yard of the hospital. While Rangers secured the outside of the buildings and 15th MEU's Marines watched the neighbouring area, SEAL climbed up in the floors and unexpectedly found Jessica Lynch on a bed. They said:" *We are American soldiers!* ". Private Lynch was saved.

Neither the Iraqi physicians, more than happy about this arrival - nor Saddam's soldiers who had fled a long time ago, made any opposition;

Overall, SEAL performed more than 300 missions in Iraq in less than two months. The most stressing was the discovery of a mass grave of 3000 bodies of Kuwaiti people who had disappeared during the 1990-91 Gulf War. All the bodies had a bullet in the skull. ❏

THE SPECIAL CRAFTS " AT THE FRONT LINE "

As of October 2000 after the attack on *USS Cole* in Yemen, the various Special Boat Teams units of the NAVSPECWARCOM were deployed and rotated in the Indian Ocean. Between 1999 and 2002 for example, SBT-12 carried out 220 maritime controls and captured more than 100,000 tons of smuggled oil. And since the beginning of Enduring Freedom, the San Diego unit boarded and searched 21 vessels, captured 18 highly-ranked terrorists trying to escape the Middle East via the Arabian Sea.

SBT-12 was also able to successfully carry out two major missions at the beginning of Operation Iraqi Freedom. In March 2003, on day two of the hostilities, ten special crafts took SEAL teams to secure the two main oil distribution platforms of the Al Faw peninsula and the offshore gas and oil terminals in Iraq. *"We were able to get SEAL and Polish GROM to the platforms, and then provided cover for them,"* said Intelligence Specialist 2nd Class (SWCC/DV or Special Warfare Combatant Crew-men) Herbert Clay, MK-V (Mark-V) assistant boat captain. *"It was vital that the oil platforms and the off-shore terminals were shut down at exactly the same time to prevent the pipes from bursting, and from causing the mission to be all for nothing. This was an important mission during the war because it prevented Saddam Hussein from sabotaging the platforms and causing a major environmental disaster similar to what he did in the first Gulf War."* The second mission involved SWCCs clearing and securing of the Khor Al Abdullah and Khor AZ Zubayr waterways, which enabled the first delivery of humanitarian aid to the port city of Umm Qasr. It was also a history making first for the MK-V. *"This was the first time in history for a MK-V to operate in a river,"* said Operation Specialist 2nd Class (SWCC) Brian Dillon, MK-V navigator. *"We were the first ones up the river and it was difficult to navigate because I didn't have any navigational charts for the river. It had never been charted before. There were numerous boat wreckages floating in the river, plus we had to deal with bad weather, from thick fog to sand and rainstorms, and extreme tidal chan-

ges. The craziest thing was we were about half way up the river when mines were discovered behind us - the same path we had just crossed - and in front of us. We stopped where we were and waited for the mine sweeper ships to clear the mines."*

Once the mines were cleared, SWCCs continued their mission of securing the river, ensuring enemy forces weren't hiding among the boat wreckage and preventing vessels from trying to pass by them to get down river. *"Overall, we cleared about 22 vessels a night,"* said Brian Dillon.

"We would put special operation forces on board to scout for enemy targets trying to escape, oil being smuggled, and to make sure the vessel wouldn't be a threat to our forces or anyone else". SWCC's helped check and clear 110 suspicious vessels of having contraband or suspected terrorists, and captured 31 enemy prisoners of war during their five-month deployment. ❏

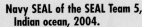

Navy SEAL of the SEAL Team 5, Indian ocean, 2004.
Although most of the maritime counter terrorist missions require light armament only, a machine gun offers a fire power welcome in case of the unexpected. This Navy SEAL has a M60E3 equipped with an Elcan M145 scope. A belt of 200 rounds is in a soft container on the side of the machine gun, another belt in a pocket eye-affixed at the belt. It's a relatively light equipment: a simple LC2 web kit over a SPEAR bullet-proof vest, knee pads and a Protec helmet.

THE "MARINE RECON"

Based on a report received at the 1st Marine Division (1 MARDIV) HQ stating that 90 T-72 tanks were progressing toward the Kuwaiti border, the division's command changed its six-month old established plans: The ground attack had to begin twenty four hours in advance.

However, some hours later, it was asserted that there were only 6 tanks and that they had been down there for twenty days! The original plan was rescheduled and thousands of vehicles killed their engines. The Marine Recon received the order just ten minutes before crossing the border.

Above. On 20 March 2003, two elements of Explosive Ordnance Disposal unit attached to a 1st Marine Division's Force Recon Platoon observe a mine field along the Iraq-Kuwait border. *(USMC Photo)*

Left. On 21 March at Oum Qasr, a few hours after operation Iraqi Freedom was launched. In front of UN-teams in charge of controlling the Iraq-Kuwait border abandoned buildings, Marine Recon of the 15th Marine Expeditionary Unit performed a last reconnaissance to try to flush out the last Iraqi soldiers. *(USMC Photo)*

Right. On the motorway to Diwaniya, centre of Iraq, Marine Recon of RCT-5, who had just reconnoitered and secured a crossroads, wait for LAV recce vehicles to arrive. *(DOD Photo)*

118

On 21 March 2003, a 1st Marine Division's Force Recon combat team assaults a building that Iraqi soldiers were defending, some kilometres near Umm Qasr. In southern Iraq, Recon faced heavy resistance several times from Iraqi Infantry units. (USMC Photo)

HEAD OF THE COMBATS

THE " MARINE FORCE RECON COMPANIES "

There are currently four companies of Marine Force Reconnaissance: the 1st Force Recon Co. based at Camp Pendleton, California; the 2nd Force Recon Co. based at Camp Lejeune, North Carolina; the 3rd Force Recon Co. based at Mobile, Alabama, consisting of six platoons; and lastly, the 4th Force Recon Co. based at Honolulu, Hawaii. ❏

The Marine Recon of the 1st Force Recon Company [1] had been deployed in Kuwait since January 2003. It was reinforced with platoons of the 2nd and 4th Force Recon Company and worked for and ahead of both the 1st MEF (Marine Expeditionary Force) of Task Force Tarawa and the 1st Marine Division.

In the early hours (0400 local time) of the offensive on 20 March 2003, the 1st Marine Division [2]'s Marine Recon captured the Safwan hills, a most important observation post in a rather flat region, while the division's Marines engaged Iraqi

From top to bottom. On 7 April 2003, before Qalat Sukkar, Marine Recon attached to the 24th MEU during its advance to Amara, eastern Iraq. The Marines aim was to neutralize three Iraqi divisions (10th, 14th and 18th Infantry divisions) facing Iran. *(USMC Photo)*

Two sergeants of a Marine Recon attached to Task Force Tarawa have just found an Iraqi on-trailer tactic missile at Kut. After they set C-4 type explosives, they are going to explode the device from a stand-off position. *(USMC Photo)*

On 12 April 2003, a Force Recon sniper team attached to 24th MEU of the 1st Marine Division observes the last Iraqi defenders before Bassorah. Force Recon's mission was to carry out reconnaissance ahead of the combat units within a 20 kilometres maximum range. *(USMC Photo)*

Above.
The first day of offensive into Iraq, 1st Marine Division's Force Recon easily captured posts and installations at the Iraqi border. Several kilometres further, UN buildings were searched, without any Iraqi resistance. *(USMC Photo)*

Right. After the capture of Nassiriya on 23 March 2003, while Marines eliminated the last strong points of resistance and hunted looters, Staff Sergeant Ben Cushing of the Force Recon detachment and Master Sergeant Gregory of 15th MEU show more than 13 millions of Dinars seized at a city's bank. *(Force Recon 15th MEU Photo)*

observation posts which were under the Marine Corps artillery fire. That same day, elements of the Marine Regimental Combat Team-5 (RCT-5), following some Force Recon of the 1st Recon Company, secured a part of the Ar Rumaylah and az-Zubayr oil fields, not far from the Army Special Forces and British Royal Marines.

Overall, 5 000 Marines of Task Force Tarawa and elements of the 101st Airborne Division entered into Iraq and advanced up north along the Euphrates River in parallel with Army V Corps. Two Recon platoons were reconnoitering the main axis of advance moving ahead of the first echelon.

Along the Euphrates River

On 22 March, Marines of the 1st Marine Division changed course and advanced up towards Nassiriya. They captured two bridges on the river during the day.

---

1. 1st Company was at full strength with six recon platoons in support of the 11th, 13th and 15th MEU, the 1st MEB and 1st MEF. As a Marine Corps Special Operations, it could work with the USSOCOM special units.
2. The 1st Marine Division worked with the British 7th armoured brigade against the Iraqi 51st mechanized division, vicinities of Bassorah.

The 3rd Infantry Division left the 2nd Marine Regiment (Task Force Tarawa) capture Nassiriya, which was defended by several hundreds of determined soldiers and tens of tanks and artillery. Overall, more than 100 Marines were wounded and nine killed during the combats. On 23 March, the 1st MEF's other units made a western by-pass of Nassiriya. In the south, the 15th MEU along with the British soldiers fought the 7th Armoured Brigade to capture Oum Qasr, still defended by elements of the Republican Guard. This harbour, located 48 kilometres south of Bassorah was a key objective to allow massive reinforcements and equipment to be delivered from the Persian Gulf. Iraqi 51st ID, which defended Bassorah, withdrew before the Marines.

On 24 March, while Task Force Tarawa was still fighting in

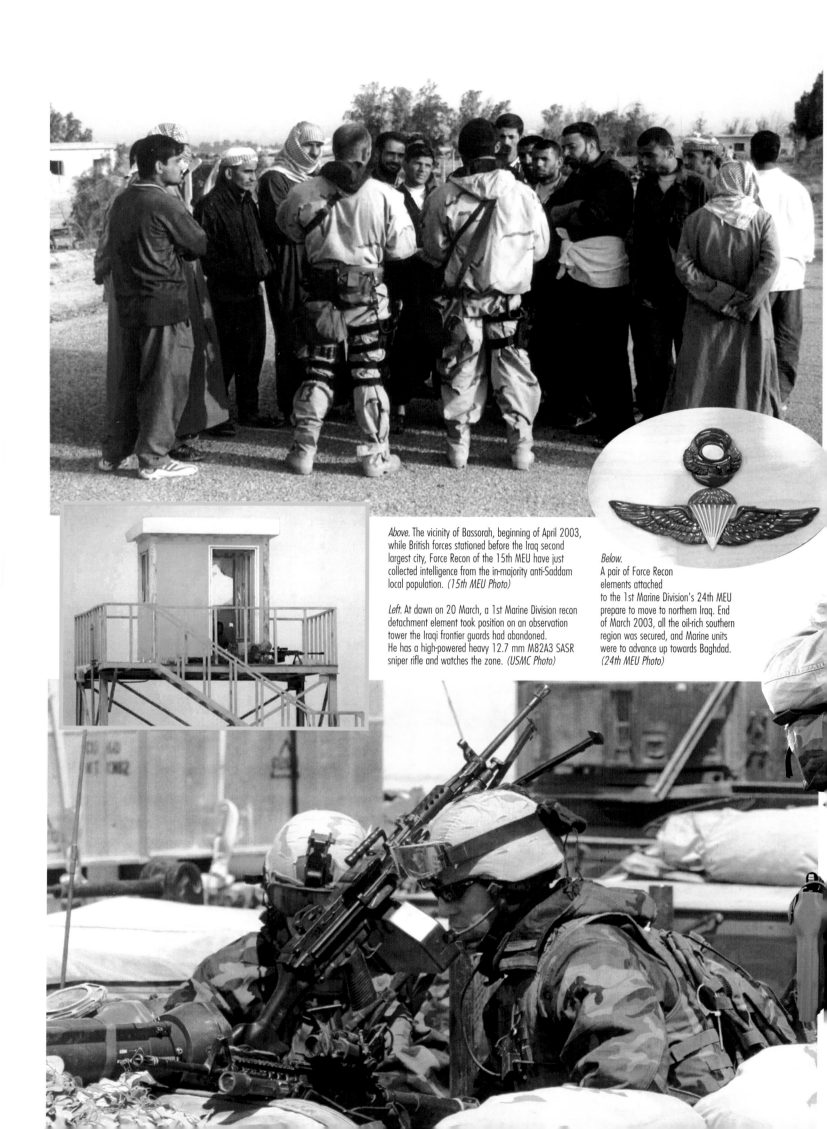

Above. The vicinity of Bassorah, beginning of April 2003, while British forces stationed before the Iraq second largest city, Force Recon of the 15th MEU have just collected intelligence from the in-majority anti-Saddam local population. *(15th MEU Photo)*

Left. At dawn on 20 March, a 1st Marine Division recon detachment element took position on an observation tower the Iraqi frontier guards had abandoned.
He has a high-powered heavy 12.7 mm M82A3 SASR sniper rifle and watches the zone. *(USMC Photo)*

Below.
A pair of Force Recon elements attached to the 1st Marine Division's 24th MEU prepare to move to northern Iraq. End of March 2003, all the oil-rich southern region was secured, and Marine units were to advance up towards Baghdad. *(24th MEU Photo)*

From top to bottom. Major military operations of Iraqi Freedom have ended. Forces Recon of the 1st Recon Company takes a shot for posterity with their vehicles and trophies taken from the Iraqis. (USMC Photo)

A Force recon Scout-Sniper pair of the 1st Marine Division advance during the first hours of the offensive towards Umm Qasr and Bassorah. The sniper has a 7.62 mm M40A3 precise rifle with Leupold scope. (USMC Photo)

Nassiriya, Marine RCT-5 fast paced to the north of Diwaniya. The next day, a huge sand storm overwhelmed the south of Iraq, which gave the Recon some time to rest a little.

Marines of RCT-1 made a western by-pass of Nassiriya, while RCT-5 made an eastern one, both units advancing towards Kut. They were to engage the "Baghdad" Republican Guard mechanized division. On its side, at the country's south edge, 15th MEU at last captured Umm Qasr harbour together with the Royal Marines of the 45 Commando and the SBS/SEAL Special Forces, as well as the Polish GROM. On 26 March, despite the sand-storm causing very low visibility, Marine RCT-1, 5 and 7 of the 1st MEF continued their advance and captured Ash Shatrah near Kut. Advance-guards, comprised of Marine Recon even passed Diwaniya. Combats continued in Nassiriya.

On 27 March, the Republican Guard's " Baghdad " division blocked the Marines' advance, while Task Force Tarawa was still fighting within and around Nassiriya,

Marine Recon, Bagdad 2003.

(see caption on page 124)

for the militiamen were continuously attacking the resupply convoys.

The day after, while US Army V Corps made a hold, Marine Regimental Combat Teams-5 and 7 had already reached the vicinities of Diwaniya and RCT-1 was fast pacing to Kut.

On 30 March, 1st Marine Division units had to stop at Qalat Sukkar to get some resupply. Marine Cobra helicopters blasted the heaviest Iraqi defence of Diwaniya.

But the Iraqi resistance in Nassiriya was going on. The American Command sent 2 000 additional Marines of the 24th MEU, several platoons of Marine Recon and SFG's Special Forces to finish with it. On 31 March, RCT-5 recaptured the Hantush airfield, north of Diwaniya that they had lost four days before.

On 1st April, it fast paced toward the Tigris River between the " Al-Nida " and " Bagdad " Republican Guard divisions.

End of the Nassiriya resistance

During the night and still in Nassiriya, American Special Forces carried out a well done media-covered operation: the rescue of Private Jessica Lynch of the 507th Ordnance Maintenance Company, captured and wounded in an ambush on 23 March. This operation was carried out by Rangers of the 2nd Battalion, SEAL of Team 8 and Recon of the 1st MEF, heliborne by US Air Force Special Operations aircraft. During this operation, the Marines made a diversion, for the Iraqi militiamen were near the hospital where Jessica Lynch was detained.

Above, from left to right. Raids against already-structured rebels began in May 2003, after the end of the major operations to conquer Iraq. Here is an operation carried out by Force Recon of the 1st Force Reconnaissance Company and Marines of the 4th Light Armored Reconnaissance Battalion, on 2 August 2003, along the Tigris River. *(USMC Photo)*

On 2 April, American ground forces launched two major attacks south of Baghdad in order to break the "Medina" and "Bagdad" élite divisions of the Republican Guard. 1st MEF units succeeded in destroying the "Baghdad" division before Kut. The Marines' recon vehicles were less than 80 kilometres from Baghdad on the east bank of the Tigris, after

Marine Recon, operation *Iraqi Freedom*, spring 2003. This Marine Recon is in MOUT (Military Operations in Urban Terrain) BDU. Because of its better protection against fire, the Nomex flight suit coverall is preferred to the traditional BDU. The FSBE AAV (Amphibian Assault Vest) originally studied for the boarding of ships or oil platforms provides a ballistic protection against any individual weapon. It also offers a carrying modular capability for magazines or other accessories pouches. The photo also shows the PVS-14 NVG, the Peltor Comtac headset which is ideal for close-combat environment, the M4 SOPMOD with Aimpoint sight, the IR PAQ-4C laser designator and the Sure Fire M900 lamp. With the "fast rope" gloves are disposable handcuffs which allowed neutralizing arrested suspects when securing administrative buildings during the capture of Baghdad.

capturing a key bridge at al-Numa-niya and the al-Numaniya air base. The next day, the RCT-1, 5 and 7 units advanced up along the Tigris valley, pushing back the Republican Guard "Al-Nida" division. However, Recon faced a heavy resistance at Al-Aziziyah, about 60 kilometres from the Iraqi capital. On 4 April, while RCT-5, followed by RCT-7, entered into Baghdad through the eastern suburbs, RCT-1 and 2, then 15th and 24th MEU advanced up along the Tigris River. Twenty four hours later, RCT-5 made an eastern Bagdad encirclement; while in the south, RCT-7 captured the Republican Guard's "Medi-na" division's command.

On 6 April, RCT-5 encirclement of Baghdad continued in order to link up with the 3rd Infantry Division. That same day, the first American aircraft landed at the international airport, soon followed by attack helicopters.

On 8 April, Force Recon advanced up through the south-east suburbs to capture Rashid air base. Farther south, Task Force Tarawa was given the order to capture Kut, then to move forward to Amara to neutralize the Iraqi IVth Corps, positioned not far from the Iranian border.

While 3rd Infantry Division entered into Baghdad by the north-west, on 9 April, Marines crossed Saddam City to enter into the eastern capital, where the Chiit population gave them a warm welcome. Then, they raced to the presidential area. Marines symbolically tore down Saddam Hussein's statue on place Fardus in centre Baghdad. In Amara, on 10 April, fortunately without any resistance, 24th MEU captured the 10th Armoured Division HQ and all its equipment. On 11 April, 1st MEF was named Task Force Tripoli while it advanced up toward Tikrit. It captured the city on 13 April. There had been little resistance; in fact, Iraqi leaders had fled. The major operations were now ending. Yet, Marine Recon presence in Iraq was just at its beginning, for 1st Recon Company, reinforced, was redeployed in Iraq in May 2003, then again attached to Task Force Scorpion as of September 20033, to be based in south-east Iraq. On the other hand, 1st Marine Expeditionary Force was engaged in support and help of humanitarian operations which slowly took place. Needs were huge.

Secure the oil-rich zones

However - as all reports certified - Marine Recon were under-employed. *"Their employment ahead of the front lines was*

Since 2004, various Force Recon detachments participated in the oil wells and infrastructure protection missions in southern Iraq, within the Maritime Special Purpose Force Platoons. Here is a fast rope training session from a Navy SH-60 Seahawk helicopter, and a "cluster" exercise near Ar Rumaylah.

(Reserved Rights)

considered as too risky ", said one of the commanders of operation *Iraqi Freedom*. Yet, on February 2004, 1st Force Recon Company returned to Iraq with the 3rd Force Recon Company in support of the 1st Marine Division's RCT-7.

On 23 July 2004, six " HAHO " Recon of the 1st Marine Division 1st Reconnaissance Battalion, jumped in the dark over Baghdad to carry out a mission against Iraqi rebels (the last jump Marines had done was thirty five years earlier, on 17 November 1969). " It was an end-to-end mission said Master Sergeant Todd Smalenberg, for we wanted to make a HAHO jump over the objective to insert clandestinely at night in order to avoid rebels and IED makers. " In November 2004, 25 Marines of the B Company's 2nd Platoon, of the 3rd Recon Battalion 4 had to carry out a secure mission of the oil wells and infrastructure, as well as protection at sea with high-performance Mark V combatant craft of the Naval Warfare Special Operations Craft and with RIBs (Ridged Inflatable Boat). They also had to carry out a ground-oil-zones reconnaissance mission in Bassorah and Oum Qasr region as well as along the Iranian border.

On 6 March 2005, 2nd and 3rd Force Reconnaissance Companies returned to Camp Lejeune after seven months in Iraq. 7th and 8th Platoons, reserve units based at Mobile, Alabama, had performed more than 350 missions in the highly tense province of Anbar. ❐

---

3. In June 2003, US Marine Corps agreed to turn over Force Recon to Special Operations Forces. As of October 2003, 86 elements of the 1st Force Recon Co. began their training with SEAL of the Naval Special Warfare Squadron One, to become fully operational in April 2004.
4. Force Recon Platoons are attached to a MEU HQ.

CONTROLLERS"
ON THE SPOT

COMBAT CONTROLLER MISSIONS

Air Force Combat Controllers are trained to infiltrate hostile areas and provide ground forces, aircraft, and headquarters commanders with vital satellite communications, command, and control links. They usually carry approximately 100 pounds of equipment consisting of weapons, night-vision goggles, oxygen equipment for High-Altitude Parachuting, rappelling equipment, state-of-the-art communications equipment, and anything else needed to complete the mission. ❏

Previous pages.
The various Army's and Marine's units reports stated the key role CCT played during Air Force Close Air Support. Less than fifteen minutes between a call from the ground, the target designation and the strike. All the more as precise ammunitions were employed in priority against the ground-to-groun missiles, artillery guns, " sensitive " targets in cities. Thus, at An Najaf and Ko the coalition's aviatio performed a grea number of clo supports, crus missile-launche and guns witho collateral damage in the surrounding houses. This was achieved thanks to the CCT.
(Photo USAF)

Conscious of the Air Force special teams capabilities, *Iraqi Freedom* planners decided to gather all Air Combat Controllers (CCT) on duty, including those deployed in Afghanistan, to integrate them into the Army, Navy and Marine units which are to cross into Iraq.

Their success in Afghanistan, coalition aircraft air-ground precision guiding, was a key factor of the decision. As a matter of fact, 85% of the air strikes were guided by CCT, and all reports confirmed their action was a key contributor to the Taliban's collapse in 2001. In October 2001, Combat Controllers were among the first thirteen American Special Forces to land in Afghanistan.

Same type of mission as in Afghanistan

For the major operation that Iraqi Freedom was, CCT were to carry out the same type of mission again: guide in US Air Force and Navy fighter-bombers. CCT teams were in all theat-

CCT from the 720th STG.
Heavily loaded, this CCT has all the tools needed to achieve his mission: ANVIS NVG binocular mounted on a MICH helmet, satellite radio and combined-arms link radio in a Raid-Pack bag, MBITR individual radio with a free-hand TASC-II helmet, M4 SOPMOD assault rifle with M203 grenade-launchers equipped with a PAQ-4C infra-red laser aiming device AIMPOINT M2, hand weapon, knife, and infra-red Strobe.

After the Afghan campaign, USAF (with some three hundred and sixty Combat Controllers) had understood the operational potential the CCT had. Thus, during the Iraqi operations, combat units demands were higher than the CCT team's capabilities. As they did it in Afghanistan with the Mujahideen, CCT were deployed in Kurdistan to support the Peshmergas advance and to conduct close air support operations. (Photo USAF)

Even if the March and April major operation have ended a long time ago, CCT team are still in Iraq. Besides the exercises they carry out counter guerrilla actions within the Special Forces detachments
(Photo USAF,

CCT WITH THE " 82ND AIRBORNE "

It was the first day of operations in southern Iraq. Staff Sergeant Josh Littlefield of the 14th Air Support Operations Squadron, detached to 82nd Airborne, was in charge of air support. His unit's mission was to seize three bridges on the Euphrates River. *"We captured the first two without any problem when, going ahead to the third, fifty Iraqi soldiers assaulted us. The first mortar round left me unconscious, while shrapnel went over my head. My comrades woke me up and asked me to manage the air support! But an RPG rocket hit the vehicle and I was knocked unconscious again for the second time! "* Moments later Littlefield came back to life. It was imperative to call for support. Under enemy fire, he spotted his Air Force comrade, ten meters further, who had the radio. *"What do I do? "* yelled his buddy.

Iraqi Freedom war surprised him for he arrived from Afghanistan where he could freely drive on roads. And there, around him, there were more than a hundred well-armed and determined Iraqis.

As he understood Iraq had nothing to do with Afghanistan, he requested a first air support. However, Baghdad's soldiers were taking women and children as shields. Therefore, coalition's aircraft couldn't strike at first, and could only fly low to scare them. On the second day, American units were still held by the Iraqi defences. Littlefield requested another air support, which this time proved more effective, for aircraft struck the buildings were Iraqis were entrenched. *"After these combats, the unit I was embedded in, changed tactics: it systematically fired mortars and guns on all possible buildings before an assault. Despite the numerous Iraqi deaths while we advanced, the lack of action impacted our morale. We wanted to fight, for time goes faster when you are in combat! "*. On 15 April in Iraq, Littlefield decided to re-enlist the same day he ended his contract, in order to come back to Iraq or Afghanistan. ❑

res of operations: in the north with the Special Forces and the paratroopers of the 173rd Airborne Brigade, in the west with the coalition's Special Forces, in the south with the V Corps forces, Marine and various teams of the Special Forces who were ahead of the conventional forces.

In the north, during the Debecka pass battle fought near between Mosul and Kirkuk, CCT succeeded in containing an Iraqi motorized rifle brigade attack by helping destroy several tanks and a dozen of armoured personnel carriers (APC) vehicles in guiding aircraft towards targets. The other armoured vehicles were destroyed by shoulder-fired Javelin missiles fired by Special Forces.

In the south, CCT were part of the *"largest Navy SEAL operation in history "*, which was to seize and protect the oil-producing infrastructure and to secure the Al Faw peninsula, southern Iraq. Air Force Special Forces were with the British SAS and SBS, men of the Polish GROM and US Marines. During this operation to take control of the refineries and pipelines, coalition Special Forces didn't have any casualties. CCT mission was to route naval gunfire and artillery, mortars, close-air support and unmanned aerial vehicle traffic *"in an extremely congested and complicated battle space"* involving air, land and sea forces, Captain John Traxler of the 720th STG later explained. During the whole Pfc Jessica Lynch rescue operation three CCT were among the deployed Special Forces. They maintained the liaison between the ground units, the helicopters in charge of the heliborne operation, the AC-130 and A-10 support aircraft hovering above the zone, and the AWAC which coordinated the air missions.

The same "language" as the others

At the end of the ground operations, and after four months in Iraq, several CCT were redeployed to Afghanistan where coun-

Above.
On 29 April 2003, Senior Airman Jared Peitras and Technical Sergeant Mark Harris assigned as CCT at Baghdad international airport search buildings where Iraqi-soldiers- abandoned-armaments may hide.
(Photo USAF)

ter-Taliban operations were going on. Soon, the three-Services-published-reports mentioned the excellent quality of the CCT/aviation actions. Subsequently, both the US Army and the Marine decided to create their own CCT.

The CCT key role in the ground and air operations of Iraqi Freedom did not stay unnoticed to the USAF HQ. As early as the fall of Baghdad, it decided to increase the strength of the CCT units: in April 2004 a class of 32 students was set up to bolster the CCT cadre to 360 elements.

"We talk Air Force language to (Navy) SEALS and to the (Soldiers) on the ground. It allows us to get more airpower into a theatre of operations in a (shorter) amount of time", said Technical Sergeant Robert Boulanger.

720th Special Tactics Group

The 720th Special Tactics Group (720th STG), consists of 21st, 22nd, 23rd and 24th Special Tactics Squadrons and the 10th Combat Weather Squadron. 720th STG is headquartered at Hulburt Field, Florida. It is a small force of less than 400 elements, who are either Combat Controllers, or Pararescuemen, or Combat Weathermen, but all considered as the élite of the US Air Force.

To earn the scarlet beret you must have attended the Air traffic control school, Army airborne school, US Air Force survival school, combat control school, scuba school, and HALO-HAHO (High Altitude-Low Opening, High Altitude High Opening) jump school.

Le 720th Special Tactics Group is one of the US Air Force Special Operations Command (AFSOC) components. ❑

ON 30 MAY 2005...

On 30 May 2005, an aircraft crashed in the province of Diyala with four Air Force Special Forces aboard. Among them were Captain Derek Argel and Staff Sergeant Casey Crate of the 23rd Special Tactics Squadron.

They were the AFSOC first deaths, with Staff Sergeant Scott D. Sather, killed on 8 April 2003, one day before the fall of Bagdad, during operation *Iraqi Freedom*. ❑

CCT From the 720th STG, Northern Iraq
Deployed in Kurdistan with the Army Special Forces, CCT were especially active in northern Iraq.
The terrain being more " green ", the Woodland BDU was preferred to the desert camo BDU, even if several sand-colour equipment show that we are in Iraq.
Radios use such as the LST-5 or the AN/PRC-177 multi-channel satellite link allows coordinating both the ground troops and the aircraft of the various Services working jointly.

131

USAFSOC IN ACTION

American, Australian, British and Polish Special Forces operations which seized more than 20% of the Iraqi territory would not have got that percentage without the almost permanent presence of USAFSOC aircraft such as MC-130 Combat Talon, MC-130P Combat Shadow air refuelers and AC-130 Spectre.

During the 24 hours prior to *Iraqi Freedom*, MC-130 and MH-53 fleet flew non-stop to set up the tens of Special Forces teams and their vehicles every where in Iraq. Only the crews experience allowed such low-altitude infiltrations deep into the country with almost no losses [1]. The Iraqis had not a clue of the size of the operations the USAF Special Forces aircraft did.

As a first step, in mid-March 2003, the 4th Special Operations Squadron with AC-130U, and the 8th Special Opera-

Previous pages.
Front view of a MH-53J Pave Low III of the 20th Special Operation Squadron. Based in Kuwait, this unit carried out night-heliborne operations to deploy tens of Special Forces teams with their vehicles and equipment in Iraq as of 18 March 2003. They had almost no casualty during these operations.
(Photo USSOCOM)

From top to bottom.
Based in Masirah, Oman, in a first time, AC-130H/U Spectre of the 4th Special Operations Squadron moved to two Saudi Arabia air bases by mid March 2003. The Spectre aircraft permanently carried out close air support from these bases. In a nutshell, they provided the continuity of the operation mode of Enduring Freedom in Afghanistan. Here, on 20 May 2003, a Combat Talon II of the 352nd Special Operations Group lands at Lakenheath air base in Great-Britain after five months in the Middle-East. *(Photo USAF)*

Close-up on an airman working on the AC-130 Spectre guns. Here he supplies a 40 mm gun. During operations, and besides some spectacular aspect of a Spectre strike, the tactical effect is impressive. *(Photo USAF)*

A RC-135 V/W Rivet Joint of the 55th Wing before a flight over Iraq for Central Command. Although this aircraft is attached to the Air Combat Command and not to the USAFSOF, the Rivet Joint aircraft carried out ELINT intelligence flights for the benefit of the Special Forces.

tions Squadron with MC-130E, left Al Masira, in Oman, to take quarter in two Saudi Arabia air bases. On their side, the 20th Special Operations Squadron with its MH-53J Pave Low III, and the 21st Special Operations Squadron, with MH-53M Pave Low III, and elements of the 193rd Special Operations Wing with their EC-130E Commando Solo flew from Kuwait.

The 57th Rescue Squadron (about fifty men) with HH-60, the 58th Rescue Squadron (75 men), the 66th Rescue Squadron (110 elements) and the 301st Rescue Squadron (50 men) were also stationed in Kuwait. On the Encirlik air base in Turkey were the 711th Special Operations Squadron of the National Guard with its MC-130E Combat Talon, and the 129th Rescue Squadron, from the reserve component, with HC-130 and HH-60G aircraft.

From 2200 to 0400 on 20 March, during the first wave of bombardments, Air Force imposed "direct firing" to its aircraft which had to fly between 300 and 3,000 feet. All flights of Air Force aircraft were modified. Thus, MH-53 Pave Low

1. A MH-53 crashed onto an obstacle; it had to be destroyed later on.

which heliborne ODA 551 had to fly between bombardments. Then, after they had dropped ODA 551 personnel and equipment in Karbala's south-western desert, the helicopters had to fly against the clock to cross the border before first light. When they entered the Kuwaiti sky their tanks were almost empty (they had only fifteen minutes of flight time left).

On 22 March, six MC-130 Combat Talon flew from the Romanian Constanza air base with 280 special forces personnel and part of their armament to Kurdistan. As Turkey had denied its territory overflight agreement, American aircraft had to fly over Iraq where air defence was sill active.

Above. End of November 2004, an EC-130H Compass Call aircraft of the 41st Expeditionary Electronic Combat Squadron takes off from the Bagram air base in Afghanistan to Iraq. During the March and April 2003 operations, the EC-130H provided the " electronic umbrella " of the special and conventional forces. *(Photo USAF)*

Below. One of the brand new MC-130 Combat Talon of the Air Force Special Operations Command fielded some time after the major ground operations in 2003. Most of the aircraft of the special operations are " worn-out ", after they very often flew to support the ground units. *(Photo USAF)*

Therefore they had to fly at mid altitude, and despite aerial manoeuvres to avoid fires, three Combat Talon were hit. One of them had two engines with technical problems and had to make an emergency landing in Turkey. The others landed at Bashur, near Irbil, where the longest runway of Kurdistan

AVAILABILITY/MISSION RATIOS

AC-130:	91%	EC-130E:	87,8%
EC-130H:	97%	HH-60G:	88,5%
MH-53M:	82%		

As of September 2003, USAFSOC understood it needed more heavy aircraft to carry out its missions. USAF Special Forces Command looked for some financing to modify fourteen C-130H in four AC-130U and ten MC-130 Combat Talon III.

Moreover, ten old HC-130H had to be modified in EC-130H and WC-130H in priority. ❏

FLYERS IN IRAQ

Overall, some 4 millions of flyers were dropped over Iraq from November 2002 until the end of March 2003. This is relatively small compared to the first Gulf War (29 millions of flyers) and during the air operation *Desert Fox* in 1998 (2.4 millions). On the other hand, from 20 March until 20 April, 31.8 millions of flyers were dropped over Iraq.

In spite of this huge number, these flyers were also improved upon, such as colour or better quality paper. Similarly, messages were more understandable by most of the people. These flyers were also highly visible, especially on sandy grounds, which allowed Iraqi to read them without taking them in hands — a key point in a state where the police role is so important.

However, this flyer-psychological action to convince the Iraqi armed forces to surrender was not a success, despite what intelligence had said about the effect such a psychological operation would have.

If the results of these flyers were not the same as in operation *Desert Storm*, it is more than likely because Iraqi soldiers had not

FRONT

BACK

FOR YOUR SAFETY
Stop repairing military fiber optic cable.
You are risking your life.
The cables are tools used to suppress
the Iraqi people by Saddam and
his regime, they are targeted for destruction.

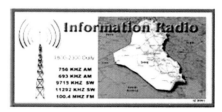

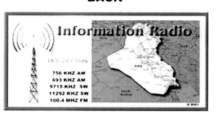

FRONT

BACK

MC-130E Combat talon II flew a lot to drop the flyers during the 2003 operations.
(Photo USAF)

FRONT

Military fiber optic cables have been targeted for destruction.
Repairing them places your life at risk.

BACK

Military fiber optic cables are tools used by Saddam and his regime to suppress the Iraqi people.

suffered of a month-long intense air bombardment campaign. Following these *Desert Storm* bombardments, Iraqi were more " receptive " to the calls to surrender. Moreover, they did not defend their country during *Desert Storm*; at the time, a lot of them were not ready to stay and die for Kuwait.

The flyers campaign of Iraqi Freedom targeted Iraq's capitulation as its priority. But the speed of the troops on ground did not give enough lead time to make the program really work. Specialists acknowledged that in most of the cases the "target" did not really understand the messages which were delivered.

Besides, an intense counter-propaganda was developed to counterbalance the psychological operations.

The Baghdad regime sentenced any soldier to death who would surrender or desert.

If overall the 3rd ID captured 2,600 prisoners, no unit capitulated. On the other hand, many soldiers left their unit on their own and abandoned their equipment.

Therefore, to make an accurate assessment of how efficient the psychological actions were on operation *Iraqi Freedom* proved to be it has been difficult, or even impossible. ❑

FRONT   020-20D

Coalition Air Power can strike at will.

Any time, Any place.

BACK

Coalition air power enforces the No-Fly Zones to protect the Iraqi people. Threatening these Coalition aircraft has a consequence. The attacks may destroy you or any location of Coalition choosing. Will it be you or your brother? You decide.

020-20D

FRONT

BACK

FRONT

BACK

Coalition forces do not wish to harm the noble people of Iraq. To ensure your safety, avoid areas occupied by military personnel.

Above.
An EC-130H Compass Call of the 41st Expeditionary Electronic Combat Squadron performs an air-to-air refuelling over Iraq.
The coalition's electronic cover was so efficient the Iraqis were not able to jam the transmissions. *(Photo USAF)*

Below.
EC-130H Compass Call are still in Iraq for they still provide electronic cover for the ground forces, and try to jam the insurgents' communications. *(Photo USAF)*

was. Combat Talon had successfully flown the longest infiltration of their history, meaning fifteen hours non-stop, of which four hours and half an hour over Iraq.

The next day, Turkey approved its territory over flight: Combat Talon in charge of the SF's heavy armament and vehicles were able to make safer flights.

For three weeks AFSOC aircraft and helicopters resupplied SF teams. In a first step they landed at night on abandoned or unprepared airstrips, then on forward bases in Iraq, like Talil airbase in southern Iraq which was operational on 4 April 2003.

In addition to A-10 and medic helicopters, USAF Special Operations Command used Talil airfield to resupply special units in central Iraq or as a transit base to go to other bases in the western part of the country that SF held since the beginning of the conflict.

Besides the mission of dropping teams in the heart of the country, Combat Talons were set up with on-board medic teams. Thus on 7 April, two Special Forces members injured near Baghdad were retrieved by a Rescue Squadron's HH-60 and heliborne to the SF's forward air base of Najaf where a medical MC-130 airlifted them.

During Iraqi Freedom, AFSOC deployed 73 aircraft (57% of its air fleet): 18 MC-130 Combat Talon, 8 AC-130H/U, 8 EC-130E Commando Solo, 8 refuelling MC-130P Combat Shadow, 14 MH-47, 18 MH-60, 16 HH-60 and 31 MH-53J/M Pave Low. Not forgetting 58 HH-60-in-majority rescue operations helicopters.

Overall, AFSOC carried out 3,711 "special" missions, which means 15% of the USAF 24,196 missions.

As soon as ground operations had begun, two MC-130 Combat Talons took off from Kuwait and infiltrated into Iraq. Aboard were ODA 554 members, two Humvee and two civilian pick-ups.

The crew were wearing NVGs and flew nap on the earth. Should they have committed any error, they would have crashed, implying the death of all aboard as the aircraft were full of gasoline and ammunitions.

The " big birds " landed in the dark on the abandoned runway of Wadi al-Kirr which was bombed several times during Desert Storm and Southern Watch. Pilots stopped their engines, teams and vehicles disembarked through the rear door. After they had made the take off check list, pilots and helicopters disappeared in a cloud of dust. The night was far from

On 6 April 2003, during operation Iraqi Freedom, one HH-60 Pave Hawk of the 301st Rescue Squadron performs an air-to-air refuelling from a HC-130 of the same Squadron.

Left.
Aboard a MC-130 Combat Shadow, an airman checks an air-to-air refuelling of a Special Forces helicopter proceeds properly. During the three weeks of offensive, the crews of the Special Operations Squadron performed hundreds of day and night missions. Iraqi Freedom was the largest air operation ever performed by the USAF special units. *(Photo USAF)*

Below.
Beginning of 2003, Pararescuemen of the 301st Rescue Squadron prepare to carry out a rescue mission of a coalition's crew. While the 110 elements of the 66th Rescue Squadron and the 50 men of the 301st Rescue Squadron were based in Kuwait during OIF, the 129th Rescue Squadron flew from the Incirlik air base in Turkey. *(Photo USAF)*

over for the crews as they still had several missions to perform in enemy territory.

It has been said that American Special Forces hated to *"enter in the battle"* without the AC-130 gunships support. This proved to be true in Afghanistan and in Iraq. As a matter of fact, as of 20 March, an AC-130 flew over the oil platforms to support the SEAL's and Polish commando's attack. Later on, a Navy PC-3 called on an AC-130 to destroy several Iraqi patrollers on the Tigris River. On 28 March, some hours before capturing H2 airfield in western Iraq, Rangers and British SAS requested an AC-130 of the 4th Special Operations Squadron to strike the air base runways as they feared the numerous Iraqi troops on the site could react. From the videoed information the Predators transmitted in real time, AC-130 repeated the tactics set up in Afghanistan end of 2001. Thanks to their sensors they were able to aim at the targets identified by the UAVs.

To repeat what had been done in 1991, several MC-130 had been equipped to be able to launch the Massive Ordnance Air Burst (MOAB) 9,525 kg bombs. However, unlike the first Gulf War, none of them were launched on Iraqi troops.

EC-130E of the 193rd Special Operations Wing, National Guard of Pennsylvania, broadcasted radio messages for 306 hours and televised messages for 304 hours; 108 radio messages were produced, 81 different flyer models were dropped within three weeks, a total of 31,800,000 flyers, equivalent in length to 120,454 rolls of toilet paper. EC-130H Compass Call flew 125 missions over Iraq.

During the last days of the operations, MC-130 became the VIP's favourite transport aircraft, thanks to its low altitude and flexible flying capability which permitted avoiding the guerrilla's rocket launchers, thus, being able to more easily approach Baghdad international airport. ❑

For weeks, Special Operations Squadron carried out night flights to infiltrate the Special Forces teams with their vehicles, to drop and deploy SEAL, Delta and Rangers, to regularly supply the various team scattered on the Iraqi territory. Here, technicians affix a pusher bar on an EC-130 Compass Call of the 43rd Expeditionary Electronic Combat Squadron at an United Arab Emirates base.
(Photo USAF)

Above.
During the last days of the coalition's offensive in 2003, the various Rescue Squadrons were permanently flying. Here, on 8 April 2003 at a forward base in Iraq, one 301st Rescue Squadron's HH-60G Pave Hawk and the crew takes off to rescue a pilot shot down near Baghdad.
(Photo USAF)

Right.
One crew member of a HH-60G Pave Hawk, here the gunner, carefully watches the ground movements during a flight over the Dhi Qar province in January 2004. Despite the end of the major ground operations in 2003, the threat of enemy fire (rebels fire actually) is still possible.

On Baghdad international airport tarmac, USAF Special Forces helicopters are to carry out a mission. On the foreground, Senior Airman Josh Crowell performs the pre-flight check of a HH-60 Pave Hawk of the 101st Expeditionary Rescue Squadron, a National Guard unit. *(Photo USAF)*

USAF PARARESCUE

THAT OTHERS MAY LIVE

The largest rescue operation implemented ever

AIR FORCE "RESCUE SQUADRONS" IN ACTION

Previous page, bottom.
Several teams of the 101st Expeditionary Rescue Squadron are part of a landing and advance in hostile environment exercise while they are deployed in Iraq. These elements are from the Air National Guard of New York State for a six-month tour. *(Photo USAF)*

Above. Beginning of April 2003, Pararescuemen of the 301st Rescue Squadron, assigned to Task Force South, return from an operation to a forward base. They have rescued an A-10 pilot, left on the photo, which was shot down by the Iraqi air defence south of Baghdad. The pilot is Major Jim Ewald of the 110th Fighter Squadron. *(Photo USAF)*

Below.
Close up on a Pararescueman of the 301st Rescue Squadron during a mission over Iraq on 6 April 2003. This mission, carried out together with helicopters of the 101st Air Assault, aimed at rescuing a wounded American. *(Photo USAF)*

From the lessons learnt from the 1991 first Gulf war, and more recently from Enduring Freedom, the *Iraqi Freedom* Air Command was to set up the largest Rescue operation of air crews since the Vietnam War.

During the March-April 2003 ground operations, three Air Force Rescue Task Forces in charge of carrying out all air crews recovery operations were to be deployed. The first Task Force (TF) consisted of the: 66th Rescue Squadron (RQS), flying the HH-60 helicopter; 71st RQS, flying the HC-130 tan-

ker aircraft; and the 38th RQS providing Pararescue jumpers (PJ), deployed to Jordan. The second Task Force, consisted of the: 301st RQS, flying the HH-60 helicopter; 39th RQS, flying HC-130; 304th RQS providing PJs deployed to Kuwait. This second TF comprised reserve units, usually stationed in Florida and Oregon.

On its side, the third Task Force consisted of the: 129th RQS, flying HH-60; 130th RQS, flying HC-130; 131st RQS providing PJs, deployed to Turkey. These Air National Guard units were from Moffett, California. These three Task Forces were collocated with A-10 units which provided close fire support when a rescue operation was to be launched.

The plan was that these TFs would move forward into Iraq as coalition forces seized Iraqi airfields. Units had to be ope-

Above.
Training is the corner stone for Rescue units to survive.
Thus, if these PJ are from the National Guard, they are also deployed in Iraq in real conditions, facing a well decided and relatively well armed rebellion. It worth noticing the diversity of equipment with the MICH TC 2001 helmet, equipped to have a PVS-14D NVG, and TASC 1 radio helmet with the Peltor Comtac communication system; The Alta and Blackhawk knee pads; the Bolle X-800T and Wiley X SG-1 glasses.
(Photo USAF)

rational as soon as supporting communications were set up. On 4 April, Talil airfield became a forward air base for a detachment of the 301st and 304th RQS and PJs. These operational short " flyovers " occurred several times, after American, British and Australian Special Operations Forces (SOF) had seized other airfields in the North and West of Iraq. This tactic allowed to dramatically reduce flying and response times.

If the Army, Special Forces and Marine Corps had no formal rescue squadrons, they did have embedded "rescue teams". Thus, the Army had several "Disaster Assistance Response Teams" (DART) formed from the 5th Battalion of the 158th Aviation Regiment.

These DARTs, called " Raptors ", were organized to move with attack-helicopters on deep attacks and to provide an immediate rescue capability for shot down aircrews. Prior to the *Iraqi Freedom* launch, " Raptors " had been equipped with several AH-64 Apache helicopters, forming into Task Force " Gabriel " attached to V Corps.

In addition, several rotary-wings from the Army Special Forces 160th SOAR had been dedicated to combat rescue operations. Special Forces were trained and therefore could be engaged to carry out Combat SAR missions.

On 3 April 2003, when returning from a rescue mission over Iraq, a Pararescueman of the 301st RQS leaves his HH-60G Pave Hawk. As soon as the coalition forces entered into Iraq, especially the Task Forces from Kuwait, they settled on the captured Iraqi airfields. By 4 April, the Talil air base was used as a forward base for 301st and 304th RQS detachments. (Photo USAF)

A pair of Pararescuemen of the 301st RQS is winched to a HH-60 Pave hawk during a rescue exercise at Baghdad international airport in July 2004. The man on the left wears an Air Rescue vest especially designed by the Eagle Company for the Rescue units, while the man on the right wears a Warrior SOS helmet, a FLC combat vest and a Molle II tactical vest.
(Photo USAF)

Left and below.
This exercise is carried out in southern Baghdad. Rescue teams are first heliborne, and then they have to advance in a hostile terrain, reconnoitre the buildings and rescue the crews. At the top right, the PJ is equipped with a MICH TC 2000 helmet with a PVS 23 adaptation for ANVS-6 or 9, a Peltor Comtac audio earset, ESS NVG system, and a M4 SOPMOD carbine with an Aimpoint ML2.
(Photos USAF)

The Patriot " threat "

On 23 March, a Patriot missile mistakenly downed a British Tornado, call sign *Yahoo 76*. After several hours searching for the crash site, a Task Force " Gabriel " helicopter repatriated the forward-based at Ali Al Salem in Kuwait squadron Flight Lieutenants Kevin Main's and David William s's bodies.

This mistake was the result of a series of navigation error and air traffic-control procedures. In fact, the aircraft had been identified as an Iraqi missile, and a Patriot shot it down

On the same day, a Task Force consisting of HH-60s, on HC-130 and several A-10 was set up on short notice to rescue Special Forces personnel near Baghdad. A-10s succeeded in striking all Iraqi fire positions, while HH-60s landed in cloud of dust to rescue all the wounded personnel. The return toward Kuwait proved difficult as the HC-130 had to fly well below the clouds to urgently air-refuel the rotary-wings who

SEARCH AND RESCUE CENTRE

The Search and Rescue Centre (JSRC) was in charge of coordinating the US Air Force recovery operations over Iraq. It consisted of 52 personnel, and was located in Saudi Arabia. JSRC was manned with recovery specialist flying helicopters, recovery controllers, signal personnel, and CSAR trained and skilled officers and NCOs.

Americans flew two types of aircraft for their CSAR missions: the HH-60 Pave Hawk helicopter and the HC-130P. These aircraft didn't launch alone on a mission: they got fire support from A-10, and even sometimes from the AC-130 " gunship ".

If medical support was required, one or several Pararescue jumpers were dispatched.   ☐

The Marine Corps had several rescue teams called "Tactical Recovery of Aircraft and Personnel" (TRAP), flying CH-53 helicopters. These aircraft would primarily support the 1st Marine Division, south of Iraq.

Along side the Air Force rescue teams based in Kuwait were two units of the Navy reserve: the 4 Helicopter Rescue Squadron, from Norfolk, Virginia, and the 5 Helicopter Rescue Squadron from San Diego, California. They deployed a total of 180 personnel and eight HH-60H Seahawk helicopters.

All these CSAR units in the region were under the operational or tactical control of the joint search and rescue centre (JSRC) collocated with the Combined Air and Space Operations Centre (CAOC), at Prince-Sultan Air Base in Saudi Arabia. CAOC, created for Iraqi Freedom, had 52 personnel assigned to JSRC coming from all services and coalition partners.

Colonel Keith Sullivan was JSRC's Commanding Officer (CO). He had direct access to the 27 rescue coordination centres within the numerous HQs and Task Forces. Because CAOC was located on Prince-Sultan Air Base, Colonel Sullivan was able to benefit from any needed air support within the quickest time when a recovery operation was launched.

For the duration of the conflict CAOC reported 55 CSAR missions. Among others, five coalition downed aircraft: crews, one F-14, one F-15 E, one F-18, one A-10 and one British Tornado were rescued.

se tanks were almost empty. Such a similar operation would be launched again on 7 April with almost exactly the same elements.

A similar error occurred less than twenty four hours later in the Baghdad area, with a flight of four F-16 CJ of the 22nd Fighter Squadron. The F-16 supported a large formation hitting targets, when a Patriot battery of the 52nd Air Defense Artillery Regiment, located near Al-Najaf, targeted it.

Unfortunately for the Patriot unit, these F-16s were equipped with an electronic system to locate and destroy enemy surface-to-air missiles. On the F-16 detection screen the Patriot site appeared as an Iraqi SA-2. Immediately the flight leader launched a missile which destroyed the radar site but, fortunately, did not harm any personnel.

On 1 April, a mechanical failure in the fuel system forced the F-14 (call sign Junker 14) crew of the Fighter Squadron 154 aboard *USS Kitty Hawk* to eject over southern Iraq. Two Air Force HH-60 of the 66th RQS (call signs Vampire 25 and 26), led by Major Chris Barnett, took off on short notice to rescue the pilots who landed 130 kilometres southwest of Karbala. The first aircraft which spotted the pilots was a A-10 led by Major Jim Stephenson of the Air National Guard who then acted as "*on the scene commander* "of the downed pilots. Guided by the A-10, HH-60s picked up the two crew men, not without some confusion, as the SAR teams were not familiar with their newly issued rescue equipment.

Team Leader, Parajumper, Iraq 2003.
This troop leader Parajumper is equipped with an intercom headset below a MICH helmet to stay connected with the HH 60 crew during the flight. He wears a HSGI Weesatch ballistic rig with additional plates, and various pouches to carry medical, optical or transmission materiel in addition to the usual ammunitions. This PJ is ready for night combat with a PVS-14 monocular night vision device (MNVD) and AN/PEQ-2 IR laser designator. The PELTOR Comtac headset protects against harmful noise levels, " normal " noises being four times amplified, while any sound above 80 DB is immediately attenuated to a harmless level allowing individual radio communication to continue. The photo also shows an Eagle Air Rescue vest specially designed for the C-SAR, here worn above a Low wizz PACA bullet-proof vest.

But the operation was a success.

The most dramatic PR (Personnel Rescue) operation took place on 1 April to rescue Private first class Jessica Lynch, captured and taken prisoner in a hospital in An Nasiriya. If Air Force rescue forces did not conduct this operation, Pararescue jumpers, among Navy SEAL and Rangers took their part in it. A rescue operation that many compared to the Son Tay raid, North Vietnam, in 1970, to try to liberate American prisoners. (Unfortunately this raid had been launched too late, the prisoners had been moved to another detention location).

Still on 2 April, an F-18 (call sign Dogwood 02) from Fighter Squadron 195 aboard *USS Kitty Hawk* was shot down southwest of Baghdad. Task Force " Gabriel " immediately launched a HH-60, soon joined by helicopters of the 301st RQS.

The aerial ballet of the " watchdogs"

Rescue teams rapidly found the wreckage of the F-18, then the body of the pilot, Lieutenant Nathan White who had died in the crash. Two weeks later, a CENTCOM spokesman officer revealed that a Patriot missile had downed White's aircraft.

On 6 April, an Air Force F-15 E (call sign Borax 56) from the 33rd Fighter Squadron crashed near Mosul, north of Iraq. Specially designed for low-level attacks, the aircraft had flown into the ground for an unknown reason. A SAR Task Force supported by A-10s was launched in order to rescue the F-15 E crew. An active enemy air defense was in the vicinity. It is why CAOC requested the support of about ten fighter-bombers as well as KC-10 and KC-135 tankers: command expected a real air battle.

As a matter of fact, the " aerial ballet " would last several hours. Enemy air defense would certainly be silenced, but the rescuers would never make contact with the two pilots. In mid-April, a Special Forces rescue team would recover the wreckage of the aircraft and the remains of the two pilots, Captain Eric Das and Weapons-Systems Operator Major

Above and left.
After they have localized the shot-down crews, climbed down on a fast rope to save time, secured the building where the crews hide, the PJ secure a security perimeter while the medic provides the medical first aid to one injured element. They then have to carry the wounded man to the HH-60 and to winch him if necessary. A rescue action remained a dangerous operation even though A-10 aircraft created a security zone around it.
(Photos USAF)

Right.
Close up on a Pararescueman who provides cover to his team's buddies by facing any possible enemy intrusion. Armed with a M203 with a Reflex Trijicon scope, this element is equipped with a Warrior SOS helmet with PVS-14 mounting, ESS NVG system, and an Eagle Air Rescue combat vest.
(Photo USAF)

Williams Watkins III. On 7 April, a SA-16 hit an A-10 damaging the right engine, the flight air control and the hydraulic systems.

Captain Kim Campbell of the 75th Fighter Squadron succeeded in flying his aircraft to Ali Al-Salem air base in Kuwait. His professionalism and calmness saved his life and the aircraft, and obviated another rescue mission.

The next day, a SAM hit an A-10 again (call sign Facing 43) during a close support operation for the 3rd Infantry Division in the south suburbs of Baghdad. The pilot, Major Jim Ewald of the 110th Fighter Squadron from the National Guard, was informed he could land at the recently secured Baghdad international airport. But thinking he could still control his aircraft, the pilot decided to go further south to land at Talil.

However, after flying about ten minutes, the A-10 became uncontrollable, and the pilot ejected. His wingman (call sign Facing 44) noted his position and immediately started the CSAR procedures.

(Continued on page 151)

Pevious page.
One or several injured people are systematically included in the scenario of a crew rescue mission, in order to make the operation more complex as real life is often even worse.
Overall, between 19 March and 16 April 2003, CAOC launched fifty five rescue missions, including five shot down coalition's aircraft, one F-14, one F-15 E, one F-18, one A-10 and one British Tornado.
(Photos USAF)

Right, from top to bottom.
On 6 April 2003, war goes on and missions add up for these crews of the 301st Rescue Squadron. They have just landed on a forward base in central Iraq and have a chat with some elements of the 101st Air Assault which provide the zone's safety. The man on the left wears a C-SAR modified HGU-55P pilot helmet, (with a helicopter pilot micro), a FLC vest and an Eagle Air Rescue over-vest with a PACA bullet-proof vest.
(Photo USAF)

Before a mission in the green zone in December 2003, these Pararescuemen of the 64th Expeditionary Rescue Squadron check their radio equipment on the Baghdad international airport tarmac.
(Photo USAF)

The various tours of duty in Iraq are also unmatchable trainings, where the adversary is always present even though it is a rebellion. Here, Pararescuemen of the 64th Expeditionary Rescue Squadron practice on the Balad air base.
(Photo USAF)

BEFORE "IRAKI FREEDOM"

Well before Iraqi Freedom, in fact since 1990, Air Force Rescue Squadrons were part of operation Northern Watch whose aim was to enforce the no-fly zone above the 36th parallel in Iraq - which means about 10% of the country - in order to protect the Kurd minority. RQS helicopters were then stationed in Turkey.

Within the framework of operation Southern Watch - the largest -, the US Air Force flew over almost the whole of the south of Iraq, up to the southern suburbs of Baghdad. The various RQS were based in Kuwait and Saudi Arabia.

When an American aircraft was shot down the answer was to launch the desert badger plan, whose aim was to target and disorganize the Iraqi C2 (Command and Control) centres in Baghdad. When a pilot was captured the plan was to move to the next level of retaliatory attacks. ❏

A wounded soldier is winched during an exercise in urban area around Baghdad by the 301st Rescue Squadron. During OIF in March-April 2003, Rescue units reported to the Combined Air and Space Operations Center, or CAOC located in Saudi Arabia. CAOC had 27 rescue centres within many HQs and Task Forces.
(Photo USAF)

Above. The most dramatic operation Pararescuemen carried out was certainly on 2 April with the rescue of Private Jessica Lynch, captured and kept prisoner in a hospital at An Nassiriya. If the Air Force Rescue units had no role in this operation, Pararescuemen were part of it among SEAL and Rangers teams. *(Photo USAF)*

Parajumper, southern Iraq, end of 2003.
PJs have various BDU. In fact, Special Forces have a real "freedom" to choose their equipment.

(Continued from page 146)

When on the ground, Ewald sheltered among reeds along a canal, as Saddam's militia threat was active in the area.

Fortunately, American soldiers of the 3rd IF who followed the descent sent a Bradley fighting vehicle to rescue him. Jim Ewald heard American voices but stayed cautious. *"Hearing the clarion call, hey pilot dude, come out, we are Americans…"* the pilot broke cover, ran to the Bradley and was pulled inside through the rear door: he was safe. Then he called his wingman on his survival radio to let him know he had been rescued by friendly troops. An hour later he was taken care of in a field hospital, then out on his way back to Kuwait in a 301st RQS helicopter. Two days later he resumed his combat missions.

At the same time, a team consisting mostly of Air Force intelligence officers and PR carried out a rescue mission in various prisons and intelligence centre buildings, looking for an

151

American pilot still missing since the 1991 first Gulf war. Captain Michael Speicher's F/A-18 went down the first night of the conflict. He never made contact with the search teams and his precise position remained unknown until the wreckage of his aircraft was found. Initially declared "killed in action", his case was reclassified "missing in action, presumed captured" in October 2001. All efforts to localize him proved useless. Years later his initials were found carved on a cell's wall of the Hakimiya prison in Baghdad. But his case remained unsolved even if all personnel missing from the 2003 combats had been found.

"Task Force Gabriel" in action

Besides SAR operations to save fixed-wing pilots, several missions were launched to rescue rotary-wing crews, because at least fifteen helicopters were lost [1], of which three to enemy actions. During the first night of combat, a Special Forces MH-53 went down in Iraq. Fortunately, the crew and the Special Forces aboard were rescued by a second MH-53. The aircraft was destroyed to prevent Iraqis from taking it. The same day, at day break, a Marine CH-46 E of the 268 Helicopter Squadron crashed in Kuwait: all fourteen American and British soldiers aboard

---

1. Besides the losses in combat, helicopter units also suffered casualties, as it was the case on 21 March, when two Royal Navy Sea Kings collided over the Persian Gulf, killing one American and six British personnel. Nine days later, a UH-1N of the Marine Helicopter Squadron 169 crashed on take off, at night, on a forward base south of Iraq. Three crew members were killed, a fourth one was saved. On 2 April, a UH-60 assigned to the 3rd Aviation Regiment was shot down near Karbala. Task Force Gabriel was alerted, but in the mean-time, an armoured unit reached the location of the accident first, where it recovered four wounded and seven dead bodies. On 3 April, an AH-1W of the Marine Helicopter Squadron 267 crashed in central Iraq. Overall, 49 Marine helicopters were damaged from enemy fires.
2. This same day, on 23 March 2003, a HH-60G of the 41st RQS crashed in Afghanistan when carrying out a medical evacuation of injured children. The six crew members were killed.

---

were killed. Still at the beginning of the operations, an AH-64 Apache of the 11th Aviation Regiment was shot down in Iraq. Task Force "Gabriel" helicopters were ready to launch a SAR operation when an Army unit reported it had recovered the crew [2].

On 24 March, a second AH-64 (call sign Vampire 12), from the 227th Aviation Regiment, went down after being shot by small-arm fires during an in-depth raid against an armoured Iraqi unit near Karbala. The other Apaches tried several times to recover the crew, but intense enemy fires kept them away. Task Force "Gabriel", planned to launch a recovery operation, but lacking fuel, had to remain on the ground on a forward base named *"Objective Rams"* about a hundred kilometres south of Baghdad. During this time, 66th RQS personnel, surprised to learn that the down aircraft

Above. Besides the rescue missions for fixed-wing aircraft pilots, there were also several missions to rescue helicopter crews. For at least fifteen rotary-wing aircraft were lost, including three of them shot down by the enemy. Overall, RQS units carried out fifty five rescue missions, saving seventy persons.

Right. Elements of the 64th Expeditionary Rescue Squadron carry out a rescue exercise, and then conduct an extract mission with a HH-60 Pave Hawk hovering above them. Operation *Iraqi Freedom* in March-April 2003 has seen the implementation of the most important air rescue force ever deployed.

was call sign Vampire 12, thought it was an error, because one of their two HH-60s also bore call sign Vampire 12. Therefore, the 66th RQS helicopters didn't take off. On its side, The 227th Aviation Regiment CO, flying a UH-60, tried to save his men. But he had to abandon the attempt because of the heavy Iraqi fires. Pilots CW2 Ronald Young and David Williams were captured. The Task Force "Gabriel" personnel were very upset not to be able to launch this rescue mission; however, they did not receive any fuel until 27 March.

During the last days of the ground operations, intelligence and rescue units searched more than ever for the soldiers captured with Private Lynch, and the pilots of the Apache shot down on 24 March. Marines of Task Force "Tarawa" eventually found the prisoners in a small village north of Tikrit. Task Force "Gabriel" helicopters flew to recover them.

The 55 recovery missions had allowed saving 70 personnel.

The recovery of Private Lynch was considered as the first successful liberation of an American prisoner of war (POW) since World War II. Iraqi Freedom was the opportunity to implement the largest recovery air force set up ever. ❏

Parajumper.
PJs' armament also varies. The Colt M4 rifle has several versions: here it is a SIR Knight's Armament, a variation of the Rail Interface System of the M4 SOPMOD.
The AIMPOINT M2 red dot sight is now largely found in the American forces. The photo also shows the COBB mount adapter for securing the USAF-typical ANVIS night vision goggle.

SUCCESS FOR BRITISH SAS and SBS

For ahead, operating around and as a spearhead

155

In March and April 2003, during operation Telic, British Special Forces (SF) were very active, ahead of the " regular " units, operating around and immediately as a spearhead. They operated in western, northern and southern Iraq.

Two reinforced Squadrons operated within the Special Forces Task Group West, with Aussies and Americans. As in 1991, their mission was to find and destroy Scud missile-launchers on the one hand, and to create sabotages to disorganize the Iraqi forces rears, on the other hand.

In the first hours of the conflict, British SF's mission in the south was to carry out strategic actions so as to capture ashore oil terminals or inland oil infrastructure, then to support the 7th Mechanised Division.

South of the Tigris River

Preceded by a couple of AC-130 Spectre aircraft which air raided the scattered Iraqi defences, five combined SBS/SEAL and Royal Marines teams were heliborne from Kuwait onto the Al Faw peninsula to secure drop zones before the arrival of the 40 Commando commandos. Five RAF's Chinook HC-2 dropped the first wave, followed by seven Marine's CH-53. In the meantime, a CH-46 crashed with the British observation-in-the-depth teams — which temporarily disorganized the assault. The first teams were under small arms firing. They quickly "cleaned" the zone, while fleeing Iraqis were bombed by the naval artillery and the Anglo-American guns firing from the Kuwait's Bubiyan Island.

Lastly, the arrival of the 42 Commando ended this Iraqi resistance. While the 40 Commando captured Al Faw, Royal Marines of the 42 Commando assaulted Um Qasr sea port. They had been preceded by some SEAL and Polish commando teams which had quickly secured the port facilities.

Above. After a successful capture of the oil infrastructures of the Fao peninsula during the first stages of the conflict, SBS carried out intelligence actions for the 7th Mechanised Brigade and the 6th Mechanised Division. *(MOD Photo)*

Previous pages.
While in western Iraq, together with Australians and Americans, two reinforced squadrons were part of the "Coalition Special Forces Task Group West" to find and destroy the SCUD missile launchers. British SF were in the southern country with the mission to seize the oil terminals, and then to carry out intelligence ahead of Her Majesty's units. *(MOD Photo)*

For seventeen days, British surrounded Basrah. SBS teams carried out a series of recons in order to spot the Iraqi defences and to *" feel the degree of resistance of the defenders "*. As a matter of fact, the British HQ left a " passage " to allow Saddam's forces to evacuate the city without any combat - and without losing face. In fact, the British army had chosen not to carry out an annihilating combat [1].

On 7 April, an SAS/SBS team was part of the Sindbad operation whose aim was to enter Baghdad's outskirts.

---

1. On 28 March, it was the only time when Iraqis tried a large scale armoured attack with fourteen ageing T-55 tanks. These tanks were destroyed by the Royal Scots Dragoon Guards Challenger II 120 mm shells within minutes.

156

"SMILE, SHOOT, SMILE"

In Iraq, the British have had a different approach than the American's, for as early as January 2003, the stabilisation phase was planned. Before their deployment to Iraq, soldiers of the 19th Mechanised Brigade had an additional training on crowd containment and were issued books on the Iraqi culture.

The Brigade left most of its Challenger tanks and its artillery in the UK, but was reinforced with light Infantry units and Civil Affairs teams, and received a Phoenix UAV battery as well as a fleet of 200 armoured Land Rover light vehicles.

Because the British didn't want to leave the image of an occupying force like the Americans', and because strength was rapidly reduced at the end of operation Telic 1 (the English contingent was decreased from 33,000 to 10,000 people), the British HQ soon decided to form Iraqi units. Iraqi Civil Defense Corps (ICDC) was integrated in the Battlegroups (end of 2003 more than 300 Iraqi soldiers were within the Queen's Royal Hussars which then had a thousand men).

Unlike the American units which stay deployed in Iraq for eight to twelve months, the British have chosen six-month rotations, which avoid routine and worn out troops.

British troops always have the objective of building good relationships with the population. Despite demonstrations and attacks in 2004 and 2005, patrols are carried out on foot, wearing berets, without sun glasses, and weapons aiming down. As a specialist reports: "it does not prevent the soldiers to be on the alert and to apply the slogan: Smile, shoot, smile ".

Combat sections have a double vehicle rotation: Land Rover for normal patrols, Warrior or Saxon for more tense periods. ❏

They entered the western suburbs ahead of the Irish Guards warriors and Royal Scots Dragoon Guards Challenger II. They then discovered numerous civilians looting the official buildings. It was a clear sign: Baath party leaders had disappeared.

Special Forces reported about their recon while the British armoured fast-paced into Basrah to seize the key points. Although militiamen were still fighting with the energy of despair, civilians spontaneously came to inform the Brits. On their side, still preceded by SBS personnel, 40 Commando Royal Marines entered through the southern outskirts. Within hours the last sporadic defences of Iraqi militia disappeared. The British had just seized the largest southern city of Iraq.

West of the Euphrates River

During the night of 18 March, several SAS Land Rover Defender vehicles fast paced into the Iraqi desert, just along the Jordan-Iraq border. The objective was to fast pace north-east toward the Anbar province and to reach the Euphrates River. At the same time the Aussies' SAS moved in parallel, but more in the south.

As of 2 April, SBS detachment stationed in Jordan entered into operations. It consisted of 40 elements and its mission was to carry out a series of sabotages and recon actions for the benefit of the coalition's aviation, in the Mosul

region. In two nights, CH-53 Pave Low American helicopters heliborned the various teams with their heavy equipment, Land Rover and Quad. While it tried to settle its position, a team of ten elements faced a motorized unit. As they didn't know whether it was Iraqi soldiers or Kurds peshmergas, SBS decided to not open fire.

Unfortunately there were superiorly equipped Iraqis. After an hour of heavy fighting, British forces had to abandon their vehicles and to withdraw in the nearby hills. The patrol leader called for support. They were retrieved during the night by a SF Chinook. However, two men were missing!

The day after, Emirates Al-Jazeera television broadcasted laughing Iraqi civilians driving a Land Rover Defender and a Quad. Baghdad also announced ten SAS had been killed that day in northern Iraq. British MoD (Ministry of Defence) had to publish a statement confirming ten " *British soldiers had been extracted from Iraq* ", but with no more information. It was only on 14 April that the operation was unveiled, as well as the story of two SBS who marched for 150 kilometres to reach the Syrian border. Something which reminded the 1991 SAS " Bravo Two Zero " story [2]

But this time, the two men were well equipped with a GPS terminal, a precise map, sufficient food, and warm clothes. They had walked over night, hiding during the day, and managing to avoid the Iraqi army surveillance posts protecting the pipelines. Thus, they had succeeded in reaching the desert areas nearby Syria. It is a PM Tony Blair's emissary that took them home from Damascus.

End of October 2003, British SAS/SBS and American Delta Forces launched a raid in the Mosul sector, in northern Iraq, to capture a key member of Ansar al-Islam terrorist group, considered as one of the Iraqi branch of Al-Qaeda [3]. During the fight to invest several buildings, SBS Corporal Ian Plank, aged 31, was killed and four other British Special Forces slightly injured. Coalition SF succeeded in capturing several terrorists, including Saudis, and killed about ten militiamen.

Under the " British Rule "

From April 2003 until end of 2004, in the four south-east province of the British-controlled zone, things were different. The Chiit population, which had suffered from the Saddam Hus-

2. In 1991, a team of eight SAS was in charge of hunting the Scud missiles. The operation was a disaster with three deaths (one KIA and two from hypothermia), and the capture of four others (including the very famous Andy McNabb). Among the team only Chris Ryan was able to escape and to reach Syria.
3. One remembers that in March 2003 American Special Forces had seized the zone this terrorist movement occupied in Kurdistan. However, many of its members were able to escape to Iran, and to come back to Iraq later on.

Above.
SBS teams carried out several sea reconnaissances of Uum Qasr harbour, just a few days before operation Iraqi Freedom began. The oil facilities of the port were captured by a combined SEAL, Polish GROM and SBS detachment after the beginning of the war. (MOD Photo)

Below.
Map showing the area of operations of the British units, and especially the Rumallia oil fields, primary and major objective of coalition's Special Forces in southern Iraq. *(MOD Photo)*

sein's dictatorship hoped for change. Several political and religious leaders, such as the Al-Dawa party or the Supreme Assembly of the Islamic Revolution in Iraq, exiled in Iran until 2003, formed militia when they came back (the Madhi army, the Badr militia...).

SAS of Sabre Squadron, southern Iraq, 2004.
Unlike the American special units, British SAS have little equipment and move only in light vehicles such as Land Rover Defender during their hit and run actions in major built-in areas, or with the British regular units when dealing with contingency objectives. Because of their " *Special Operation Capable* " characteristic, and like their US counterparts, SAS have a large liberty to choose and to wear their individual equipment.

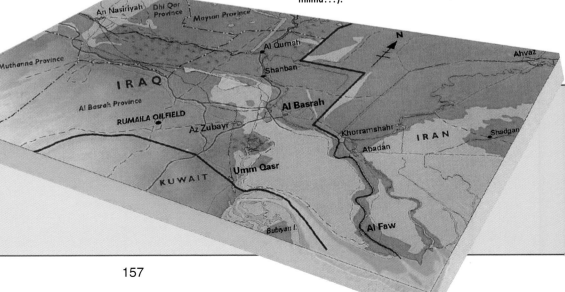

Left and below. With the capture of Uum Qasr harbour, coalition's Special Forces secured Iraq's only deep-sea port which allowed delivering military equipment and humanitarian aid. It was a joint Special Forces, Marine Recon and SBS action coming from land, while SEAL, Special Boat Teams and GROM commandoes arrived from ashore. *(MOD Photos)*

Right.
As of 2 April, a forty-element SBS detachment based in Jordan went to operations. Its mission was to perform sabotages and a series of intelligence actions for the coalition's aviation in Mosul's area.

If at the beginning people did not support them, things changed within two years. That is why the British formed "action" teams with Iraqi Chiits in order to infiltrate these "become-popular" movements, and certainly to increase the SAS and SBS strength.

As of 2004, about twenty SAS (24 according to some) operated in the Basrah region. They had to identify the " routes " Chiit rebels used, and if necessary, to eliminate the militiamen. As English Secret Services were certain that orders came from Iran, they wanted to "secure" the border with the nearby neighbour.

Sometimes things went wrong. Thus, on 19 September 2005 in Basrah, two SAS disguised as Arabs in a civilian vehicle were spotted at an Iraqi police check point. After a car chase, (the two Britons killed a civilian and injured several others during the chase) they were eventually arrested and "*beaten up* ". Police officers found weapons, explosives and communications gear in their vehicle. "*At first, the official version was that they were*

on their way to join other SAS surveying a Moqtada al-Sadr party leader's house, and not to make the car explode in the middle of a market as the Middle-East media proclaimed, said a SF expert. This action was part of counter-terrorism. As it was clearly said, SAS were in charge of hunting Iraqi extremists and neutralizing them. "But this time it was a different story, for the SAS followed an Iraqi police officer known to systematically torture his prisoners. After the first small arms firefight, SAS decided to give up.

They presented themselves as British soldiers, showing an English flag. But no sooner they were arrested than they were put in jail, interrogated, and beaten up.

Save the SAS at any price

As soon as the British heard of their arrest, Brigadier John Larimer's HQ designed a rescue operation.

Less than an hour later, a first VCI Warrior patrol was launched and took position around the police station. However, the Shiit crowd threw Molotov cocktails. Three British soldiers were injured while they got out of their vehicle.

Speed was the key factor for the life of an SAS counts for almost nothing in Iraq. This time ten Warrior armoured vehicles and one Lynx helicopter, with sharp shooters aboard, surrounded the building. Two officers tried to negotiate with the police officers inside the building. The latter spoke at length and eventually refused to release the prisoners. Then, everything went fast. The British stormed the police station and at the same time beat off the hundred assailants around the vehicles. All Iraqis who tried to resist or to take a weapon, police officers included, were killed. However, the British found an empty police station; the two SAS had been moved to a nearby house by militiamen of the Moqtada al-Sadr's Mahdi army.

The latter had accomplices in the police ranks. The British immediately launched another operation to free the SAS.

SAS of Sabre Squadron, 2004.
This Her Majesty's Special Forces has a M4 carbine.
Here is a Canadian DIEMACO C8-FT version of it, which replaced the mechanically less reliable L85A1.

The DPM desert BDU is often used with other greenish camouflages. Combat vests vary, from the Arktis 1604 model worn here, to the Blackhawk TAC-V eagle or Omega, a more " exotic " one for British troops.

During the night of 18 March, several SAS Land-Rover Defender vehicles moved into the heart of the Iraqi desert, just along the Jordan-Iraq border. The objective was to fast pace north-east towards the Anbar province and to reach the Euphrates River. To resupply teams in the Iraqi territory, the RAF used C-130 Hercules, in addition of Chinook and Puma.
(RAF Photo)

SAS and SBS have been in Iraq since the major ground operations in March 2003. Here are two Land-Rover Defenders of an SAS team opening the road for a British Army convoy.
(MOD Photo)

Doors were forced, defenders killed, and the hostages freed alive [4]. As of this date, the relationship between British forces and the Basrah Shiit authorities would never be the same.

Some also say SAS would also be in Bagdad at the beginning of 2006. There would be a sixteen-man detachment forming the new secret unit called Task Force Black.

This unit would consist of Delta Forces, SAS and CIA " action " elements. SAS would thus be part of the Marlborough operation (launched in July 2005), whose aim is to eliminate terrorists which operate in the Middle-East.

Certainly a long run operation...   ❒

As of October 2005, relationships between British forces and the Bassorah Iraqi authorities deteriorated. Even more when they realize the Brits have been hunting some local police elements - Chiit in majority - for months, alleged to be closely linked to the Chiit militias. Her Majesty's HQ then decided that SAS would watch the police's " death squadrons ". Here, on 19 September 2005, two SAS were captured by the police, then beaten up and subsequently handed over to a Chiit militia. They were rescued some hours later.
(MOD document)

---

4. According to Moqtada al-Sadr supporters, he wanted to exchange the two English for Sheikh Ahmad al-Fartoussi, captured the previous Sunday by the British forces.

Opposite page, from top to bottom.
Series of images showing an operation in Bassorah by a SAS team against Chiit militiamen in 2005. British Special Forces first encircled, and then captured them without collateral damages.
(WZK Studio Photo)

SAS of C Squadron, Bassorah, spring 2004.
The British Army focused on deploying communications systems to the lowest level. Thus, every Infantry man had a PRR (Personal Role Radio) delivered by Marconi-Selenia and equipped with an EarSet microphone, the device being almost invisible. This SAS wears a TAC-V1NU vest, light and aired for hot climate. The Diemaco C8 carbine is equipped with a Trijicon NSN ACOG scope which allows short range sniping in urban environment.

(Document MOD)

AUSTRALIAN SAS TOOK CO

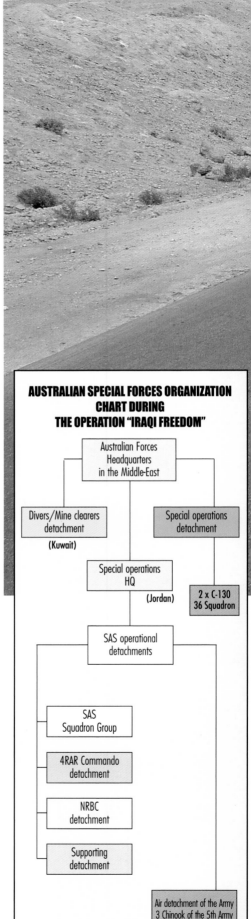

As of August 2002, Australian armed forces HQ was ready
to set up a joint command structure for a possible deployment
" to fight terrorism wherever it may be ". It is also true it already had
the previous Afghan deployment experience of operation Slipper in 2002.
The Australian high command knew it would join an American-led operation
against Iraq.

December 2002, *" the dice was cast "*: Canberra government requested the Chief of the Joint Staff to form a task force. On 10 January 2003, Prime Minister John Howard announced he was to deploy troops in the Middle East *" in order to help the diplomatic efforts aiming at a peaceful resolution but also to make Iraq disarm "*. He also added that the country *" prepares to deploy for military operations, should that be necessary "*.

Operation Bastille began. Australian diplomats crossed the region to gain the approval to deploy in the Iraqi neighbourhood countries. On 23 January 2003, *HMAS Kanimbla* left Sydney with some of the SAS's and support units' hea-

Previous pages.
One of the SAS motorized team had just stopped in the Iraqi desert during the last days of March 2003. At this time, the Scud threat -— the stationed in western Iraq coalition's Special Forces first mission — had disappeared. It is worth noting that they were scattered on the four cardinal points to be ready for any threat.

Above, right and below.
Besides the SAS teams heliborne during the first hours of the conflict and placed in observation, the Australian Special Forces Task Group also deployed a twenty or so 4x4 vehicles to carry out reconnaissance operations at the heart of Iraq, their WWII elder English brothers in arms did in Libya against the German-Italian forces.

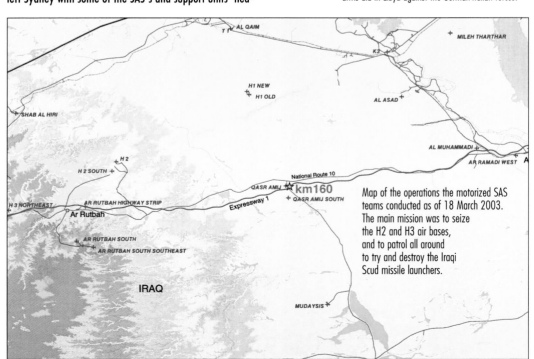

Map of the operations the motorized SAS teams conducted as of 18 March 2003. The main mission was to seize the H2 and H3 air bases, and to patrol all around to try and destroy the Iraqi Scud missile launchers.

AUSTRALIAN SPECIAL FORCES ORGANIZATION CHART DURING THE OPERATION "IRAQI FREEDOM"

- Australian Forces Headquarters in the Middle-East
  - Divers/Mine clearers detachment (Kuwait)
  - Special operations detachment
    - 2 x C-130 36 Squadron
  - Special operations HQ (Jordan)
    - SAS operational detachments
      - SAS Squadron Group
      - 4RAR Commando detachment
      - NRBC detachment
      - Supporting detachment
      - Air detachment of the Army 3 Chinook of the 5th Army Aviation Regiment

Australian Special Forces Task Group played a significant role
in achieving the western Iraq strategic objectives.

vy equipment, while SAS, 4RAR commandoes, RAAF personnel and support units flew to the United Arab Emirates and Jordan. On 25 February, some 2 000 Australian soldiers arrived in the Middle East, not only within operation Bastille, but also within operation Slipper which continued [1]. This Australian force consisted of a Special Forces detachment named Special Forces Task Group (SFTG), the Combat Service Support Group, a diver explosive ordnance group, several F/A-18 Hornet fighters, a C-130 Hercules transport aircraft detachment, Chinook helicopters of the 5th Aviation Regiment, and *HMAS Kanimbla* with an Army air defence unit and landing crafts aboard.

Canberra made a statement during the whole operation Bastille, that, although its units were part of the coalition, they remained under Australian command.

---

1. *Operation Slipper was moved to the Indian Ocean with the deployment of* HMAS Anzac *and* HMAS Darwin *frigates, as well as an AP-3C maritime patrol aircraft. There were no special units on the Afghan territory at this time.*

From top to bottom.
During the capture of Al-Asad air base, Incident Response Regiment teams specialised in NRBC warfare performed reconnaissance and searches of weapons of mass destruction (WMD), with 4RAR commandoes in support. On this photo, a combined SAS/4RAR team searches the base.

Close up of one of the Long Range Patrol Vehicles (LRPV), Australian-SAS-specially-studied-4x4-vehicle. LRPV had been successfully deployed in Afghanistan during operation Slipper; they were again deployed there in 2005.

The hunt for the Scud

On 18 March 2003, operation Bastille became Falconer with the Australian government announcement that its forces would join those of the coalition against Iraq.

Australian special units in Jordan, with American Rangers of the 75th Regiment and British SAS/SBS forming a Sabre Squadron, had almost a month to get used to the terrain and to train, day and night, to drop into the Jordanian desert from Chinook of the 5th Aviation Regiment and from the C-130 Hercules of 36 Squadron.

Australian SF also carried out exercises with their American and British counterparts (called Full Mission Profiles Exercises) to mirror their operational methods and to find ways of communication for the transmissions and the reconnaissance modes of action.

First Gulf War's images of Scud missiles fired on Israel and Saudi Arabia were still in the minds of the coalition HQ. Therefore, as for the Rangers or US Special Forces or British SAS, the Australian Special Forces primary mission was to find and destroy the Iraqi strategic missiles that intelligence reports had said were in Western Iraq.

To this aim, SAS Squadron was supported by 4RAR commandoes reinforced detachment (see 4RAR chapter), but also by several NRBC teams from the newly formed Incident Response Regiment, a NBC warfare specialist.

Based in a Jordanian base nearby the Iraqi border, the Special Forces Task Group forward command worked with the US Special Forces HQ-West, and Her Majesty's SAS liaison cell.

Below.
This map gives the location of the various SAS " ground-observing-teams ". Neither the Beduins of the area, nor the militiamen looking for " special commandoes " detected them. Beginning of April, these teams assaulted " km 160 " and captured it.
(DOD Photo)

Right, from top to bottom.
During all the operations, Special Forces were supported day and night by three CH-47 Chinook helicopters that provided equipment to the SAS deployed in Iraq territory.

Training made the difference

Mid-March, SFTG was ready. On the 18th and under its government's order, it entered into Iraq by land and by air. At 2100 sharp, SAS Long Range Patrol Vehicles (LRPV) crossed unseen the Iraqi border posts and various bunkers and trenches. It was not until 30 kilometres within Iraq that the SAS faced an enemy convoy.

The Iraqis opened fire but were immediately overwhelmed and encircled by the Australians firing from aboard their vehicles. Thirty minutes later, the Iraqis were all captured and those injured medically treated by SAS first aid specialists. This first encounter did not jeopardize the spear head teams' mission which seized H2 air field at dawn without meeting any resistance.

The same night, while the ten or so LRPV fast paced in the Iraqi desert, three SAS combat teams were heliborne with USAFSOC MH-53J more than 600 kilometres within Iraq. After an air refuelling and difficult night flight conditions, Pave Low dropped the Australian SF not far from Ramadi to observe the enemy's movements at the crossroad of the two most important Iraqi highways.

These Australian SAS were much closer to the capital coalition's ground element; their presence remained undetected by the Beduins. During the last days of the ground offensive, the SAS left their caches and neutralized the last strong points of the zone.

(Continued on page 168)

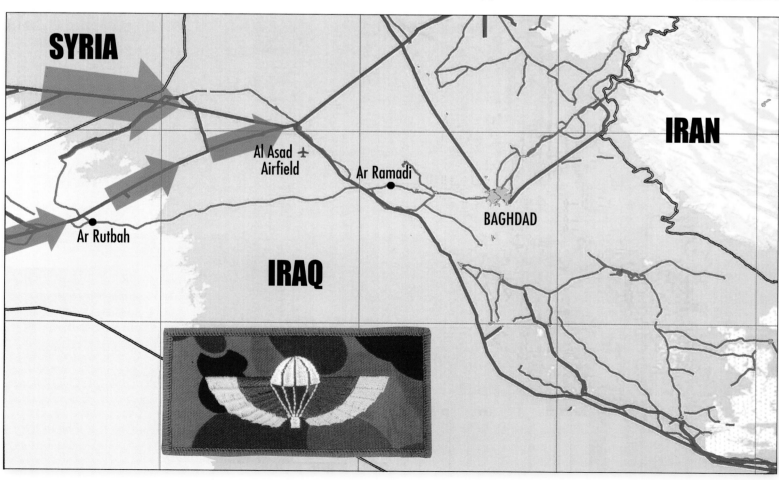

On 18 May 2003, SAS were welcomed home by their families, Australian PM and their comrades as they got off RAAF aircraft at Campbell Barracks base. If most of the Special Forces Task Group returned to Australia, several teams remained in Iraq and in Jordan to be part of the counter-terrorist operations.

SPECIAL OPERATING FOR THE AUSTRALIAN HERCULES

Based in Jordan as of 25 February 2003 with the Special Forces, two RAAF C-130 Hercules of 36 Squadron were part of all "assault drops" exercises and other trainings of resupply before operation Iraqi Freedom began.

If CH-47 Chinook carried out operations as early as 19 March to drop equipment for Sabre Squadron elements, Hercules flew their first mission in Iraq on 30 March, with a refuelling of vehicles on the Talil air base.

This Iraqi base became the central base of all the coalition's Special Forces after it was captured. One of the Hercules landed at Al-Asad air base as soon as it was captured by the SAS. On 13 April, an Australian C-130 was one of the first aircraft to land at Baghdad international airport. ❑

(continued from page 165)

The ground detachment mission for the second night was to capture a well defended transmission station centre. After a reconnaissance and the encircling of the defences, the SAS carried out a " fire ball " tactic attack which consisted in opening a passage into the external line of defence, then to request the destruction of the radio station.

One hour later the fight was over, the defenders surrendered one after the other. Not only did this destruction prevent the Iraqi command from giving orders to its troops, but it also sent a clear message to Baghdad's leaders about the coalition's capabilities and on how close to the capital the Special Forces were.

The SAS continued to extend the radius of their patrols, rapidly winning more terrain. They maintained surveillance on the main highways to intercept the Scud or the more classical convoys. The Iraqis tried to oppose SF during the first week of the conflict. But every time they were overrated by their opponents' fire power and training level. The third day a SAS patrol faced several hundreds of Iraqi combatants. Firefights lasted for several hours during which they were under heavy machine gun attacks, rocket launchers, grenade launchers and sniper rifles. However, the Iraqis were overwhelmed by the coalition's aviation strikes.

SAS in foxholes

" Two days later remembered an SAS Regiment Sergeant, *my patrol suddenly faced ten or so light vehicles with about fifty Iraqi aboard armed with machine guns, rocket launchers and mortars. There was only one solution: run and force them to abandon their vehicles. Mounted machine guns forced them to lower their* heads and several were injured. Most of the Iraqis fled, but some managed to set a mortar ready and started to fire on one of our LRPV.

Fortunately, one of our Troopers destroyed the mortar with his Barret [12.7 mm calibre sniper rifle]. "SAS took advantage of it to overthrow the last enemies and capture their vehicles.

Later on, this Trooper received the Medal for Gallantry for his professionalism and bravery. On 23 March, a " more static " team was given the mission to capture " km 160 ", which it was observing, an important crossroad on the Jordan to Baghdad motorway. More than 200 soldiers were defending it. The SAS directed the air bombardments by lighting the targets with laser designators for forty eight hours.

They then launched an attack to silence the last existing positions. But they had a big surprise: the defenders had disappeared. In fact they took advantage of the sand storm to abandon their positions. At the end of the first week of operations, the Australians understood the Iraqi opposition in their area had been neutralized.

Intercept fleeing leaders

The Iraqis had ceased to mount coordinated operations against the Special Forces. It was also clear that the Scud threat was no

Right and below.
End of March, Special Forces West HQ gave SAS the order to expand their zone of operations up to 200 kilometres west of Baghdad. Motorized teams made reconnaissance and searches in several villages, and tried to gather intelligence from the population about fleeing leaders and WMDs.

longer existing (actually it had never existed) and that the strategic part of the conflict was also over. It allowed the SAS to carry out road block missions to try to capture fleeing Iraqi Baath leaders as well as foreign volunteers trying to reach Baghdad.

At the end of March, the Australian government approved a coalition's request to expand the Australian Special Forces areas of operation.

This new area included the largest Iraqi air base of Al-Asad, 200 kilometres west of Baghdad. On 11 April, the whole SAS Squadron was mobilized to capture this air base. 4RAR and Incident Response Regiment commandoes joined them. The Australian SF " cleaned " the huge air base for thirty six hours, while RAAF's F/A-18 fighters provided CAS (Close Air Support). They successfully seized more than 50 Sukhoi and MiG aircraft which were well

camouflaged and had not been detected by coalition's aviation reconnaissance. Once the air base had been cleaned- which became the Australian SFTG forward operations base -, SF quickly repaired a runway to allow the landing of a C-130 of 36 Squadron.

During these day and night operations, three CH-47 Chinook of the 5th Aviation Regiment provided the SAS with resupply. During the last days of combat, just before Saddam Hussein's regime collapsed, the Australian SF carried out patrols toward Ramadi and arrested all fleeing Iraqi elements. And while three SAS teams went to Baghdad to protect the Australian diplomatic personnel [2], the other SAS returned to Jordan to their rear base.

One month later, on 18 May 2003, they were welcomed home by their families and Australian PM when getting off the RAAF's aircraft at Campbell Barracks base.

However, if operation Falconer officially stopped for the SAS, one team remained permanently in Baghdad together with other Australian units, within the framework of operation Catalyst, to carry out counter-terrorist operations. ❐

2. Two weeks later, SAS and 4RAR commandoes were relieved in line by a light detachment consisting of 75 elements, partly from the 2nd Royal Australian Regiment, and with four LAV vehicles from the 2nd Cavalry Regiment.

ACTION FOR THE 4 RAR SP

DUTY FIRST

ROYAL AUSTRALIAN REGIMENT

In March 2003, during the second Gulf war, the Australian armed forces command decided to focus its deployed forces in the Middle-East almost only around Special Forces units. They are then designated as Special Forces Task Group (SFTG). If the spearhead of this special unit — consisting of 500 personnel - was the Sabre Squadron of the Special Air Service Regiment, the Quick Reaction Force (QRF) consisted of 80 people of the 4th Battalion of the Royal Australian Regiment (Cdo).

Mid-February 2003, the Special Forces Task Group commandoes along with a NBC Defence detachment and various supporting elements boarded in Sydney, were heading towards Jordan to deploy under the auspices of operation Bastille. Beginning of March, all SFTG elements were deployed on the Jordan's border.

Almost no opposing forces.

The QRF main role was to support the SAS teams; if one of these teams got into strife with more numerous enemies and couldn't disengage on its own, Chinook of the 5 Aviation Regiment could immediately heliborne more heavily armed 4 RAR's

Previous pages.
A few days after their deployment near the Iraqi border, 4RAR commandoes train in the Jordanian desert and carry out commando exercises to seize strategic objectives.
Less than ten days later, heliborne and riding their 4 x 4 vehicles, they will do it in real life.

Above and left.
4RAR elements search buildings and small forts on an abandoned Iraqi air base. For the second time since the Vietnam War in 1968 and 1971 (at that time, 4RAR was a light Infantry unit and not a commando one), soldiers of the 4th Battalion of the Royal Australian Regiment carried out war operations in Iraq.

Following pages (180 and 181)
Series of images shot in the Iraqi and Jordanian deserts during the *Bastille* and *Falconer* operations. In Jordan, it was the last " rehearsals " before the operations in Iraq. During the Falconer operation, 4 RAR (Cdo) commandoes supported the Australian SAS teams " in a wall mode ".

commandoes to support them. However, all SAS teams were able to manoeuvre on their own far inside Iraq without meeting strong resistance or opposition. Within days, there were able to forbid large portions of the motorway which goes from the Jordan border up to Baghdad. They even seized two major airfields in the desert, which American and British Special Units transport aircraft were able to use afterwards.

To make things better, the Australian SFTG HQ decided to "release" 4 RAR commandoes in parallel with SAS teams in the Iraqi desert.

Thus, on 15 April 2003, during the first days of the offensive, 4 RAR teams captured the largest Iraqi air base of Al-Asad, west of Iraq. A first reconnaissance ensured the defenders had left their positions and had fled. The commandoes'

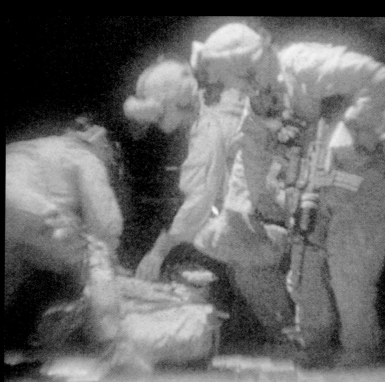

Above and left.
A pair of 4RAR commando advance (for the Australian military reporter photographer) in an Iraqi-army-abandoned building.
By the beginning of February 2003, 4 RAR commandos are on alert, and ten days later, 80 elements forming Bravo Company fly
to the Middle-East: operation Bastille begins. After several operations at the heart of Iraq, they returned home. Then, 4 RAR (Cdo) reported to the Special Operations Command, with the SAS Regiment,
the Incident Response Regiment, the Special Operations Combat Service Support Company and the 126, 152 and 330 Signal Squadrons.

TO BECOME A 4 RAR (CDO) COMMANDO

Commandoes' basic training lasts approximately nine months. It does not include the advanced trainings they need to take later on. Civilians who want to join must take a two-month *"special forces accelerated training"* in addition to the aforementioned nine months.

Before becoming a real commando and integrating the 4 RAR (Cdo), the applicant has to follow various courses: commando training; special forces weapons course; Special Forces roping course; commando urban operations course; commando parachute course, including water insertion; commando amphibious operations course; combat first-aider; commando signaller; demolitions course.

In addition to these courses, and after one year serving as a commando, other basic trainings will be required: precision firing, mortar firing, climbing, operations in cold and mountain zones, reconnaissance, foreign languages and navigation. Some of these will become the commando's specialities. Then, the commando will be considered as fully operational and will be eligible for specific counter-terrorism training.

As a NCO (Non-Commissioned Officer), after years in a unit, this commando may be eligible to various trainings: climbing teacher, parachute instructor (automatic opening), closed-combat instructor, chief of demolition workshop, survival training instructor, close-quarter fighting techniques and tactics instructor, mountain warfare instructor, NBC warfare and armament, leader of a platoon, leader of an infantry platoon.

Above.
During operation Falconer, 4RAR (Cdo) assault teams carry out
heliborne operations from Chinook of the 5th Aviation Regiment.
After the successful SAS/4RAR combined operations in Iraq,
the Australian command decided to deploy SAS and commandos
almost systematically during counter-terrorist operations,
as here in Afghanistan.

Right.
To move in the desert, and in addition to the 4x4 Defender,
4RAR commandos are equipped with 6x6 Quads
for quick transport towards the forward bases
and reconnaissance.

vehicles then raced on the kilometres of tarmac to capture one
after the other more than 50 MiG jets, camouflaged under
palm trees or half-covered with sand, and almost 8 million kilo-
grams of explosives.

No sooner the *"public-relations"* series of photographs was
taken than the commandoes worked on filling in the craters
the coalition aircraft bombs had made. With two bulldozers
found on site, they succeeded within less than twenty four hours,
in repairing the runways sufficiently to allow the first coalition
C-130 of the 36 Squadron to land.

Assault landing in Baghdad

Two days later, the first Hercules C-130 of the 37 Squadron
landed at the darkened Baghdad international airport. Immediately a 4 RAR commando fanned out from the rear door of
the aircraft to set up a security zone around the Australian C-
130 - whose engines were still on, in order to quickly take off
in case of danger.

For fifteen minutes, commandoes wearing NGV (night goggle vision) as the night was particularly dark protected the

183

Above.
In one of the major Iraqi air bases in western Iraq in April 2003, 4RAR commandos have just discovered a huge two-seat combat trainer MiG-25PU/RU Foxbat hidden in palm tree field.

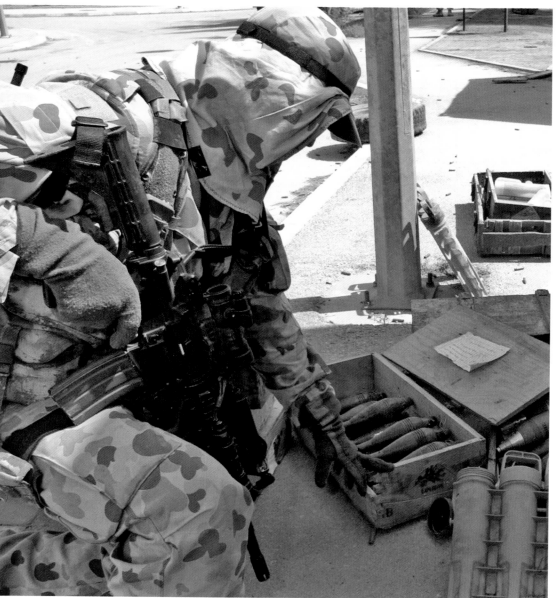

Left.
On 15 April 2003, a 4RAR commando checks there is no IED in a mortar ammunition box after an Iraqi major air base in the northern country has been captured. Iraqi resistance against the Australian commando action was almost nonexistent.

teams unloading tons of medical and first-aid supplies. Once the aircraft was empty commandoes embarked in the Hercules C-130 which took off immediately after and disappeared in the Iraqi night.

Gathered in Jordan, 4 RAR (Cdo) commandoes and their supporting elements were repatriated in May to their Holsworthy base in Australia, where they were received with all the honours deserved by the victorious.

That same month the Special Operations Command was officially created. ❏

THE 4 RAR (CDO) ARMAMENTS

Although 4 RAR is under the command of SOCOMD, Because of 4 RAR (Cdo) role being both conventional and unconventional (CT), the unit uses a large variety of equipment to meet the demands of both tasks.

Although standard issued F88 Austrian Steyr assault rifles and F89 Minimi Light Support Weapons are in the unit's armoury, much of it is being replaced by the latest generation of M4A5 Carbines and shortened ParaSAW variants of the famous Minimi.

For its CT role the venerable H&K MP-5 family of machine pistols are used along with SiG P226 and P228 pistols and Remington 870 shotguns.

In terms of sniping capabilities, the unit use the current issued SR-98 and Accuracy International's X-18, with the AW50 12.7 mm (.50 cal) Anti Material Rifle (AMR) being introduced in 2003. ❏

Patrol on foot in the desert along the Iraq-Jordan border.
4RAR commandoes, with the American Rangers and Australian SAS,
carried out several screening actions against fleeing Iraqis.
In 1997, it was decided the light Infantry 2/4 Royal Australian
Regiment would become a commando unit.
And in November 1999, the 4 RAR was declared operational.

185

AUSTRALIAN CHINOOKS AT

During operation Falconer, Chinook of the Townsville-based (Australia) 5th Aviation Regiment, provided a part of the personnel and equipment airlift to the Joint Special Operations Task Force-West's Special Forces units to the forward operating bases. Of course, Chinook primary airlift was provided to SAS and commandoes of the Australian 4RAR.

5th AR helicopters were deployed at the beginning of 2003. They first took part in a series of exercises in the Jordanian desert with the Australian, American (Army SF) and British Special Forces in order to get used to the various techniques and to harmonize procedures.

During the night of 19 March 2003, Chinook dropped the first Australian SAS reconnaissance patrols in Iraq, and provided the logistical support during all the actions.

Despite its age, the Chinook provided missions at the heart of Iraq. The Chinook has the capacity to lift up to 11.7 Tons, carrying internal and/or external loads, or 30 combat troops. Besides, and in several occasions, SAS conducted Chinook heliborne assault missions (including their 6x6 vehicles) along the roads towards Syria to try to capture fleeing Iraqis.

HE HEART OF THE OPERATIONS

THE COALITION'S
SPECIAL FORCES

All coalition's participating countries provided Special Forces (SF) detachments. In reality, these SF's primary mission has been to provide their own national forces with protection, and to carry out intelligence actions over their zone.

Only a few actually had offence missions against the guerrilla. Among them were Australian and British SF that we dealt with in previous chapters. However, several countries deployed significant Special Forces.

Polish SF were on the front line

The first operation the media covered took place at the beginning of the war, in March 2003, when Polish Army GROM commandos and Polish Formoza Navy group took the Iraqi port of Umm Qasr, together with the American SEAL and British SBS. In

Page 188, From top to bottom.
In the port of Umm-Qsar, GROM Special Forces and Polish Formoza combat divers have just captured Iraqi sailors of a small minelaying ship. (US Navy Photo)

Czech Republic detachment was in the Bassorah region under British-led command. Among it were ten or so Special Forces of the SOG special unit. (Photo MOD)

Page 189. A Polish commando of 1 Pulk Specjalny Komandosow (1st Regiment Special Commando) in a joint blocking of an area operation with Infantry units in the Sunnit region of central Iraq. (Polish MoD Photo)

Above and left, from top to bottom. First media-covered operation at the beginning of the war in March 2003. Polish GROM and the Formoza Navy group combat divers are ready to seize the Iraqi port of Umm-Qsar with American SEAL and British SBS.
(US Navy Photos)

Norwegian Special Forces teams, here Rangers of the HR Jegerkommando, were very discreet during all their deployment in Iraq until September 2005. At least it was true for the twenty officers and one hundred and seventy soldiers of the Engineer Company. (Forsvardepartementet Photo)

Right. Among the first Italian Special Forces in Iraq in summer 2003 for operation Antica Babilonia were the paratrooper carabinieri of the " Tuscania ", followed by the " Col Moschin " and the COMSUBIN GOI (Raiders Operating Group) combat divers. (Esercito Photo)

Bottom right. During the second quarter of 2005, Estonia deployed in Iraq a light Infantry ESTPLA-11 platoon of 34 soldiers, including five Special Forces personnel (ESTPLA Photo)

summer 2003, the Polish contingent deployed within the Multinational Division-Centre, a quieter sector than the « Sunnit triangle ». This Special Forces contingent still comprised of GROM teams. 2004 was a difficult year for the Polish forces. The mood was not enthusiastic because there was a gap between the peacekeeping mission originally announced and the on site chaotic situation. Moreover, the units formed for the deployment lacked cohesion and the selection of the volunteers had not been at the right level. As an expert said, « rediscovering war for an army whose only experience had been the cold war within the Warsaw pact » was not easy, all the more so as in Poland the deployment had no popular support.

Beginning of 2005, some 5,000 Polish soldiers were still stationed in Iraq. Six months later, mid-August 2005, this number was down to 1,500, with a rapid response battalion consisting of paratroopers and special forces, of which ten or so GROM personnel and thirty or so Army Special Forces. The plan is to have the Polish contingent deployed in Iraq until 2007.

In 2005, there were several national Special Forces detachments. Some of the 450 Bulgarian soldiers were from the 5th Infantry Battalion and about twenty were from the Special Forces. The contingent was under Polish command, and so was the Armenian detachment with about ten SF. Thirty six Bosnian mineclearing specialist sappers were integrated in a Marine unit at Fallujah; Azerbaijan had an Infantry company with 150 men and a group of ten special forces in the Anbar region. In April 2005, the Georgian « Shavnabada » (also known as the 3rd Battalion,

1. In February 2006, there had been seventeen soldiers and four Polish civilians (of which two journalists) killed in Iraq since April 2003.

POLAND

بولندا

Series of Photos showing
the various GROM
and Formoza commandos
operations against
the Iraqi rebellion in southern Iraq,
from March 2003
until September 2005.
Unlike other coalition's
special forces,
the Polish SF always
worked with their American
and British counterparts.
(GROM Photos)

Above and right. Macedonia decided to deploy 33 men forming a Special operations detachment attached to the national Ranger battalion. *(MK MOD photo)*

11th Brigade) Infantry battalion was attached to the American 3rd ID in Baghdad. Its 550 men were responsible for the Rashid hotel and Iraqi parliament security. Beside, Georgia had a 300 man commando battalion deployed near Baqubah.

In May 2005, the Fijian government decided to deploy an additional 90 soldier contingent to support the UNAMI (United Nations Assistance Mission in Iraq). Still in 2005, a 3,600 soldier contingent from South-Korea arrived in Iraq. Mid-July it was downsized to 3,300 to avoid duplication in operations. A Special Forces Battalion was among the Korean forces deployed in Iraq. However, as for the Japanese contingent, Koreans worked at the rebuilding of the country and unlike Australia, Poland and Great Britain, did not participate in the military operations.

In September 2005, Danish forces were still in Iraq, carrying out control operations in Bassorah with British forces.

On 19 September, the Danish held three check points after the British had been able to rescue their two SAS that the insurgents had captured.

The Danish contingent mission (downsized to nineteen elements in September 2005 from 1,400 in the spring of the same year) was to provide security around the camps and supply convoys on the roads of southern Iraq. It consisted of an Infantry Com-

A GROM element provides Polish authorities with protection during the time a convoy of light vehicles has stopped. *(GROM Photo)*

Above and below. Within the Romanian contingent was a significant Special Forces detachment whose elements made rotations between Iraq and Afghanistan. Thus, these commandoes acquired a strong counter-terrorist experience. *(Ministerul Apararii Nationale Photo)*

pany, military police groups, and several teams of the Army Special Forces and Civil-Military affairs. According to the authorities, and although it had not been revealed to the media for a long time, Danish forces had five "serious" firefights.

During the second quarter of 2005, Estonia deployed 34 soldiers of the light Infantry platoon ESTPLA-11, including five Special Forces personnel. A month later, the 380 soldiers of the Salvadorian « Cuzcatlán » battalion were relieved by 360 men of a combat battalion. At the same time, Albania had 120 soldiers in Iraq, including ten or so Special Forces elements. During summer 2005, Japan had more than 600 soldiers under Australian command (they were previously under Dutch authority). It is worth noticing that, at the date of writing, 200 Japanese were still in Kuwait. The Japanese contingent consisted of a company of Rangers providing security around the other units.

Since the deployment of the coalition's forces, Latvia has had 136 soldiers in Iraq, consisting of an Infantry company and a Special Forces Troop. Lithuania has had 120 men, including ten Special Forces. Half of them were integrated in the Danish-led battalion, the others in the Polish-led division at Al-Hillah. Macedonia decided to deploy 33 personnel forming a special operations detachment attached to the national Ranger battalion. End of July 2005 the fifth contingent of SF arrived in Iraq.

Within the Polish-led division, the Mongolian detachment consisted of 130 soldiers forming an Infantry company, a paratrooper Troop and an Engineer Troop.

In September 2005, there were still 90 soldiers of the Czech Republic in the Bassorah region under British-led command. There were about ten members of the SOG special unit; other soldiers trained the Iraqi police. By the beginning of 2006 Slovakia had 100 pioneers of an Engineer unit in the Multinational Division Central-South, and two teams of Special Forces in charge of the closed security.

Left. Light vehicles of a combined Infantry-commando Polish unit patrol in the Sunnit region. *(Polish MoD Photo)*

Since summer 2005, Iraqi Special Forces formed a combat Brigade. Coalition made a lot of efforts to train thousands of Iraqi soldiers to become commandos, with the Jordanian Special Forces support. These Iraqi SF were then part of all combats against the insurgents.
(DOD Photo)

Between 2005 and 2006 Romania had a significant Special Forces detachment together with its other 863 soldiers in Iraq: an Infantry battalion, an Engineer company, a Military Police company, an independent Infantry company and a medical group.

Until November 2005, there were still 950 Ukrainian soldiers in Iraq (500 left the country in spring 2005). Two paratrooper companies were part of the contingent.

« Latin » Special Forces

From the third quarter of 2003 and until mid-April 2004, Spain led the Diwaniya based 3rd Brigade Combat Team within the Multinational Division Central-South. As far as the Spanish units were concerned, this Brigade consisted of a Headquarter and Headquarter Company, a motorized Infantry Battalion, several platoons of Special Forces from the Spanish Legion; it also had a Honduran Special Forces battalion, a Salvadorian SF battalion, and a Nicaraguayan SF company. South American troop's missions were to provide security to the convoys and to deploy the humanitarian aid policy to the local population. However, by the beginning of 2004, Madrid decided to withdraw its contingent. By the end of April, Spanish SF provided security to the columns of vehicles returning to Kuwait.

Italy's case was different. By the beginning of 2006, Italy had the coalition's third biggest contingent. In February 2006, there were 2,650 soldiers, including several GIS (Carabinieri), GOI (Raiders Operating Group) and « Col Moschin » teams, Rangers Alpini and elements of the 185th RAO, the Air Force intelligence acquisition unit. Actually, Italian Special Forces were first to arrive in Iraq on 15 July 2003. Then, the parachute carabinieri arrived

A Polish contingent stationed in the " Sunnit triangle " quiet sector, had a rapid response battalion consisting of 1 Pulk Specjalny Komandosow (1st Regiment Special Commando) commandos and ten or so GROM elements. *(Polish Mod Photo)*

followed by the COMSUBIN combat divers. Operation Antica Babilonia (Ancient Babylon) began.

The Italians were a part of the Multinational Division South-East. A GIS team, ten or so men of the « Col Moschin », and as many combat divers of the famous GOS of the COMSUBIN were permanently on duty to carry out the « special » missions, including gathering intelligence. One of the focal points was the Nassiriya battle of April 2004 against the militiamen of the Mahdi army. On April 5, when hundreds of militiamen seized the city's bridges and set up barricades and blockhouses everywhere in Nassiriya, Italians were given the order to retake the bridges and the control of the city. With the "Bersaglieri", the « San Marco », a squadron of Cavalry of the Regiment of Savoy, the paratroopers of « Tuscania », Italian Special Forces also had teams of the GIS carabinieri and « Col Moschin ». Overall that meant 600 personnel. The first two bridges were recaptured after hours of combat. There were fifteen injured soldiers on the Italian side and in between 150 and 200 deaths on the Iraqi side. In July 2005, the Italian contingent had 3,038 soldiers, including 2,945 stationed in Iraq.

According to Rome HQ, Italian strength should be downsized to 1,600 men in July 2006; then it would become operation Nuova Babilonia (the New Babylon).

Iraqi counter-terrorist forces

Although they were not part of the coalition's units, the coalition-created Iraqi Special units deserve to be mentioned. They operated with national detachments.

The 2,000-commando Iraqi special operations force was formed in July 2004.

Four months later, it had 600 men, which meant two battalions: the 36th commando battalion, an élite Infantry unit, and

Above. Polish Army commandoes deployed in Iraq trained Iraqi soldiers. Here, Infantrymen learn how to disembark from a Polish helicopter. *(Polish MoD Photo)*

Right. Since summer 2003, Albania has constantly shown a pro-coalition support. It had a small contingent in Iraq, including ten or so Special Forces members. *(DOD Photo)*

Below. Estonia is a pro-American country which has deployed several commando teams in the Multinational division central. *(Estonian MOD Photo)*

the counter-terrorist battalion. A third battalion was formed at the end of 2004.

Iraqi SF began to operate in all the coalition's zones as of summer 2004. In November, they had formed the 1st and 2nd battalions, plus a support battalion, the 36th battalion commando and a counter-terrorist battalion. After some training in Iraq and in several Arabic countries [2], units were launched in several operations, in particular in Fallujah, Najaf and Samarra.

American Special Forces selected volunteers out of the National Guard and the Iraqi army. Volunteers went through a series of tests lasting fourteen days. If the counter-terrorist unit was created from scratch with Kurd combatants, the 36th Battalion commando strength was formed from one of the Iraqi National Guard Battalion which distinguished itself during the battle of Fallujah in November 2004.

In August 2005, the Iraqi Special Forces formed a Brigade under the command of Brigadier General Najah Hasan al-Shamary. Its various battalions were imbedded in the Iraqi Army's Divisions and Brigades, in particular in the 2nd Brigade of the 2nd Division in the region of Kirkuk, the 3rd Brigade of the 3rd Division in the region of Al-Shigar, and the 2nd Brigade of the 1st Division deployed west of Baghdad.

In 2004 there were up to 27 different contingents within the coalition. However, their strength was symbolic for most of them and their mission was low profile. ❐

2. *This training was provided by the coalition's Special Forces of the Combined Joint Special Operations Task Force-Arabian Peninsula (CJSOTF-AP), especially for the American, British and Australian units. It took place in several camps in Jordan with the support of the Jordanian Special Forces, in Egypt, Saudi Arabia and in the United Arab Emirates.*

SPECIAL FORCES DEATHS IN IRA

Private First Class Nichole M. Frye

Specialist Charles E. Bush

Master Sergeant Robert M. Horrigan

Master Sergeant Joseph J. Andres

Captain Jeffrey P. Toczylowski

Master Sergeant Anthony R.C. Yost

Sergeant 1st Class Trevor J. Diesing

Master Sergeant Kelly L. Hornbeck

1. Private first class Nichole M. Frye assigned to the 415th Civil Affairs Battalion was killed when an IED struck her convoy on 16 February 2004, in Baqubah.

2. On 19 December 2003, Specialist Charles E. Bush was assigned to the 402nd Civil Affairs Battalion. He was killed in a convoy between Baqubah and Balad, when his vehicle was hit by an IED.

3. Master Sgt. Robert M. Horrigan of the US Army Special Operations Command died on 17 June 2005 in a firefight with rebels while in a combat operation on the Syrian border. He was previously assigned to the 1st Battalion, 7th Special Forces Group.

4. Master Sergeant Joseph J. Andres, US Army Special Operations Command in Iraq died of injuries he sustained on 24 December 2005 during a combat operation in central Iraq. Originally assigned to 3rd Battalion, 1st SFG, he served at USASOC since December 2003.

5. Staff Sgt. Paul C. Mardis, B Company, 3rd Battalion, 5th Special Forces Group, died on 15 July 2004 from injuries sustained on 20 May from an IED near Mosul.

6. Sgt. 1st Class Lawrence E. Morrison of the Civil Affairs and Psychological Operations Command died in Baghdad, Iraq, on Sept. 19, of injuries sustained earlier that day in Taji, Iraq, when an improvised explosive device detonated near his vehicle. He was detached from the 490th Civil Affairs Battalion and had been in Iraq since spring 2005.

7. Master Sgt. Richard L. Fergusson, C Company, 2nd Battalion, 10th Special Forces Group, killed himself in a car accident near Samarra on 30 March 2004. He had been in Iraq since February 2004.

8. Corporal Timothy M. Shea assigned to the 3rd Battalion, 75th Ranger Regiment, was killed when a homemade bomb detonated near his position in Husayba, Iraq, on August 25, 2005.

9. Captain Jeffrey P. Toczylowski was assigned to 1st Battalion, 10th Special Forces Group. He was seriously injured as a result of a fall from a helicopter during a combat infiltration; he was airlifted to a military treatment facility in Germany where he was pronounced dead on 3 November 2005.

10. Master Sergeant Anthony R.C. Yost was assigned to 3rd Battalion, 3rd Special Forces Group. He was killed by the explosion of an IED in a building he was searching in Mosul on 19 November. He had served ten years with 10th SFG before joining 3rd SFG in March 2005.

11. Sgt. 1st Class Trevor John Diesing, Headquarters Company, US Army Special Operations Command, was killed when a homemade bomb detonated near his position in Husayba, Iraq, on August 25, 2005.

12. Master Sgt. Kelly L. Hornbeck, 3rd Battalion, 10th Special Forces Group, sustained injuries when an IED hit his patrol vehicle, he died on 18 January 2004.

13. Master Sgt. Ivica Jerak, Headquarters Company, US Army Special Operations Command, was killed when a homemade bomb detonated near his position in Husayba, Iraq, on August 25, 2005.

14. Sgt. 1st Class Brett Eugene Walden assigned to the 1st Battalion, 5th Special Forces Group, died on August 5, 2005, in Rubiah, Iraq, when a civilian fuel truck collided with their HMMWV while performing a convoy mission.

15. Master Sgt. Michael L. McNulty of the US Army Special Operations Command was killed on 17 June 2005 in a combat operation on the Syrian border.

16. Major Charles R. Soltes, assigned to the 426th Civil Affairs Battalion, was killed on 13 October when an IED detonated near his convoy vehicle near Mosul.

17. Sgt. 1st Class Mickey E. Zaun assigned to the Headquarters and Headquarters Company, US Army Special Operations Command, died from injuries sustained in a collision between two armoured vehicles in Mosul, on

January 28, 2005.

18. Staff Sgt. Michael Owen, 9th PsyOps Battalion, 4th PsyOps Group, was killed by an IED on 15 October 2004 in central Iraq.

19. Sergeant Regina C. Reali was assigned to the 351st Civil Affairs Command. She died when her vehicle was destroyed by an improvised explosive device near Baghdad 23 December 2005.

20. Major Paul R. Syverson III, 5th Special Forces Group was killed on June 16, 2004, when a mortar rounds hit camp Anaconda.

21. Sergeant Cheyenne C. Willey was assigned to the 351st Civil Affairs Command. He died when his vehicle was destroyed by an improvised explosive device near Baghdad 23 December 2005.

22. Staff Sgt. Aaron N. Holleyman assigned to the 1st Battalion, 5th Special Forces Group, was killed in action on 30 August 2004 when an IED detonated near his Humvee near Khutayiah. He had been in Iraq since January 2004, for his second tour.

23. Sgt. Major Michael B. Stack, C Company, 2nd Battalion, 5th Special Forces Group, was killed in action on 11 April 2004 when his convoy was ambushed near Baghdad.

24. Command Sgt. Maj. Edward C. Barnhill assigned to the 431st Civil Affairs Battalion died of a heart attack on 14 May 2004 in Baghdad.

25. Corporal Jonathan J. Santos, 9th PsyOps Battalion, 4th PsyOps Group, sustained injuries and died after his vehicle was hit by IED on 15 October 2004 in central Iraq.

26. Lieutenant Colonel Mark P. Phelan was assigned to the 416th Civil Affairs Battalion. He died on 13 October 2004 when an IED detonated near his convoy vehicle in Mosul. He was responsible for public health within the battalion.

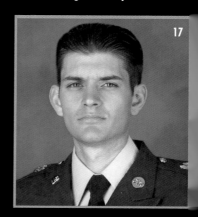

Sergeant 1st Class Mickey E. Zaun

Staff Sergeant Aaron N. Holleyman

Staff Sergeant Paul C. Mardis

Sergeant 1st Class Lawrence E. Morrison

Master Sergeant Richard L. Fergusson

Corporal Timothy M. Shea

Master Sergeant Ivica Jerak

Sergeant 1st Class Brett Eugene Walden

Master Sergeant Michael L. McNulty

Major Charles R. Soltes

Staff Sergeant Michael Owen

Sergeant Regina C. Reali

Major Paul R. Syverson III

Sergeant Cheyenne C. Willey

Sergeant Major Michael B. Stack

Command Sgt. Maj. Edward C. Barnhill

Corporal Jonathan J. Santos

Lieutenant Colonel Mark P. Phelan

AKNOWLEDGEMENTS

I would like to thank Michel GOYA for his knowledge of Operation *Iraqi Freedom* and his various analyses of the Iraqi conflict, Harry PUGH for his help during "the hunt for information", Laurent CIEJKA for his persistence to achieve the book, Yves DEBAY for his photos taken at the heart of operation Iraqi Freedom and his courage after his many captures both by the American units and the Iraqi militia! I also want to acknowledge Philippe AZALBERT, Jerome BRÉGÉRE, Laurent BRULÉ, Yann LABBÉ, Laurent JURQUET, Aurélien PUCHAL, Aurélien MOREL, Lionel SKARZYNSKI for the many hours spent in a photo studio in BDU!
Pascale Garnier deserves all my thanks for her endless hunt of misspellings and redundant sentences
I would also like to especially thank David SADOK without whom this book would not be so real!

BIBLIOGRAPHY

— *Master of Chaos,* Linda Robinson,
Public Affairs, Perseus Books Group, Cambridge, 2004

— *On Point, The United States Army in Operation Iraqi Freedoom.*
Col. Gregory Fontenot, Lt. Col. E.J.Degen, Lt. col. David Tohn. Naval Institute Press,
Anapolis, 2005

— *Plan of Attack,*
Bob Woodward, Simon & Schuster, New York, 2004

— *Shadow Warriors,*
Mir Bahmanyar, Osprey Publishing, Oxford 2005

— *Special Operations in Iraq,*
Mike Ryan, Pen & Sword Books Ltd., Barnsley, 2004

— *The war after the war, lessons learnt from twenty months of stabilization operations in Iraq*, Major Michel Goya,
Revue Doctrine CDEF, Paris 2005

Design and lay-out by Eric MICHELETTI and Jean-Marie MONGIN
© *Histoire & Collections 2006*

All rights reserved. No part of this
publication can be transmitted
or reproduced without the written consent
of the Author and the Publisher

ISBN: 2-915239-64-9
Publish number: 2-915239

© *Histoire & Collections 2006*

A book published by
HISTOIRE & COLLECTIONS
SA au capital de 182 938, 82 €
5, avenue de la République F-75541 Paris Cédex 11

▶ N° Indigo 0 820 888 911
0,118 € TTC / MN

Fax 01 47 00 51 11
www.histoireetcollections.fr

This book has been designed, typed,
laid-out and processed
by *Histoire & Collections*,
fully on integrated computer equipment

Printed by Zure
Spain, European Union
April 2006